Therapy Services

Therapy Services
Organisation, Management and Autonomy

John Øvretveit
Brunel University, Uxbridge, Middlesex, UK

Routledge
Taylor & Francis Group

LONDON AND NEW YORK

First published 1992
Second printing 1996
Reprinted 2004
by Routledge,
2 Park Square, Milton Park, Abingdon, Oxon OX14 4RN

Transferred to Digital Printing 2006

Library of Congress Cataloging-in-Publication Data
Øvretveit, John. 1954–
    Therapy services: organisation, management, and autonomy/by John Øvretveit.
        p.   cm.
    Includes bibliographical references and index.
    ISBN 3-7186-5245-5 (hard). -- ISBN 3-7186-5246-3 (soft)
    1. National Health Service (Great Britain) 2. Hospitals--Great Britain--Rehabilitation services. I. Title.
    [DNLM: 1. Health Service--organisation & administration--Great Britain. 2. Therapeutics--Great Britain. WB 300 096t]
    RA412.5.G7087 1992
362.1'78'0941--dc20
DNLM/DLC
for Library of Congress   91-35418
                                                                            CIP

Publisher's Note
The publisher has gone to great lengths to ensure the quality of this reprint but points out that some imperfections in the original may be apparent

Contents

Preface

Although few in number relative to medicine and nursing, the "therapy professions" have much to contribute to improving health and preventing illness. At present, demand exceeds supply. In the future, the need for these services will be even greater, with changes in demography and treatments, and a greater emphasis on promotion and prevention. How are the therapy professions to respond, given the limits to finance, training and pay?

In the past these professions concentrated on developing their practice base. Social scientists focused on relationships between these professions and medicine. Neither fully recognised the importance of organisation and management to the professions, or to effective service delivery.

This book shows the practical and theoretical significance of organisation to these professions. In the UK, these professions owe their shape and size to the NHS, and to state support for their services and autonomy. Effective organisation and management is essential for the NHS to make the most of this scarce and valuable resource.

The book argues that these professions must respond more positively to the new "public welfare markets" that are emerging in the UK (and elsewhere) if they are to secure their futures and ensure that people benefit from what they have to offer. It reports recent research that helps therapists to understand the changes and to decide how to respond.

The book draws on twenty-five years of applied organisational research with therapy professions, and gives an insight into a unique method of social research developed at the Brunel Institute of Organisation and Social Studies. The theoretical approach focuses on "formal" organisation and seeks to understand how institutional structures are created and their effects. It understands people's feelings and behaviour in relation to their social situation, and seeks to help create social institutions which bring out the best, rather than the worst, in people. This approach is particularly relevant to therapy service organisation and management, because the relationship between the therapist and the client, which is so important to helping the client, is enhanced or destroyed by the right type of organisation and management.

I am not embarrassed to declare my allegience to the NHS and to its values of free access to health care according to need. But improvements are necessary, especially to ensure that access is fair, as well as free. This means that priorities must be defined, through "political" as well as clinical processes, for determining need, and that services are properly organised to meet priorities.

This book shows that attention to organisation and management, and to securing finance in the new "public market" can ensure that the people who need therapy services get them. That, with the right organisation these professions, unencumbered by the history and tradition of their "sister" and "brother" professions can continue to develop the innovative responses to health (and social) needs that have distinguished them in the past.

Acknowledgements

My thanks to the Brunel Institute of Organisation and Social Studies and to the managers and practitioners with whom I worked for making possible the research which is reported here. Few research institutes in the UK could have provided me with the interdisciplinary environment in which to develop the ideas. My thanks also to Anna, Rick and Mary, without whose support the book would never have been written. Thanks also to Stephanie Robson and Mark O'Callaghan for their comments on drafts, and to Professor Maurice Kogan.

BIOSS Research: A General Note

BIOSS (Brunel Institute of Organisation and Social Studies) is an applied research institute within the School of Social Sciences at Brunel University. The Health Services Centre is based within BIOSS and has undertaken research into health and welfare service organisation for twenty-five years. Its members carry out field research, consultancy and local workshops. They have developed and published a substantial body of knowledge about health services and professional organisation.

Services Provided by the Health Services Centre

Members of the Health Services Centre are available to help staff develop their organisation and analyse organisational problems. It is through this work that we also develop usable knowledge and methods for solving organisation and management problems.

On-site workshops, training programmes and consultancy services are offered. National workshops are held at Brunel University which are publicised by mailing to each district.

The programme of on-site workshops and research into therapy service organisation and management continues, applying and refining the formulations presented in this book. For further details about fees and the services provided by the Health Services Centre, contact:

John Øvretveit
Co-director
Health Services Centre
Brunel Institute of Organisation and Social Studies
Brunel University
Uxbridge
Middlesex UB8 3PH, UK

Tel. Uxbridge (0895) 256461
(or 081 940-4049)

Chapter 1:   INTRODUCTION

The management team met to consider the structure of the two merged units. After agreeing the options for the directorates and nursing organisation, the meeting turned to 'the paramedics'. One of the assistant general managers shifted in his seat, eager to get onto works and support services and the issue of external contractors. He deferred to the professional-patient care ethos, but asked impatiently , 'who is in this group anyway?'

The chairperson gazed around the table for help. 'Good point, do we put psychology in with them?' One general manager suggested that all paramedics should be part of directorates, but before he could start talking about teamwork again, the community manager mentioned the 'income generation potential of this group'......'Perhaps we should ask them to tell us where they want to be?' A visible shudder went through the group at the thought of a series of lectures on the important contribution of each 'undervalued' group , and of sitting through the District/Unit service debate again.

The chairperson, a practical man, wanted the basics 'Who are they and what do they do?' There was a pause as people began to realise that this issue was going to take time, which they did not have. Images came to mind of basket weaving, toe nail clipping, shoes for the disabled (like someone had at school), tonsils, ink-blot tests, and the food police. 'Lets call them therapists'. The chairperson look relieved, 'Alright, where shall we put them? How many are there and where do they work?'

1: INTRODUCTION

The above caricatures health manager's understanding of "therapy services". It also conveys the priority accorded to these services during health service restructurings. This book is about how these professions have developed in the British NHS and about their future in the new "public markets".

The book has a practical and a theoretical purpose which reflects the method of research on which it is based. The practical purpose is to help managers decide how best to organise and then manage therapy services. The theoretical purpose is to use research into the organisation and management of one group of health professions to contribute to social scientific knowledge about professions.

This introduction explains why the term "therapy professions" is used, why this group of professions was chosen, and why their organisation and management is of practical and theoretical interest. It gives an outline of the book and describes the research method and sources. It then gives a "thumb-nail" sketch of each profession.

The "Therapy Professions"

What do the following professions have in common : clinical psychology, chiropody, dietetics, occupational therapy, physiotherapy, and speech therapy? At first sight not much. Indeed members of these professions argue that being grouped together is an historical accident, reflecting administrative ignorance and organisational politics or convenience rather than an understanding of their work.

Certainly there are significant differences between these professions in their work, pay, status, skills, knowledge, and other social attributes. However, there are also similarities. Practitioners from these professions all work in direct contact with clients for some, or all of the time; members of the public can refer to them directly; they can work as private practitioners outside state services; they are regulated by their professional associations, and most by the state; and they are few in number relative to medical and nurse practitioners. There are similarities in the choices open to them about their future organisation, and in the implications of these choices. In relation to their organisation and management they are usefully considered separately from nursing, medicine and other health professions.

However, the purpose of this book is not to distinguish one group of professions from medicine and nursing, or from each other. Social scientists have for too long been accomplices to aspiring or existing professions searching for characteristics which are said to differentiate one group of workers from another. These characteristics, such as skill, knowledge, or length of training, are not different in kind to those of other occupations.

This book shows that it is in their organisation, and in the different forms of authority delegated by the state, that professions differ from other occupations, and from each other. In addition, that the current changes in health services will have a profound influence on the division of labour in health and on the future of health professions. The book uses evidence of the organisation and management of these professions to advance these and other theoretical propositions.

The practical aims of the book

Why write, or read, a book about these professions as a group, and about their organisation and management?

Deciding the best organisation

First some practical reasons. Chapters 4 and 5 show that the 1990 UK government health and social service reforms make it possible to organise and manage therapists in ways which were not possible before. General managers and profession-managers want to know more about the options open to them, and about what type of management is needed for these professions in the quasi-markets which are emerging.

Although few in number, therapists have a growing part to play in meeting the changing health needs of populations. In addition to their innovatory work in the acute sector, they are developing new and flexible ways of caring for older people, and for people with permanent disabilities or long-term illnesses. They are also developing new approaches to rehabilitation, and to health education promotion and prevention. These are priorities of the nineties and beyond.

In some senses they represent the "acceptable face" of alternative medicine, not because they accept the controls put on them, but because of their knowledge of, and integration with other welfare services and their concerns for proof of effectiveness and equality of access. There has never been a greater demand for their services. In any other market bankers would be falling over themselves to invest in a service sector with such potential.

Given the small numbers and high demand, it is important that the NHS makes the best use of this scarce resource, and creates the conditions to help these profession to continue to innovate. To achieve this, professions have to be organised and managed in appropriately for the health needs of an area.

In some Districts these professions are poorly organised: their skills are not used to the best effect, therapists have left their jobs and the profession, and there are fewer new entrants. There is a danger that purchasers and providers, preoccupied with other matters, may recognise the contribution of these professions and the conditions they need to thrive when it is too late. In the frequent reorganisations of the 1990s it is important that decisions are made about the organisation and management of these professions with an understanding of the options open, and of the likely results of different choices.

Opportunities of Contracting

The effect of the UK health reforms is to make one management option less viable for these professions. In the 1980s a balance between general- and profession-management was achieved through joint-management arrangements, a British compromise which was rarely defined. Clarity of management requires that a choice is made between one of the two extremes of general management (with professional advice), or profession-management. Rather than ruling out profession-management the reforms make this choice now more attractive to general managers because contracts can give them the control they need.

Better Profession-Management

This leads to another of the practical reasons for considering the organisation and management of these professions. Where profession-management is retained or developed, managers recognise that they need to improve their skills and develop new ones to manage their services in the new "market" environment. This book aims to help profession-managers to understand the implications of the new "market". It discusses the management methods which they need to know about and use if they are to be successful and are to secure the future of their profession.

The Theoretical Aims

There is a social scientific reason for focusing on organisation and management. There is little research reported about the organisation of these professions, and this book aims to add to this knowledge. It shows that a study of the organisation and management of these professions can bring new insights into the nature of professions. It proposes that:
- Professions are social institutions for organising workers to acquire and apply specialist skills to meet needs, and to pursue their member's interests,
- Professions differ from other associations of workers, not in the expertise, knowledge or other characteristics of the workers, but in being authorised by the state to decide and regulate aspects of their work and conditions of work,
- Certain characteristics such as skill, length of training, etc. are only relevant insofar as they can be used by the profession to persuade the public and the state that the profession should be self-directing in a range of activities,
- One of the most persuasive arguments for state regulation is danger to the public of incompetent practitioners, together with practical ways of discriminating competence.
- Professional organisation has a greater influence on the shape of the profession than any other factor,
- We can learn about professional autonomy through a study of professional organisation at the national and local levels.

2: AN OUTLINE OF THE BOOK

The theoretical theme is the nature of the autonomy of the therapy professions, and how their autonomy has, and will change. The practical theme is how therapists are organised and managed, and how future organisation must be designed for the emerging "public markets". The link between the themes is the concept of "business autonomy".

The rest of this chapter gives a brief summary of each profession. Chapter 2 then outlines some theoretical approaches to studying professions, and considers one in detail: Freidson's theory of medical dominance and professional autonomy. The chapter substantiates its criticisms of this theory by giving details of professional organisation at the national level. It argues that state regulation does not provide professions with control over work or conditions of work. It proposes that a study of professional organisation is needed to contribute to knowledge about professional power, authority and autonomy, and of its effects for citizen and social well-being.

Chapter 3 develops these arguments by describing changes in the organisation of physiotherapy and clinical psychology at the local level since the 1970's. It shows the influence of NHS organisation on these professions, and how different forms of autonomy are institutionalised in NHS management structures.

Chapter 4 looks to the future and considers the implications of the 1990 NHS and social service reforms for the therapy professions. It argues that the starting point for organisation and management must be an understanding of needs, and of the responses and resources available to meet those needs. It shows that, in the new UK "welfare markets", needs are perceived by purchasers and by therapy providers. It discusses different ways of financing therapy services. This sets the context for examining models of organisation for therapy services in Chapter 5.

The models described vary from full-integration with NHS teams, to independent-solo or co-practice. The chapter considers criteria for choosing between models, and the advantages and disadvantages of each. It argues that therapists do have a choice, and that they may exercise this choice, especially in the frequent provider reorganisations that will occur in the nineties.

The details of any therapy management structures depend on the work which therapists do, and should facilitate this work. Chapter 6 presents an analysis of therapist's work and of practitioner autonomy and accountability. Chapter 7 considers the role of therapy managers which follows from these analyses of therapist's work, and of public markets. It shows how therapist managers can tell if they are "full-managers" where general managers have a management role. It considers whether there is a "post-district therapist" role for managing therapists in different provider Units.

One of the main reasons for therapists to take organisation and management more seriously are the emerging "public markets". Chapter 8 outlines how to develop a business strategy in the special circumstances of these "markets". It argues that strategy should determine management structure, rather than vice-versa. It discusses structures which provide the necessary independence for therapists, and a career structure, but also allows for staff deployment in relation to needs and the market.

The two most important future management tools for therapy managers are contracts and quality methods, which are discussed in Chapter 9. It shows how to prepare and negotiate a contract with an "internal" or "external" purchaser.

Purchasers want to quality specified in contracts, and then want proof of the quality of the service. A discussion of quality assurance shows the high cost of poor quality, and that quality depends on efficient processes, as well as staff commitment and attitudes. It shows how professional staff can be motivated to prove and improve the quality of their service, which is necessary if the service is to be competitive.

The state, as virtual monopoly employer of therapists in the UK, has shaped these professions in influencing pay, grades and career structures. Chapter 10 considers how organisation structure provides or frustrates career progression, the effects of grade definitions, and implications of more flexible arrangements in the future.

Chapter 11 provides a summary, and outlines the theoretical conclusions and the practical conclusions for the future. It describes different types of autonomy and argues that the future of the therapy professions depends on their developing "business autonomy" inside and outside the NHS.

3: RESEARCH METHOD AND SOURCES

The practical and theoretical themes of the book arise from a particular type of research method. The method aims to contribute to social scientific knowledge through using social scientific methods and theory to help people solve practical problems in organisation. The method, a problem-focused and collaborative applied research method called "social analysis", is a variant of action research. The latter is an approach little known or used in the UK, but more common elsewhere. The research method is described in Appendix 1, and the research sources are listed in Appendix 2.

4: WHAT IS A "THERAPY PROFESSION"?

Putting aside, until the next chapter, the question of whether these occupations are "professions", why was the generic term "therapy profession" chosen? Why are only six such professions considered? The answers to these questions are mostly pragmatic.

First, three of the professions refer to themselves as therapists. Second, all of the professions could be said to be engaged in therapeutics, defined as a curative or remedial art and science.

It is true, however, that medicine and nursing engage in therapeutic practices, and these are the two professions from which those in question wish to distinguish themselves. Also, strictly speaking, some of these professions are not well defined as therapy professions. There is a debate within health psychology as to whether psychologists should leave behind them their "clinical roots" and spend less time on direct client-contact work in favour of organisation development, research, evaluation, training and consultation.

This debate is present in all of the six professions, in part because of the widening gap between demand and numbers of trained therapists. Some of the debate is about the role and management of assistant therapists and technicians. Dieticians for their part are spending less time as "therapists" advising individual clients, and more time as consultants to others and as teachers. Chiropodists emphasise the "surgical" element of their work and also feel that "therapist" does not describe them well.

The term "therapy profession" is considered by the author to be the least bad of the alternatives: "Professions Supplementary to Medicine" is now "Allied to Medicine", and sometimes "Complementary to Medicine", reflecting professional sensitivities and growing independence. One of these phrases could be used, but they are too lengthy, the anagrams are inelegant ("PAMs"), and in view of their future role, it seems an unnecessary restriction to define these professions in relation to medicine.

Why then leave out other professions who consider themselves therapists, or who engage in therapeutic practices? Why leave out art and music therapists, opthalmic opticians, radiographers, and others? Mainly because most of the author's research was done with the six professions listed. The research itself reflects the way in which they are grouped or thought about for organisation purposes. As the caricature in the chapter introduction suggests, issues of health service organisation are mostly considered in terms of medical specialities, nursing and support services. The "therapy professions" do not fit in neatly. It was because they and their managers wanted to explore different possibilities that the opportunity arose for much of the research on which this book is based.

These pragmatic reasons for selecting the six professions do not invalidate the practical and theoretical aims of the book. The practical organisation and management issues at stake are similar, and in this area each profession can learn much from the others. The similarities and difference in the "sample" are sufficient to explore, and I will argue, prove the theoretical propositions.

5: PROFESSION PROFILES

The following gives a "thumb-nail" sketch of the six professions and their work.

Chiropody

Chiropodists treat conditions of the lower limb and foot. They treat and educate patients with foot ulcers, nail problems, warts, corns and "mechanical" problems which cause some of these conditions. They work mostly with the elderly, where they can help maintain mobility, and with physically handicapped people and with children, where early detection and treatment can prevent later problems. They undertake minor surgery and can prescribe certain restricted medicines.

In 1990 there were about 3,500 chiropodists employed in the NHS (1,336 in 1975 (DHSS (1976); in 1950 the NHS employed 30 full-time, and 388 part-time, out of 3792 members of the Society of Chiropodists (Cope report (1951)). In 1990 the average health authority of 200,000 populationemployed about 15 chropodists. State registration is a condition for employment by health and local authorities, and to become state registered (S.R. Ch.) a person must have gained a qualification which is recognised by the Chiropodist's Board of the Council for Professions Supplementary to Medicine (hereafter CPSM). This involves a three year training after "A" levels at one of the 14 chiropody schools, leading to a diploma or BSc degree.

The membership of the Society of Chiropodists was 5,570 in 1990. The society is a registered trade union, representing members individually and collectively, as well as an educational association which validates training and promotes research. It is also a professional association, acting to promote standards and discipline members. Others who do not belong to the society work part or whole time in private practice, and are not state registered. The next chapter considers the significance of state registration as one of several types of regulation.

Dietetics

Dietitians assess and advise clients and patients about their diet, and teach dietary treatment and prevention. They also advise other professionals and catering departments about the role of nutrition in health. They work in acute medicine, in primary health care settings and in hospitals for the elderly, as well as in mental health and handicap services.

In 1990 there were about 1,550 dietitians employed in the NHS (484 in 1975 (DHSS (1976)). An average health authority employs about 6. As with chiropody, state registration is a condition for employment by health and local authorities. A four year training after "A" levels leads to a degree (or a diploma after 2 years, if the person starts with a degree), which is accepted for state registration if it is from one of the 9 centres recognised by the Dieticians Board of the CPSM

There are 2,800 members of the British Dietetic Association, a registered trade union as well as an educational and professional association. Some work part- or whole-time in private practice, and are not always state registered.

Occupational Therapy

Occupational therapists work with people who have a physical or mental illness or disability to help them overcome the effects and adjust to everyday living. They teach ways of building physical and psychological strength, and how to cope with disability. They have a role in most types of rehabilitation, as well as in preventing admission, and work with all client groups.

In 1990 there were about 7,000 occupational therapists employed in the NHS (2,036 in 1975 (DHSS (1976)) which is about 22 employed by an average health authority. There are considerably more occupational therapists employed by Local Authorities than any other of the professions considered here (1,400 including unqualified). A small but increasing number are now in private practice.

State registration is a condition for employment by health and local authorities. To become state registered a person must have gained a degree or diploma qualification which is recognised by the Occupational Therapists Board of the CPSM in conjunction with the College of Occupational Therapists and, where appropriate by a degree awarding body. Training lasts 2-4 years after "A" levels, depending on the type of course.

The British Association of Occupational Therapists is a trade union with more than 11,000 members, which includes unqualified, as well as state registered and qualified members. The College of Occupational Therapists is part of the Association and has an educational and professional role.

Physiotherapy

Physiotherapy is the use of physical means to prevent and treat injury or disease, and to assist rehabilitation. The methods used include massage, manipulation, mobilisation, electrotherapy, and hydrotherapy. There are more working in acute and hospital settings than the other professions considered here, and they often require specialist facilities and equipment. Over the last ten years more have been working in health centres and in people's homes, especially to help children, the elderly, and people with menetal health problems and learning difficulties.

They are by far the largest of the "therapy" professions: in 1990 there were about 13,500 physiotherapists employed in the NHS (5,298 in 1975 (DHSS (1976)), which is about 50 employed by an average health authority. As with chiropody, dietetics, and occupational therapy, state registration is a condition for employment by health and local authorities. To become state registered a person must have gained a degree or diploma qualification which is recognised by the Physiotherapists Board of the CPSM, which involves a 3-4 year training after "A" levels.

The Chartered Society of Physiotherapy has 24,500 members, and has an educational and professional role, as well as being a trade union. There are over 3,000 physiotherapists in private practice or private hospitals.

Speech and Language Therapy

Speech and language therapy is concerned with the assessment, diagnosis, treatment and management of those with a communication disorder. In 1990 there were about 3,500 speech therapists employed in the NHS (930 in 1975 (DHSS (1976)), about 13 employed by an average size health authority. They have voluntary regulation by the College of Speech Therapists through registration with this association, and will soon have state registration. To be employed as a speech therapist by a health authority a person must have acquired a qualification which is recognised by the College, which is a 3-4 year degree, or a 2 year postgraduate diploma if the person already has a degree.

There are 6,000 members of the College of Speech Therapists. The Manufacturing Science and Finance Union represents speech therapists in NHS wage negotiations.

Health Psychology

Clinical Psychology is the application and development of psychological theory and methods to promote health and to cure or prevent illness. Psychologists have traditionally worked with people with mental health problems or learning disablilites, but now work with all client and patient groups. There is a debate within the profession about how much work should be done with individual clients, as opposed to working with groups, "through" carers or other professionals, or working on evaluation and organisation development and in other ways. The term "health psychology" is used to convey this wider application of psychology.

In 1990 there were about 2,000 clinical psychologists employed in the NHS - about 8 in an average health authority. Unlike all the other professions considered here (apart from speech therapy) they are regulated only by their professional association, the British Psychological Society (BPS), through listing as a "Chartered Psychologist". To be employed as a clinical psychologist by a health authority a person must have acquired a qualification which is recognised by the BPS. This is a postgraduate diploma, which takes 2 or 3 years training, after a first degree in psychology and usually practical experience as well.

There are 2,300 members of the British Psychological Society's Division of Clinical Psychology. The BPS could represent their member's interests in formal wage negotiations: being a body incorporated by Royal Charter, and registered as a charity (not as a company since 1966) does not prevent this. However, the BPS decided not to perform this role and its members are represented by Manufacturing Science and Finance Union (MSF). The reason for this decision was, amoungst others, *"to avoid conflict of interest when advising government and other bodies about the role of psychology. It enables the society to consider firstly what is in the public interest and then secondarily what is in its members interests, whereas the role of the trade union must necessarily be the other way round."* (BPS Deputy Exec. Sec. Personal Correspondance, 1991).

The idea of a professional association putting the public interest before that of members of the profession is not one that has governed the decision of profession's disciplinary bodies, and is a notion which we will consider in the next chapter.

	Chiropody (Ch)	Dietetics (Dt)	Health Psychology (CP)	Occupational Therapy (OT)	Physiotherapy (PT)	Speech Therapy (ST)
Numbers						
Membership of Professional Association	5,500	2,800	2,300	11,000 (2,000 unqualified)	24,500	6,000
Employed by the NHS	3,500	1,550	2,000	6,000	13,000	3,500
In an average NHS district	15	6	8	22	50	13
Employed by Local Authorities	15(?)	10	35(?)	1,400 (inc unqual.)	?	25(?)
Private Practice or Private Hospitals	1,500(?)	257	100(?)	?	3,000	35(?)
Training						
Training Entry Qualifications	3 GCSE 2 "A" Level	3 GCSE 2 "A" Levels	Psychology Degree	3 GCSE 2 "A" Level	3 GCSE 2 "A" Level	3 GCSE 2"A"Level
Length	3 years	4 years (2 if have degree)	2-3 years	3 years	3-4 years	3-4 years
Exit Qualifications	Diploma or Degree	Degree or Post-Grad. Diploma	MSc or Degree	Dipolma or Degree	Diploma or Diploma	Degree
Regulation	State Registration	State Registration	By profession Chartered	State Registration	State Registration	By Profession (soon SR)
Pay						
Just Qualified	12,095	10,630	12,000	10,170	10,170	11,187
Highest	24,180	24,180	44,143	25,050	25,050	28,674

Notes
1 Figures are approximate.and are rounded averages from different sources.
2 Main sources are professional associations (August 1991), and Pay Review Body Report for Nursing Staff, Midwives, Health Visitors and Professions Allied to Medicine, (Jan 1991).
3. Entry qualifications for most all are a minimum of 5 GCSE, and 2/3 "A" levels for school leavers.

Chapter 2: *PROFESSIONAL AUTONOMY AND ORGANISATION*

'Most of the commonly cited attributes of professions may be seen either as a consequence of their autonomy or as conditions useful for persuading the public and the body politic to grant such autonomy.'

(Freidson (1970a))

1: *INTRODUCTION*

The questions of how best to organise and manage workers who have specialist expertise, and how to regulate the power which arises from that expertise are questions of increasing importance in modern society. New occupations have emerged to apply scientific advances and to meet (and create) needs which were not previously recognised. These changes have put strain on traditional forms of organisation for regulating occupations and for employing memebers of different occupations. Nowhere has the change and challenge to organisation been greater than in the British heath sector, and in the NHS, which employs a greater variety and number of professions than any organisation in the world.

This chapter considers some of the social scientific issues raised by a study of therapy professions. It notes some of the theoretical perspectives used to study professions, and presents one theory which explains the position and history of the "therapy professions". The chapter derives hypotheses from this theory and tests these against the research evidence, presented in this and the next chapter.

2: *THEORETICAL ISSUES AND PERSPECTIVES IN THE STUDY OF PROFESSIONS*

The study of occupations and professions has a long history in the social sciences. Early studies addressed the question,"what is a profession?" Many American sociologists, reflecting the interests of different groups in their society debated at length the different possible defining characteristics of "a profession" and of "a professional" (Cogan (1953)).

Social scientist's preoccupation with defining the distinctive features of professions was modified with the rise of occupational groups all claiming professional status and advantages. The central theoretical issue became, "to what extent do different occupational groups exhibit some, or all of the characteristics of an "ideal-typical" profession?"

This approach generated research into whether there was a "natural history of professionalisation" for occupational groups aspiring for the higher status and income which came from being a recognised profession (Hall (1968)). There were also studies of a parallel, but contrary, trend - the possible "deprofessionalisation of professionals" with the growth of capital-intensive technologies and managerial techniques in professional work. (The "professionalisation"/"deprofessionalisation debate"(Jackson (1970), Haug (1973), Larson (1977)).

The approach also led to studies of particular types of professions, such as "semi-professions" (Etzioni (1969)), and to studies looking at occupational groups in a particular field of work. These studies were less interested in the traditional definitional questions and more interested in the relationship between particular fields of work and with occupational characteristics. The "faith of the counsellors" (Halmos (1965)) was a phrase used to characterise similarities in orientation of professionals in personal services.

There were also studies focusing on individual professional practice. The Chicago school of symbolic interactionism produced empirical research into working practices in various occupations and street trades, and showed similarities rather than differences between professionals and ordinary "tradesmen" (Becker (1961)). One strand of this approach led to a study of the meanings and interpretive processes occurring in individual professional practice. Later ethnomethodological studies developed this microsociology of individual meanings in particular situations, such as in GP consultations (Dingwall (1976)).

More recent studies, some of which arose out of the Chicago school, used a "power perspective" to look at competition between and within professions for markets and privileges (Freidson (1970), Johnson (1972)) Two questions this perspective addressed were, "how did this field of work come to be organised as a profession at this time in this society, and, "what is the relationship between the state and professions?" Appendix 6 presents a detailed review of these main perspective and studies.

One of the foremost studies within the "power perspective" was Freidson's study of professional dominance (Freidson (1970a)(1970b)). The following considers this theory in more detail because it is the theory of greatest relevance to the "therapy professions" which are the subject of this book. It is also close to being a general theory of professions - something which is lacking in the field. It avoids the shortcomings of the "definitional" studies, the narrowness of the microsociological studies, and seeks to explain the differences between professions.

3: PROFESSINAL DOMINANCE AND AUTONOMY

First, Freidson's theory about professions in general. His central proposition was that,*"From the single condition of self-direction or autonomy I believe we can deduce or derive virtually all the other institutional elements that are included in most definitions of professions"* (Freidson (1970a))

His second proposition was that an occupational group is more likely to be self-directing in its work when achieves a "legal privilege" which protects it's work from being undertaken by other occupations. By this he meant state licensing arrangements, like state registration in the UK.

Third, self-direction is only possible if an occupation can control the production and the application of knowledge and skill in its work. "Full autonomy" is not possible if others can criticise or evaluate the way in which members of the profession conduct their work. Freidson also linked codes of ethics to autonomy, regarding them as, *"A formal method of declaring to all that the profession can be trusted and of persuading society to grant the special status of autonomy."*

Freidson's main argument was thus that,*"most of the commonly cited attributes of professions may be seen either as a consequence of their autonomy or as conditions useful for persuading the public and the body politic to grant such autonomy."* (Freidson (1970a) p 135)

Medical Dominance

However, the main subject of Freidson's 1970 study was medical dominance. He proposed that a clear distinction should be made between a profession which is dominant in a particular field, and others. He came close to offering a definition of "a profession", not in terms of "autonomy", but in terms of "dominance":*"One might call many occupations "professions" if one so chooses, but there is a difference between the dominant professions and the others ..... in essence the difference reflects the existence of a hierarchy of institutionalised expertise."*

His central argument was that the only "truly autonomous" occupation in health services was medicine, and that it's autonomy was sustained by the dominance of it's expertise in the health division of labour.

Hypotheses & Research Method

A logical criticism of Freidson's theory is that the central concepts of the theory -autonomy, dominance and control - are not defined. For example, his only definition of autonomy is a dictionary one, simply as self-direction in work and freedom from evaluation by others. A further criticism is that he does not substantiate his argument with empirical evidence about different professions.

However, Freidson's theory was an important advance and moved attention away from what professions said they did, to a more independent study of the social structures and processes which upheld their power. One of the aims of the research programme which this book draws on was to test and develop Freidson's theory. To do this the research derived the following hypotheses from Friedson's theory:

Hypothesis 1: Characteristics of professions which are said to distinguish them from other occupations derive from their autonomy. (eg status, pay, expertise, length of training, codes of ethics, etc.)
Hypothesis 2: "Legal privileges" create a protected market for professions.
Hypothesis 3: "Legal privileges" are the basis for autonomy and self-direction.
Hypothesis 4: Autonomy will only be found where a profession can control the production and application of skill and knowledge in its work.
Hypothesis 5: Autonomy will not be found if people outside the profession can understand, criticise and evaluate the work.
Hypothesis 6: There are differences between a "dominant" profession and other related professions, which reflect the existence of a hierarchy of institutionalised expertise.

This chapter considers the evidence for and against the above hypotheses by looking at the structures and processes at the national level which regulate and control the medical and therapy professions in the UK. In particular, do "legal privileges" create a protected market for professions, and are "legal privileges" the basis for autonomy and self-direction? Do they function as a state-supported "closed-shop"?

4: PROFESSIONAL AUTONOMY AT THE NATIONAL LEVEL

Three main forms of "professional organisation" exist at the national level:
- associations of members of the profession,
- structures for regulating training and the practice of a profession (e.g. state registration councils) and,
- structures for negotiating the pay and conditions of service to be offered by state employers.
We will see that professional associations are involved in different ways in creating and operating structures established by the state for the last two purposes.

The Nature of Occupational Control over Pay and Conditions of Work

The expansion of state welfare services in the UK during the 1960s and 1970s led to an increased union role for many professional associations. It led to national structures for negotiating the pay and conditions of work of the professionals employed in these services. As Dimmock (1979) noted,*"It was the government's desire to establish an ordered machinery for collective bargaining, as a corollary to the introduction of the NHS, that emphasised the ambiguities of the role of the British Medical Association. The continuous rule-making processes which constitute collective bargaining are different in kind from the spasmodic ad hoc negotiations that tended to characterise the BMA's previous relations with the state."* (Bosanquet (1979) p 208)

The pay and conditions of work which state employing authorities offer are negotiated and decided at a national level through a variety of different structures. These structures indirectly influence both the division of labour by setting minimum qualifications for employment, and career and management arrangements by establishing grade definitions based on specialist experience or management responsibilities.

These institutional structures and the increase in professional union activities have sometimes produced competition between professional associations and multiple-occupation trade unions. In national negotiations over pay and conditions of work, some professions are represented solely by their association(s), which have recognised trade union status and have established local steward systems (e.g. medicine and physiotherapy). Some professions are represented by one or more professional associations, and by one or more unions (e.g. nursing). Some professions are represented solely by a multiple-occupation trade union, while the professional association is not a recognised trade union (e.g. clinical psychology).

The following describes the structures for nursing, medicine, physiotherapy and clinical psychology. The evidence from the UK refines Friedson's proposition. None of these professions "controls" their pay and conditions of work. Each influences decisions about pay made by the state at the national level in different ways, and through different mechanisms.

Medicine and Nursing

When the NHS was created in 1948, medical and nursing professional associations represented their members in negotiations with employers (Regional Hospital Boards) and the state (Ministry of Health) on Whitley Councils established for each of these occupations (Levitt (1976), Dyson and Spary (1979), Parry and Parry (1976)). The medical profession felt that this structure and the decisions which were reached were unsatisfactory. Stevens described the profession, in 1951, as viewing itself as being,"tied to a politically dependent service", and that,*The Ministry of Health as the employer and source of income could not by itself commit government funds in addition to those already granted for the NHS by the Treasury."*(Stevens (1966) p. 130).

After a long and complex series of political manoeuvres (Parry & Parry (1976) pp 218-222, and Stevens (1966)) involving a Royal Commission, doctors were removed from the system of direct negotiation between their representatives and health departments on their Whitley Council. In 1963 a permanent independent review body was set up for doctors and dentists to, "advise the Prime Minister on the remuneration of doctors and dentists taking any part in the NHS." This review body based its recommendations on evidence from doctor's representatives, from the DHSS, and on changes in cost of living, state of recruitment and comparisons with other professions.

The evidence is that neither the state or the occupation "controls" the pay and conditions of service of members of the medical profession. An independent review body is a particular type of structure, which arrives at recommendations through a complex process. As Stevens (1966) remarked, *"The creation of review machinery could be seen as a successful attempt by the medical profession to overcome some of the penalties of being state servants ...... the Review Body removed from the Ministry's jurisdiction the vital but unpleasant decisions regarding the level of professional remuneration for the most powerful and important group in the health service."* (p 137).

The profession does, however, entirely control a the state fiananced merit award system which makes awards for contributions to medical knowledge and practice. ("National statistics" reported by the Guardian newspaper (17/2/88) showed that in 1987 one consultant in three (total numbers 6,500) held an award worth between £5,790 to £29,550, and that two-thirds of consultants retired with such an award).

Nurses were represented by their professional associations in direct negotiations with employers and the state in the Nurses and Midwifes Whitley Council. In response to widespread dissatisfaction and the threat of strike action, an independent review body was created on 1982, but members of the occupation are suspicious about state influence in the body, and the status of its "recommendations".

In the cases of both the doctors' and nurses' review bodies the government ultimately determines the finance available for pay settlements, which in turn is influenced by public expenditure policies. Frequently District Health Authorities are not provided with additional funds to meet the pay awards which are decided.

Physiotherapy

The way in which pay and conditions for physiotherapists in the NHS are decided is different. Physiotherapists were represented by their professional association, together with other therapy professions, on a "Professional and Technical" Whitley Council. The influence of the professional association over its members' pay, grade definitions and conditions of work is thus limited by the requirement that this Council reaches settlements agreeable to a number of occupations. This is similar for the other therapy professions.

Clinical Psychology

In the case of clinical psychology the profession's influence is weaker, not only because of the structure of a multi-occupational Whitley Council, but also because it is represented by a multi-occupational union: previously The Association of Scientific, Technical and Managerial Staff (ASTMS), now the Manufacturing Science and Finance Union(MSF).

The professional association (not a registered trade union) has little influence over pay, grade definitions and conditions of work. As with physiotherapists, union representatives aimed to negotiate the best short-term settlements, and used grade definitions as bargaining counters in their strategies.

The result is that employing authorities are constrained in the descriptions of the posts they can offer by the wording of grade definitions, and the "career structure" of the profession is built on a series of definitions negotiated for short-term expediencies (BPS, DCP Newsletter correspondence (1981-1983)). It is of note that clinical psychology is one of the few professions, apart from the medical profession, which has arrangements for awarding pay on purely professional criteria in its top grade award and assessment procedure.

Thus in the UK where the state is the main employer, none of the therapy professions or medicine "controls pay and conditions of work" (Freidson (1970)). Each exerts different degrees and forms of influence through structures and mechanisms at a national level. Decisions made at this level, however, constrain the types of employment and levels of pay which employing authorities offer, and determine career structures within the occupation. The decisions are also affected by government public expenditure policies.

In short, the state decides pay and, influences a variety of aspects of the occupation through its role as employer. In this instance the institutions and structures at the national level clearly provide for control of occupations by the state, rather than for control by occupations of pay and conditions of work.

Central control over pay is not only of significance in setting general levels of pay and differentials, but also in deciding grade definitions. Grade definitions affect the career structure of the profession and can have a profound long-term influence (chapter 10). Of particular significance are high-level clinical practitioner posts which provide opportunities for career progression within clinical practice. Pay flexibility introduced by the 1990 reforms (chapter 4) will take some time to have an effect.

A general concern of professions is that organisations frequently reward management roles more highly than practitioner roles, and experienced practitioners are drawn into management to increase their pay, and are "lost to the profession" (Øvretveit et al(1982)). Each of the therapy professions tried to establish practitioner grades to provide a clinical career structure, with varying success. Central determination of these grade definitions and pay levels is a slow process, and in effect provides central government with control over the long-term shape and nature of the profession.

The Nature of Occupational Control over Practice and Training

How much control, then, do professions have over fields of work? Do they operate a state-supported closed shop? The following shows that at the national level there are a variety of structures and rules for regulating training and the practice of different professions. Until recently there was no state support for regulating clinical psychology, and the type of regulation which now exists (by "charter") is different to that for other therapy professions.

Medicine and other therapy professions have a complex involvement with the state in establishing and administering state regulatory structures and rules. Often state regulation is exercised through the rules and structures of professional associations, or by involving members in state structures. The following describes the exact details and mechanisms of these regualtory structures.

First the different types of state regulation of practice: The strongest type is that of making the practice of certain activities by the unregistered a criminal offence ("functional prohibition"). For this to happen, which produces a form of state-authorised monopoly, an unambiguous definition of the activity is necessary. The difficulties of doing this are illustrated in the case of psychotherapy (see the Foster report (1971) and the Seighart report (1978)).

To prohibit certain activities, however, is not to prohibit others from carrying out other activities commonly undertaken by the profession, so even the strongest form of regulation does not establish a pure monopoly. The second type of state regulation is to make it an offence for the unregistered to represent themselves as a registered practitioner, usually through a "protected title".

The following describes the type of state regulation of two of the six therapy professions of this study and compares these with medicine.

Doctors

The Medical Act of 1958 established the current General Medical Council (GMC) to set up a register. (This Act has been amended by subsequent Medical Acts). The GMC has the usual functions of a statutory registration authority: a) keeping and admitting to the register, b) disciplining for "unprofessional conduct" by removal, and, c) setting qualifications for admission.

The exact form of regulation was established in a section of the Act (almost unchanged since 1858) which makes it an offence for an unregistered person to "wilfully and falsely" represent themselves as registered. The offence is not that of practising medicine without being registered, but of assuming a name or a title which implies registration. [1]

There is no "functional closure" of the profession, but the regulation is stronger than "protected title" because of the following restrictions: non-registered practitioners may not charge for "medical or surgical advice" but may do so for treatment which does not constitute "an operation"; non-registered practitioners may not hold a "public medical appointment"; only registered doctors may prescribe "restricted drugs"; only registered doctors may sign various "certificates".

Professions Supplementary to Medicine

---

[1]Physicians did at one time establish a monopoly of practice through the licensure of practitioners in a Royal Charter in 1518. Power was given to the Physicians' Guild (chartered as the Royal College of Physicians) to try, imprison, and/or fine those who infringed the rights granted in the Charter (Malherbe (1979)) However, these powers were limited after the Bonham case in 1610, where Bonham claimed damages against the College for false imprisonment. This established the principle that an association itself did not have the power to infringe the rights of individuals in law, and laid the basis for, and revealed the need for, public control of licensure. Subsequently the powers of occupational associations were limited, although, as was shown above, members of the occupation were usually the majority in the special councils, which were set up by the state to regulate the occupation.

The "Professions Supplementary to Medicine Act of 1960" (PSM Act) established the Council for Professions Supplementary to Medicine, which provided the legal, financial and administrative framework for the eight Statutory Registration Boards for each of the following: Chiropodists, Dietitians, Medical Laboratory Technicians, Occupational Therapists, Orthoptists, Physiotherapists, Radiographers, and Remedial Gymnasts. The composition of the Council was 7 medical members on a Council of 21, and 6 medical members on the Physiotherapists Board of 17 members.

The Boards have the usual functions of, a) keeping and admitting to the register, b) setting qualifications for the register, and, c) disciplining. In the case of b), the Board decides the qualification, and it is the professional association whose qualification is assessed and which undertakes the work of monitoring standards and quality of training. (The majority of members of the Boards are also members of the main professional association).

The Act regulates the practice of the professions by making it an offence for those not registered to use the title "State-registered Physiotherapist", but there is no prohibition of practice by unregistered practitioners.

Regulation of registered physiotherapists also existed through codes of conduct. These codes were originally laid down by the BMA when it set up a Board of Registration of Medical Auxiliaries in 1936. The codes were carried over into the state registration scheme of 1960 on the insistence of the medical profession. The codes state that:
a) A patient's illness should be diagnosed or treated solely on referral from, or while having direct access to, a doctor (except in emergencies);
b) Diagnosis and treatment should be limited to what the practitioner has been trained to do;
c) The practitioner should be prohibited from presenting themselves as someone who is able by experience or training to treat disease.

Infringement of this code (which is additional to "professional misconduct") is likely to bring a registered practitioner to the attention of the disciplinary committee of the Board. For further regulation of the professions covered by the PSM Act, it would be necessary to amend the Act. This has been attempted by chiropodists, who hoped to attain "functional closure", but the attempt failed because of the difficulty of providing an unambiguous definition of a chiropodist or of chiropody treatment.

Speech therapists were to be included under the Act, but opted-out on the grounds that they were a "free-standing" profession in their own right, as much related to education as to medicine - complementary, rather than supplementary, to medicine. This also explains why clinical psychology was not registered under the Act.

Clinical Psychology

Clinical psychologists do not have state registration, but recently established a professional charter. A condition of employment in the NHS, stipulated by Whitley Council regulations, is the possession of a qualification set by the professional association, which also regulates training. Unqualified persons can and do undertake private practice. Recently there was considerable debate about state registration, and an increasing political awareness within the profession about the advantages and disadvantages of state involvement (BPS correspondence and members' polling (1984/85)). A decision was made in 1987 to establish the title of "Chartered Psychologist" and a chartering council has been in operation since 1990.

5: EXTENT OF OCCUPATIONAL CONTROL AND AUTONOMY IN THE UK

The purpose of the above descriptions was to show the exact nature of regulation, the variety of types of control which exist, and differences between professions. How does this evidence extend or qualify Freidson's theory of occupational control?

Firstly, state registration is the only form of institutionalised control used in the UK which approaches "regulating" content of work, but none of the regulations and structures described actually defines content of work. Full "functional closure" is difficult because of the problems of unambiguously defining content, and none of the therapy professions or medicine hold a complete monopoly over an area of work.

In the UK, Freidson's statement that professions establish monopolies over work jurisdictions with state support is inaccurate: the state only regulates who may undertake certain activities by prohibiting untrained persons from performing these activities.

Secondly, state regulation provides for a variety of forms of occupational control. "Functional closure" is where an Act of Parliament makes it illegal for an unqualified person to carry out certain activities or a strategic aspect of work. None of the professions considered was or is governed by this form of regulation, although medicine has acquired sole rights to perform operations, prescribe drugs and to sign various certificates. Acts usually only provided for "protected title", which make it illegal for an unqualified person to represent themselves as registered.

Thus an Act of Parliament "regulates" the practise of the profession by non-members only in the sense that it specifies the circumstances under which unregistered practitioners may be liable to prosecution in a court of law. State registration involves members of the occupation in the regulation of registered practitioners' professional conduct (disciplining for "unprofessional conduct"), setting qualifications for registration, and approving training establishments. This leaves the choice and balance of power with the consumer, or rather for those who can afford private services.

Clinical psychologists in state or private practice whose conduct is "unprofessional" or "negligent" may be subject to sanctions by their professional association. However, the sanctions of these associations do not have the force of those associations or councils empowered by regulatory Acts to discipline practitioners. Consequently the control of the occupation over its own members and of certain standards is less than that of medicine and the other therapy professions.

State regulation of qualifications and training establishments also takes different forms. In medicine, physiotherapy and other therapies the state registration councils undertake this work. In psychology the professional association is the only body to regulate training, with no state powers.

Finally, it could not be said that any of the occupations themselves exerted the forms of "control" described. In the regulatory councils each profession had different representation, and thus the degree to which "the profession" exercises control varies. The forms of state regulation described are not operated exclusively by each profession, but involve representatives of the state and usually members of other occupations.

6: SUMMARY & CONCLUSION

Freidson established an approach to the study of professions which emphasised the strategies and structures of professional control and organisation. Unlike previous studies he did not account for differences between professions and occupations in terms of characteristics of the work, or of the workers, or in terms of profession's statements. Rather he considered the way in which professions exercise power over both the practise of certain activities and the conditions of practice.

The approach directed attention to the ways in which individual professionals and their associations sought to control:

a) *other occupations*: to prevent encroachment on valued work activities, and to ensure that others carried out work which was necessary for members of the occupation to carry out their work;

b) *others who practise* the occupation: to protect the reputation of the occupation, and to regulate manpower supply to maximise job security, income and status;

c) *clients*: to ensure a stable market and demand for services, to make work easier by ensuring compliance, and to "protect" members from unwanted client demands, criticisms and complaints;

d) *employers*: to maximise income and gain the best terms and conditions of work, and to protect members from employers' demands.

There are four main weakness to Freidson's theory. Firstly, few empirical details of the mechanisms or structures of "control" are presented to substantiate the theory. Secondly, ambiguous definitions of "control" and "autonomy" make it difficult to confirm or refute the theory. Thirdly, the one example given of state support for "occupational control" was that of state registration, and this only provides for one limited form of "occupational control". Fourthly, state involvement enhances the "control" of the occupation over certain matters, but also provides for control by the state over aspects of the occupation. The conclusion of this chapter is that professional "control" and "autonomy" are not as absolute, or as strongly promoted or supported by the state as Freidson suggested.

To substantiate these criticisms, the chapter presented documentary evidence of details of the national structures and regulations applying to medicine and the therapy professions These details were also presented to develop and apply Freidson's analysis of professions in the context of the UK.

The details of these structures and regulations showed that no professions in the UK "controlled" the content, pay or conditions of their work, or were "truly autonomous". Further, that the division of labour between occupations in welfare services was not defined by state registration. In certain cases these regulations prevented non-qualified practitioners from undertaking certain activities, but they did not define work, and only indirectly structured a division of labour.

A description of the structures showed that "occupational control" in the UK at the national level is a subtle and complex phenomenon exercised in a variety of ways through different structures and regulations. Occupational associations alone do not have powers to prevent the practice of certain activities nor the use of particular titles.   Their powers of "control" are through convincing clients and employers that membership is an assurance of quality and standards, and through setting qualifications and accrediting training programmes.

The requirement of membership produces larger associations, which in turn are able to exercise greater influence over employers, members and non-members. "Medical Dominance" at the national level is mainly through the profession influencing the manner in which state regulations of other professions were established (Larkin (1982)).

State regulation of an occupation usually provides the occupation with control over the use of a title (state registration "protected title"); over disciplining for unprofessional conduct or negligence (loss of title); over defining and assessing qualifications for the title, and over training schools. Direct control (i.e. "protected function") is hampered by the political and technical difficulties of defining the work of the occupation. Control is thus of initial entry and of misconduct only.

Occupations exercise only indirect institutionalised control of the practice of the occupation through regulating training and education. Over a longer term, this defines the work of the profession and its place in the division of labour by equipping practitioners with skills and knowledge which were thought to be necessary to practise the occupation. Employers are thus indirectly limited in this way by the judgments of the profession as to the work which its members should undertake.

The main conclusions of the chapter are thus,
1) State regulation through licensing does not assure professional autonomy and a protected market in the absolute way in which Freidson suggested.
2) The state only acts to regulate in this way when parliament is persuaded that practice by unqualified or incompetent practitioners is a danger to the public.
3) Professional influence at the national level is complex and indirect - mostly through the professional association influencing training and qualification requirements. (Only clear negligence, not incompetence, would result in removal from the register).

Evidence of the actual structures and processes of state regulation in the UK does not support Freidson's theory that autonomy is upheld by state licensing arrangements,or that these structures institutionalise medical dominance. If these structures do not provide professions with the control which Freidson suggested, how then is it possible to account for the division of labour which undoubtedly exists in, for example, a hospital? How is it possible to account for differences in the autonomy of practitioners in each profession?

The next chapter turns from national organisation to local employment organisation. It proposes that it is profession-managers and practitioners who determine the content of work and a division of labour, not state regulation. That it is the management structures and processes established by employing authorities which institutionalise professional autonomy and control in the UK, and which has a greater influence over the nature of each profession than any other factor.

Chapter 3: THERAPY SERVICE ORGANISATION IN THE NHS, 1968-1990

'Lack of knowledge about the consequences of organisational change resulting from restructuring and exclusion from a strategic influence in the process of change makes allied health professions vulnerable to a substantial reversal of both power and prospects'
Boyce (1991)

1: INTRODUCTION

Organisation affects client care, work satisfaction and the long-term shape of a profession. There is much to learn about how it does so from the NHS reorganisations of the last 20 years.

To further explore professional autonomy in the therapy professions, this chapter considers professional organisation at the local level. It presents research into the NHS management structures of two therapy professions and summarises the changes in autonomy which have taken place since 1968. In so doing it also provides a context for discussing, in the rest of the book, the consequences of the 1990 NHS reforms and provider restructurings for the future of the therapy professions.

2: PUBLIC SERVICE REORGANISATIONS,1968-1990

The research below shows that changes in NHS organisation before 1990 had a profound effect on the therapy professions. Since the beginning of the 1980s the NHS has been in a state of continual change, and the rate of change will increase with more frequent organisational restructurings in the 1990s. Therapy professions have had to respond in different ways to maintain or advance their interests, or face being ignored or submerged by the changes. Before 1990 the changes with the biggest impact were the 1974 and 1982 reorganisations and the 1985 introduction of general management.

1972-74: NHS Unified Structure & Tiers of "Consensus Management Teams"

The 1974 NHS reorganisation created 14 Regional Health Authorities, and Area Health Authorities, and they drew together previously separately-managed services (DHSS (1974) HRC(74)35). This reorganisation introduced the concept of "functional" or "profession-management", with professions headed by area heads of services, as well as multidisciplinary management and planning teams ("Grey Book" (1972)).

1980-82 District Health Authorities and Units of Management

The two main aims of the 1980-82 NHS reorganisation were to make services more responsive to patients' needs, and to speed up decision-making at local levels (DHSS (HC(80)8)). The Area Health Authorities created in the 1974 NHS reorganisation were replaced by smaller District Health Authorities (DHA's) covering populations ranging from 87,000 to 700,000. DHA's drew together related services in Units of Management ("Units"), which were managed by multidisciplinary Unit Management Teams. The reorganisation emphasised maximum delegation of authority by DHA's to Units, with no intervening levels of management.

1983-85 General Management

A government-commissioned management inquiry (The "Griffiths Report" (1983)) supported the aims of the 1980-82 reorganisation, but argued that team-decision making hampered their realisation and diffused accountablity. It recommended General Managers at Regional, District, and Unit levels to be accountable for running the service, advised and assisted by other officers and teams.

Most of the recommendations were adopted in a 1984 government circular (DHSS HC(84)13), which called upon RHA's and DHA's to create General Management posts, and to review the need for District "functional" or "profession-managers" and District-managed services. The circular proposed that DHA's develop management budgets and hold managers accountable for their performance against agreed objectives.

3: RESEARCH INTO THERAPY ORGANISATION 1968-1990

These reorganisations were times where professions at the national and at local levels manoeuvred to maintain and defend their interests, as well as those of their clients/patients. They were times where structures unfroze, where power was applied, and where deals were done before structures were set for the next few years. The following considers research into the organisation of therapy services between 1968 and 1990. The assumption is that we can learn about the nature of professional autonomy and about professions by looking at how they are organised. Our initial questions are, exactly what effect do decisions about therapy organisation in the NHS have on the the autonomy of these professions, and on their size, shape and nature?

The following considers the organisation of two of the therapy professions in detail: physiotherapy and clinical psychology. The reasons for this choice is that research data over 22 years is available about the organisation of these professions, and that most of the author's research was conducted with these professions. Together, their organisation and the changes are broadly similar to those for the other four therapy professions. The research method used to gather most of the data reported below is described in Appendix 1. The main research undertaken is listed in Appendix 2.

Format for Presenting the Research

The following first presents relevant statements from government and other reports which influenced decisions about therapy management structures at local levels. These are relevant to testing Freidson's proposition that professional autonomy is supported by the state.

This is followed by field research into organisation between 1968 and 1980, mostly undertaken by researchers using the same conceptual framework and research method as the author, and then by the author's research since 1980.

Research into three areas is reported: 1) the overall management structure of each profession within an employing authority; 2) the role and institutionalised authority of head profession-managers, and 3) the autonomy of practitioners after qualifying, and after 20 years of practice.

The focus is institutionalised structures, authority and autonomy (roles, relationships and rules which are explicit, agreed and instituted by employing authorities). This data gives evidence of the exact nature of different type of institutionalised autonomy, and makes it possible to trace changes in autonomy.

4: SUMMARY OF RESEARCH INTO THE ORGANISATION OF PHYSIOTHERAPY 1968-1990

Government Reports and Recommendations
Management Structures

The recommendations to the then new Area Health Authorities in the early stages of the 1974 NHS reorganisation were that physiotherapists be, "accountable to a consultant in physical medicine or may be a direct appointee of the AHA" (Grey Book (1972) p.84)). It also proposed that staff (of any profession) with related skills could be grouped in departments under a head of department, e.g. a therapy department.

These recommendations did not constitute government support for a District profession-management structure headed by a profession-manager, but suggested a number of possibilities. Previously a DHSS working party report, published in 1973, recommended that,"*Members of remedial professions should coordinate, organise and administer their own services.*" (McMillan Report (1973)).

Interim official guidance from the DHSS in 1974 proposed that AHAs should make arrangements for, "*The remedial services to be organised on a District basis*" (DHSS (1974) HSC(IS)101), and that AHAs should designate a senior physiotherapist to advise DMTs and to ensure that professional standards were maintained.

A later DHSS report (The Winterton/Perry Report (1977)) recommended extending the designated district physiotherapist role which had emerged to manage all NHS physiotherapy services in a District. Most of the recommendations of the report were issued as official guidance by the DHSS in 1979 (HC(79)19), and, by 1981 the Physiotherapy Journal reported that 115 out of 222 health Districts had appointed a full-managerial District Physiotherapist.

However, in 1984 the Griffiths' reorganisation circular (HC(84)13) called for a review of all "functional" District head of service posts. A number of official DHA statements of structure (e.g. Northern Region Documents 1985) either abolished the role, or reduced it's authority. Many changed the role from a full-manager of all physiotherapists in the District to an "advisory" role, typically accountable to a Unit General Manager (UGM) for "service provision", and to a District General Manager (DGM) for "professional advice".

Since 1974, then, government recommendations changed from proposing, 1) medical consultant management of physiotherapists (with the option of direct appointment of a physiotherapist-manager) (1972), to, 2) arrangements for District organisation of physiotherapists with an advisory profession-leader (1974), to, 3) a full-manager head of profession with a separate physiotherapy management structure (1979). Recommendations in 1984, although not referring specifically to physiotherapy, reduced the number of District posts and District functional organisation. Thus, over the years, government recommendations supported an increase, and then a decrease in institutionalised management autonomy and control.

Practitioner Autonomy

There were also government recommendations which affected practitioner autonomy. In 1962, following concern about the standard of physiotherapy treatments, the then Ministry of Health issued guidance for doctors,"*Doctors should prescribe physiotherapy with the same precise therapeutic indications in mind as they have when prescribing drugs .....All too often therapy is prescribed in general terms and the important details such as frequency and progression of treatment, as well as arranging for attendance at medical review clinics, are left to the discretion of the physiotherapists.*" (HM(62)18)

This statement effectively institutionalised medical control over physiotherapist practitioner autonomy. However, in 1977, in response to various changes, the DHSS issued guidelines which recognised a degree of independence for physiotherapists, "*In referring patients to therapists, doctors should give the diagnosis, where possible, and set out the aims of treatment with a note of limitations and contra-indications to a particular form of treatment.*" (HC (77) 33)

Of all the therapy professions, government recommendations about the organisation of physiotherapists by employing authorities were the most numerous, possibly because of the relatively large numbers employed and because of the close relationship to medicine. The recommendations have also been the most specific, and were widely used by members of the profession to advance their claims to autonomy within Districts.

Field Research 1968-1980

Two programmes of social-analytic field research into physiotherapy organisation were undertaken between 1968 and 1980 by Rowbottom et al (1974), and then by Jaques and Tolliday (1978). The research provides evidence of significant changes, and of variations in management and practitioner autonomy over this period, which were summarised in Øvretveit (1985).

Rowbottom (1973) reported that,"*Work in a number of field projects, confirmed in conference discussions, has suggested that the following large groups of paramedical staff are in most situations organised hierarchically under the management of medical consultants.*"

He listed a superintendent physiotherapist and head occupational therapist as the "intermediate" management level "below consultants in physical-medicine". The main field work reported by Rowbottom was a study of a physical medicine department in a teaching hospital. Rowbottom (1973) represented the structure thus (Fig. 3.1):

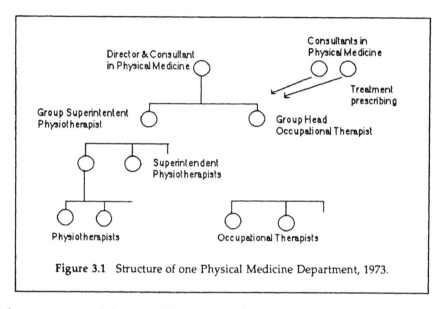

Figure 3.1 Structure of one Physical Medicine Department, 1973.

Robottom reported that one of the three consultants in physical medicine (the Director) was accountable for,*"the provision of all physiotherapy and occupational physiotherapy services to meet the prescribed requirements of medical staff of the hospitals of the group"*, and that all the physiotherapists (about 46) and occupational therapists (about 15) were seen as accountable to him.*"All three consultants would have the right to prescribe treatment in respect of their own patients to be carried out by physiotherapists and occupational therapists, as indeed would other consultants in respect of theirs."* (pp. 108-109).

This is the only detailed study of a physiotherapy or occupational therapy management structure at that time. The only evidence provided to verify the above statement that this structure existed at other sites in the country is "confirmation" in unspecified conference discussions. The following alternative was also reported,*"Where for example there is no appointed Director of physical medicine, then the physiotherapists and occupational therapists seem extantly not to gravitate to another consultant, but to stand on their own, or be regarded as subordinate to another administrator"* (Rowbottom (1973)).

The features of the first structure which give us evidence of management and practitioner autonomy at the time are:
1.Physiotherapists were grouped together with occupational therapists for management purposes;
2.The management structure was headed by a member of another profession - the medical profession;
3. The overall structure was an hierarchical managerial structure;
4. Individual practitioners were managerially accountable to a superintendent, and ultimately the consultant, and subject to the "treatment-

prescribing authority" of consultants, who were authorised to override their treatment decisions if necessary.

The second set of findings were reported by Jaques and Tolliday (1978). They presented the results of research,"*carried out during the past ten years by members of HSORU in field-work projects and in research conferences. Some hundreds of individuals have been seen, many of them on repeated occasions over many years, as new organisational patterns were tested.*"(p 157).

No further methodological details were given, but models of organisation for different departments were described, some of which were successfully implemented in two London health Districts (HSORU Doc. 1642).

One model described a department of ten qualified physiotherapists managed by one superintendent, with full-managerial authority, and who was a direct appointee of the health authority. This "profession-manager" was described as being subject to the "monitoring and coordinating" authority of both the medical top-level district community physician over matters of "service provision", and the district administrator over "administrative standards". A variation of this model was described of two or more department heads in a district, one acting as a district therapist with "coordinating" authority in relation to other heads. A second model was described as,"*suitable for some few situations in very large Districts, with a large complement of therapists in many departments (for example, one District with some 80 qualified therapists in twelve departments and a training school with nearly 200 staff).*"

In this model a district therapist would have managerial authority over heads of departments. In each model medical consultants were not described as having managerial authority in relation to practitioners, but their authority was unspecified, "*The research Unit has not yet succeeded in defining clearly the differences between prescribing and referral. It is recognised that to use the term "prescribing" for all referrals for treatment from a doctor to a physiotherapist has too narrow a feel.*"

No evidence is provided of the number of departments which were organised according to each model. However, Jaques and Tolliday's report clearly shows marked changes in managerial and practitioner autonomy compared to the structures reported earlier by Rowbottom (1973). Although there is no documented evidence, it is likely that the changes were made in response to the recommendations made by central government for self-management by the profession.

The models described physiotherapists as being grouped together in departments separate from occupational therapists, and without medical consultants with full-managerial authority over staff. In terms of practitioner autonomy, Jaques and Tolliday's (1978) model suggests general acceptance that physiotherapy managers had managerial authority in relation to practitioners, and that consultants no longer carried "treatment-prescribing authority" with rights to override the practitioner's treatment decisions.

The only other detailed research evidence available at that time is from a study by Alaszewski (1977) of management arrangements for the remedial professions in two health Districts, based on interviews with one District Administrator and three heads of department, and "internal memorandum on an experimental management structure". The report describes a "DHSS-encouraged" attempt to create an integrated therapy management structure, and reports the failure of the experiment and a structure with a superintendent physiotherapist as managerial head of department.

Summary of Research Findings for Physiotherapy 1980-88

Research by the author and a colleague using the same method as the above authors found that managerial structures had existed in the past, usually with consultants in physical medicine as managers of therapy departments (Øvretveit (1985), details of research in Appendices 2 and 3). In most sites, managerial autonomy had developed as a result of superintendent Physiotherapists taking-over managerial duties with the agreement of consultants. The one exception was at a site where a consultant was the main user of the department, where the consultant was involved in staff appointments, and full managerial authority was not exercised by the superintendent.

The research found that between 1980 and 1982 physiotherapists employed by health authorities were grouped together for management purposes in one or more departments, headed by superintendent physiotherapists. In most Districts there was more than one physiotherapy department, each headed by a superintendent. Where district physiotherapist roles existed the authority of the role over other superintendents varied from fully-managerial (e.g. Nottingham, Mansfield) to coordinating, or "advisory".

The responsibilities and authority of district physiotherapists varied, largely depending on the number of physiotherapists in the District (the range covered Bassetlaw DHA which employed 11 physiotherapists, to Nottingham DHA which employed approximately 110 staff). Most district physiotherapists were accountable to district medical officers (DMOs) and some to district administrators.

These findings were corroborated in a questionnaire survey of all head physiotherapists in the country, undertaken by Henly and Harrison (1981).

The survey showed that most heads were accountable to DMOs (who were members of the DMT); could present papers at DMT meetings, and had right of access to employing authority meetings, and some received DMT agendas and minutes.

The author's research into management structures between 1983-84 involved four workshops with district and superintendent physiotherapists, and drew on other workshops and research into the 1982 reorganisation and 1984 Griffiths' reorganisation. The general conclusion from this work was that where district physiotherapist roles had been created, Unit management had reduced their authority to switch staff between Units. District physiotherapists in workshops in the mid-1980s reported structures changing their accountability from District-level officers to unit general managers (UGMs), and requiring the agreement of UGMs to changes in staff allocation and to the funding of new posts.

Physiotherapy Management Autonomy-Summary

Up until 1982, approximately half of the health authorities in England had established forms of profession-management for physiotherapy, with district head profession-managers. The advent of Unit management in the 1982 reorganisation, and unit and district general managers after 1985 reversed the trend. Where district heads were retained, their authority over budgets and staff was reduced.

All the evidence suggests that by 1986 there were few single head profession-managers with exclusive managerial authority in relation to all physiotherapists employed by a health authority. Sometimes a profession "leader" monitored standards, but the highest level profession-managers were within Units of management and were managerially-accountable to general managers for everything apart from individual case-work. A common management structure was one or more profession-managers, managing practitioners (most with "Case Autonomy", discussed in chapter 6), and themselves managerially accountable to Unit managers for all work apart from case-work.

Practitioner Autonomy

In early 1980 practitioners were managed by superintendent physiotherapists, but the authority of superintendents varied. The examples discussed in the field project workshops in 1982-84 established that managers commonly refused to question or override experienced practitioners' case decisions, or to instruct them on how to provide a particular treatment.

However, managers did commonly assign and review administrative and non-case-work duties and tasks, which caused serious and widespread problems of high workload because practitioners were unable to negotiate case-work reductions with consultants, and managers were also reluctant to do so, refusing to allow practitioners to start waiting lists (report to CSP (1982)C.3300).

Practitioners in the eight Regional workshops in 1983 agreed that their autonomy could be characterised by the concept of "Case Autonomy", described in Chapter 6, and subsequent workshops did not refute this description. However, the research established that experienced practitioners had not acquired the degree of autonomy characterised in chapter 6 as "Practice Autonomy", which was found for experienced psychologists.

The author's field research did not involve specifying doctor's referral authority at particular field sites, and no other evidence is available of their institutionalised authority in different settings. However, field research provided a number of examples of common practice. Workshop participants reported that hospital doctors usually referred patients with a "physiotherapy please" note, or left it to the physiotherapist assigned to the ward to decide which patients to treat. No examples were reported of detailed prescriptions, or of doctors requiring physiotherapists to stop treatments against therapists' own judgments. The details of the research are presented in Appendices 2 and 3.

5: SUMMARY OF RESEARCH INTO THE ORGANISATION OF PSYCHOLOGY 1968-1990

Government Reports & Other Recommendations

No government circulars or detailed recommendations were issued about psychology organisation, possibly because of the small numbers employed (439 in 1971 (DHSS (1978)); 995 in 1980 ((BPS (1980)); 1105 in 1981 (Watts (1985)); and 1419 in 1985 (Scrivens and Charlton (1985), 1734 posts-14% vacancy rate). In devising their management arrangements, employing authorities were guided by references in general circulars to "paramedical" or "scientific and technical" staff, and by the Trethowen Report (1977) on clinical psychology. The Trethowen Report recommended that psychologists be grouped and managed within Area Departments of Psychology, with a Head of Department,"...*administratively responsible to the Area Team of Officers and would need to cooperate with the Area Medical Officer in the coordination of services within the Area*" (para. 5.3.6).

The Report also recommended that specialities within the department be headed by Principal Grade Psychologists, and that,*"We would not expect those in the grade of Principal Psychologist to have to account to the head of department on matters of purely professional judgment. Below Principal level, however, we consider that all clinical psychologists should be directly accountable to a professional superior."*

In 1981 the professional association issued guidance to its members proposing that, *"Ideally the head of the District department should be accountable to the authority, reporting to it through one of the management team, who would need to carry some general coordinative and monitoring functions on behalf of the authority in relation to other heads of department."*
(BPS, May (1981) p 8.1)

Survey research (Scrivens & Charlton(1985)) found that the average District employed 8 psychologists (range 1-40 ; only one of the 189 Districts did not employ a psychologist). There was a "District service" in 158 Districts, (with a psychologist "designated as District psychologist" in 138 Districts), and 63 of these services were, "organised and budgeted at a District level", 95 organised at a Unit level.

Field Research 1968-1980

Research evidence of structures which existed before 1974 is scarce. Some psychologists interviewed by the author reported that psychologists in mental illness and mental handicap hospitals were often managed by consultant psychiatrists. The only detailed research on structures which existed prior to 1974 was an interview with one psychologist reported by Rowbottom (1973) who,*"...argued that they are indeed independent therapists, with their own patients, received by referral from consultants or general practitioners, and as such are not eligible to be managed, or instructed on clinical matters by consultants or anyone else."* (p 115).

Rowbottom's discussion suggests that psychologists were members of a group of "paramedical" staff, which were different from the group which included physiotherapists, and were,*"not normally subordinate to consultants, though they may or may not be subject (in contrast) to their direction on treatment or services required."*

However, later discussions in the North West Thames Project in 1973 established that the Senior Clinical Psychologist in the group was,"accountable for her work to the Consultant Psychiatrist", and "an immediate subordinate" of the Consultant, as well as being subject to the "monitoring and Coordinating authority" of the hospital secretary (Doc. 1376).

A study of the Ealing Psychology Department in 1976 clarified changes in the authority of consultants in relation to psychologists. The research documentation shows that consultants at this site longer managed psychologists, and that their prescriptive authority had changed,"*The psychologist referred to decides the appropriateness of the referral, the best way to handle the problem and how to report to the referrer.*" (Doc. 1945).

These findings were found to be representative of other departments in the Region at a workshop held during 1976. Two workshops held by Rowbottom in 1978 and 1979 (documented in Kat,B.(11/5/78), and in Doc. 3044) showed that group management in Area departments existed in a number of Areas, and no examples of prescriptive authority relations were reported.

Summary of Field Research into Psychology Organisation 1980-1990

Management Autonomy

The following summarises the author's research, which is presented in more detail in Appendix 3. District psychologists and heads of departments raised a number of issues at workshops led by the author during the mid-1980s (listed Appendix 2). A major problem was how to change psychologist's sessions to provide a more balanced overall service (i.e. one where psychologists were meeting requests and needs from parts of the District where they did not already work). They reported three factors which limited their ability to provide a more comprehensive service, and which provide evidence of the extent of psychologists' "management autonomy" and control.

First, heads were uncertain about who had authority to decide new posts and how they should "present the case" for new posts. Because they were rarely permanent members of Unit and District Management Groups, their awareness of available funds, and their ability to put and argue their case, were limited. It was common that heads were required to put proposals to Unit Management Groups to incorporate in their plans, rather than direct to District management. Thus head's ability to gain new posts for the profession was limited by their not being included in the main management bodies.

Second, the head's ability to transfer psychologists' sessions or use of time between Units was constrained by the requirement that significant changes could be vetoed by the Units concerned, and that funding arrangements had to be agreed. Previously the influence of Unit management had not been as formalised or extreme. Staff or session transfers were carried out without notifying Units, and psychologists had moved between Units without difficulties.

A third factor was head's desire to get individual psychologists to agree to changes, and often the agreement of a committee or department meeting. No instances were cited of a District psychologist enforcing disciplinary procedures to carry through a change, although in principle District psychologists had this authority, and would have been supported by higher management. Thus, both the head psychologist's and other psychologist's understanding of professional autonomy limited the head's management autonomy. Heads did not exercise structural and institutionalised authority, but relied on persuasion and group pressure in departmental meetings to influence psychologists to change their practices.

Where this was unsuccessful, heads did not pursue the matter and psychologists were not prevented from following their own interests and priorities. In situations where the main management structure was a departmental group meetings (e.g. Bexley (1980)), meetings often failed to consider or agree the specialty designation or siting of new posts, and usually failed to agree changes to sessions within the group. The research revealed only three departments (Birmingham, Essex, Macclesfield) with a clear policy for renegotiating significant changes in working practices within the group. Thus the type of "service self-management" in psychology failed to limit practitioner autonomy, and almost always resulted in an imbalanced overall service.

However, towards the end of the 1980s there were indications that three developments could limit practitioner autonomy. The first was the costing of psychologists' sessions provided to Units, and the availability of this information to heads and UGMs. This made it necessary to negotiate changes with UGMs, the latter representing one limit to management and practitioner autonomy - most UGMs could veto such changes.

The second development was the requirement routinely to collect management information on each psychologist's activities, which also made it possible to question individual psychologist's use of time. The third was the move to institute regular performance appraisals of individuals and services. These three developments are systems for increasing practitioner accountability and impinge on their autonomy. Should heads or UGMs wish to exercise structural authority to limit or direct practitioners, the systems provide information which makes it easier for them to do so.

A summary of findings about management autonomy is that psychologists in NHS Districts were either grouped together in one department, or in a number of specialty departments, each headed by a psychologist. Many were titled "District Psychology Services" but the meaning of the term and the authority of the District psychologist varied.

Some Districts did not have a District service, but instead, a number of psychology departments, which were coordinated by a District Psychology Committee (e.g. Hampstead). In all cases, heads were accountable to UGMs, and UGMs could veto head's proposals for new posts or changes to sessions. This placed clear limits to psychologist's management autonomy because proposals had to be agreed at Unit level before agreement at District levels.

Practitioner Autonomy

There was conclusive evidence that senior grade psychologists had "Case Autonomy", "The right to make assessment and treatment decisions in casework without those decisions being scrutinised or overridden, unless negligence is suspected." (Øvretveit(1984)). It was less clear whether just-qualified psychologists had this autonomy, although most psychologists argued that they did. No examples were found in the research of instances where psychology managers overturned case decisions, although there were three examples of instances where psychiatrists did so. Staff performance appraisals did not examine individual case decisions.

The limits to practitioner autonomy were less clear and varied between departments. It was usually stated that psychologists were,"not accountable to managers for matters of purely professional judgment", but distinctions were made between judgments in casework and judgments about the type of service to be provided and about the balance between areas and fields of work. Management information about work activity was increasingly being used to question types and areas of work, and to set targets.

It was clear that most employment contract limits prevented psychologists from practising in other Districts, and, where there were job descriptions, some specified specialties or sites of work. Some psychology department policies had administrative procedures for travel or study leave, but none defined the type of work to be undertaken, sources of work and balance of activities between individual case, group work, teaching, consultancy, research, planning, etc.

The field studies and workshops found that psychologist's practitioner autonomy is defined by their head's authority to impose changes to their sessions and use of time. There were no "critical incidents" documented where higher management was required to support the head's authority, and the few times where heads have carried changes through they did so by gaining practitioners' agreement and without threatening or invoking disciplinary procedures.

There is considerable evidence that many senior and all principal grade psychologists had practice autonomy to, "decide the balance of activities and details of practice within a particular field, without those decisions being questioned or overridden unless policies or contract is infringed" (Øvretveit(1984)).

There is also evidence of a "personalised service" and client/practitioner choice, where clients are dealt with by one member of the department, who may choose not to take on a case, and each party may choose to terminate involvement if no progress is being made.

Profession-Management Autonomy

At the local level the degree of influence and control exercised by a profession depends on the nature of the management structure for the profession, and the role of the profession-head. "Profession-management" autonomy is determined by three main organisational factors:

(1) Size of Professional "Grouping"
The number of members of the profession within a professional grouping.

(2) Nature of Professional Grouping
Whether the grouping is, at one extreme,
(a) a "management division" made up only of members of the profession, each of whom is not subject to the authority of other professions outside the division,
(b) an "intermediate professional grouping", made up only of members of the profession who are subject to both the "managerial" authority of general managers, and "professional superiors", who have authority over "professional managers", or,
(c) a "professional interest group", made up of members of the profession, but each of whom is managed by staff who are not members of the profession (sometimes called a "specialty").

(3) Role and Authority of Professional Heads
The extent of management autonomy depends on
(a) whether the head is sole manager of members of the profession within the grouping,
(b) their authority in relation to other members of the profession employed by the organisation, and,
(c) their formal position within a Unit structure.

It is possible to define the extent of the "profession-management autonomy" of a profession within one organisation at a particular time by reference to these three factors. This makes it possible to compare the autonomy of different professions in different organisations, and at different times.

6: SUMMARY & CONCLUSIONS

What conclusions can be drawn from this research for understanding the autonomy of therapy professions up to 1990? Do these conclusions modify Freidson's theory of professional autonomy?

The research provides further evidence to support the criticisms of Freidson's theory made in the last chapter. Professional "control" and "autonomy" are not as absolute, or as strongly supported by the state in the particular ways which Freidson suggests. The research shows that,

1) In the UK, state employing authorities provide professions with different types of autonomy and control through their management arrangements,
2) There are differences between professions in their autonomy,
3) There have been changes over the last 25 years, notably a decline in the management and prescribing authority of the medical profession over therapy professions, and a replacement of top-level profession-management with general management.

The research presented in the last Chapter showed the institutional structures through which a profession exercises influence and control, at the national level: through a professional association and through structures for state regulation, training, and for negotiating pay and conditions.

Practitioner Autonomy

Practitioner autonomy is considered in more detail in chapter 6. The research found that it is determined by:
(1) The Limits to Discretion. The constraints, directives, and standards set at national, District, Unit and Division levels, which exclude certain activities, and require certain actions in specified circumstances.
(2) The Authority of Superiors. The authority of one or more superiors (managers and other staff) in relation to siting of work, task or case assignment and review, performance appraisal, and disciplinary authority.

The size and nature of therapy professions in the UK have been profoundly influenced by the way they are organised in NHS. The NHS was virtually a monopoly employer of therapists. Their total numbers were determined more by the influence of profession-managers and their ability to "create posts", than by demand for or supply of therapists. These managers also determined work jurisdictions and negotiated boundary disputes with other professions.

The way therapists are organised both reflects the local and national power of each professional group, and itself reinforces or diminishes their power. NHS reorganisations over the last 25 years first increased, and then decreased therapists autonomy. In the remaining chapters we consider the effects of the most recent 1990 NHS reorganisation.

Chapter 4: THE 1990 REFORMS & THERAPY SERVICES

'You mean every minute of our time has to be financed?'

Everyone at the meeting turned to the head therapist for an answer. She had just outlined the implications of the 1990 reforms.

'Well someone paid for our time before, its just that the money comes from a different place......and we have to, um..., 'sell' the service'.

There were some glum faces. Recent years had taken their toll on the District service and the group was demoralised. What if no one wanted to 'buy' the service? They also feared going back under medical control, in things called 'Directorates'. It was all very confusing.

'One thing I don't understand. We all have employment contracts with the health authority - they've already bought our services! What if we don't get enough contracts to pay for our time? The can't sack us can they? And if they can't, why should we bother with all this marketing stuff, we've got enough to do as it is, what with Helen off on maternity leave and.........'

Some of the group began to look more relaxed. Others were wondering if they would have to organise collections, like the nurses did last year. Everyone else looked even more confused. Finally there was a pause. They waited for their head to speak.

'Yes, well, strictly speaking I suppose they wouldn't sack anyone. We ought to check our conditions of notice though - they could give us notice and then offer us new contracts. But if we get stroppy, or ignore it all, we might get problems when the General Hospital becomes a Trust. You see, either the General will employ its own therapists, or it will buy-in from us. We've got to make it worth their while to buy from the District service....We've got some PR to do'.

Of that there was agreement, and then, thankfully, the tea came.

1: INTRODUCTION

The 1990 UK public service reforms made it possible to organise therapy services in many different ways, both within and outside of the NHS. The reforms followed ten years of gradual erosion of the autonomy which therapists had gained in the seventies. At first the reforms were viewed as another "threat" to beleaguered therapists and to public service values, but it became clear that the new public "markets" also opened up opportunities.

This chapter lays the basis for describing future therapy service organisation and management in the rest of the book. It considers the implications of the reforms and discusses the nature of the emerging UK public "markets".

2: THE 1990 REFORMS

The NHS and Community Care Act of 1990 gave the government legal powers to carry out most of the reforms proposed for NHS hospital and community services in, "Working for Patients" (DoH (1989a)), and for social services in, "Caring for People" (DoH (1989b)). These reforms followed those proposed for primary health care in, "Promoting Better Health" (DoH (1987)), which led to new contracts for family doctors and dentists in 1990, and preceded the 1991 proposals for health promotion (DoH (1991)). The following outlines the changes which affect therapy professions.

"Working for Patients" and Therapy Services

The reforms created new Regional Health Authorities (RHAs) to manage District Health Authorities (DHAs) and Family Health Service Authorities (FHSAs - for primary health care) in the Region. The new DHA's main role is to assess the needs of the population in the District for different health services, and to purchase health services from its own hospitals and community services and other providers to ensure that the health needs of it population are met. Some speculate that DHAs and FHSAs might merge.

The aim is to separate purchasing health care from providing it to enable purchasers to focus more clearly on needs and value for money, and less on problems of organising the "delivery" of health care. It also creates a "public market" for health care where providers compete for contracts, and where a greater diversity of providers is possible. The NHS review in 1988 considered giving citizens purchasing power through a voucher system, but this was rejected in favour of purchasing on behalf of citizens by a state District Authority, or a GP. The reforms bring the NHS closer to the Canadian rather than the US system.

The separation of purchasing and provision is not complete, not least because many hospitals and community health services are managed by the purchasing DHAs - these providers are referred to as "Directly Managed Units" or DMUs. To bring about further separation (and for other reasons) the government encouraged NHS hospitals and community services managed by a DHA to apply to become NHS-Trusts. NHS-Trusts are corporate entities that are still tied to the NHS by being managed directly by the Secretary of State. They have some independence to decide their organisational structure, employ staff, staff pay, retain surpluses, sell and buy land and buildings, and to borrow capital up to a set limit (DoH (1989c)).

The reforms led to providers being financed for different service through contracts with purchasers. Providers (ie mainly DMUs and NHS-Ts, but also private and voluntary organisations) compete for contracts, and their contract performance is monitored by purchasers. To begin with contracts were based on the number and source of referrals from GPs and others in the previous year. Referral-led purchasing is likely to continue, with DHA purchasers trying to influence GPs to refer to DHA-preferred services. Provider's financing and management and the highly regulated public "market" are discussed in more detail below.

The reforms also made it possible for larger general medical group practices (primary health care "family doctors") to become "fund-holding practices". In 1991 about 300 had chosen to do so, and were allocated a budget by their FHSA to buy certain hospital and community services for patients registered with the practice. Some of these budgets are used for therapy services. GPs can employ their own therapists part or full-time; they can buy from a private therapist; or they can contract a DMU or NHS-T based therapy service. In some cases part of NHS therapy budgets have been transferred to a fund-holding practice. The future debate is likely to be, not how many GPs will be fund-holders, but what proportion of the NHS budget they will gain from DHAs (and hence what portion of therapy budgets will be transferred to GPs). "Market" regulation takes many forms, two being DHA's influence over referrals by GPs (eg limits to extra-contractual referrals outside the District), and purchasing by fund-holding GPs.

Other NHS reforms of significance for the therapy professions are requirements for providers to demonstrate clinical audit and quality assurance processes, as well as Regional financing of training, pay flexibility, and flexibility to use helpers, aides, and technicians.

"Caring for People" and the Therapy Professions

Many of the reforms for local authorities and social services were similar to those for health services: purchaser-provider separation, contractual funding, encouragement for a wider range of services to give greater client choice, better management and value for money, and quality initiatives (DoH (1989b)). Implementation was slower and was affected by uncertainties about future local government organisation and financing.

In addition to local authorities being able to purchase therapy services, other changes of significance for therapists are Care (or Case) Management, and the transfer of social security "board and lodgings" payments to Local Authorities. The latter was scheduled for 1993 and gives local (and health) authorities an incentive to develop services to support people at home, rather than using private nursing and other homes where their housing fees are paid out of a separate social security budget. Therapists have an important role to play in such services, especially with demographic changes in the 1990s.

Care Management is a method for organising mostly social care for a person who needs services from a number of agencies. It was originally proposed in the Griffiths review of community care (Griffiths(1988)), and a variety of models exist for different client groups, some giving Care Managers limited purchasing powers (Øvretveit (1991)). Care managers may begin to purchase therapy services, especially where health and social services are jointly provided for a client group. With training, some therapists may be employed as Care Managers by either a local authority, a health authority, an NHS-T or a voluntary agency.

The changes with the biggest immediate effect on therapy services are NHS Unit restructuring, and financing through contracts. This process is accelerated in Units applying for trust status, and where mergers take place. Most restructurings also have in mind, or are for the purpose of, decentralising financial and management responsibilities and authority, especially when introducing resource management.

3: UNIT STRUCTURE

To examine the implications of these changes for therapy organisation the book uses the following convention and terms to represent Unit structure (Figures 4.1 & 4.2). For the purpose of this book a "Unit" means a both a Directly-Managed Unit (DMU) managed by a purchaser District Health Authority, as well as an NHS Hospital Trust (NHS-T). The term "Unit general manager" (UGM) will also be used to refer to a chief executive of an NHS hospital trust.

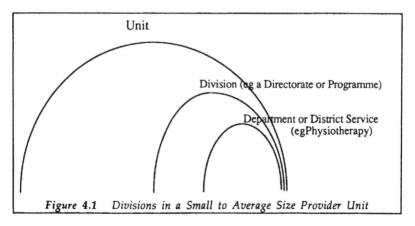

Unit

Division (eg a Directorate or Programme)

Department or District Service (egPhysiotherapy)

Figure 4.1   Divisions in a Small to Average Size Provider Unit

Figure 4.1 shows the main management Divisions within a Unit (ie a DMU or a NHS-T). In some Units these Divisions are mostly Clinical Directorates (eg surgery, orthopaedics), or Programmes (eg in a Mental Health Unit,

Programmes for the elderly, continuing care, rehabilitation, and acute services). Some Units use the term "programme" to describe a service which involves staff from a number of management Divisions. In this book the term "Programme" is used to describe a management Division, managed by an assistant general manager. "Division" is thus a general term describing the primary sub-Units of management within a Unit.

In larger Units, such as a single-Unit District, a Division may be as large as a Unit in a small District (Figure 4.2). These Divisions may encompass a number of Directorates (eg a Division of the Unit is an acute hospital, another Division a community service, etc.). The size of Divisions and Directorates (in terms of annual budget) is relevant to whether one or more therapy service can be a Division in their own right, a subject discussed in the next chapter.

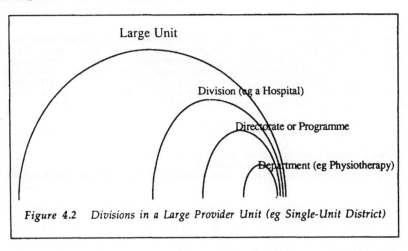

Figure 4.2   *Divisions in a Large Provider Unit (eg Single-Unit District)*

The influence of therapists in a Unit is affected by the number of therapists grouped together relative to other staff. The head of the group in a small unit is likely to be at a higher level in the structure than if they were in a large unit. If therapists form a combined department their collective influence is greater (one of the options considered in the next chapter).

In Units where the structure is not clear, or in flux, a clue to the future structure may be gained from how the Unit defines services for contracts agreed with District (or Area) or other purchasers. Market-orientated Units are restructuring to "package" services is a way which is attractive to purchasers, and which allows them to manage these services to deliver on contracts and compete. We will consider shortly whether therapy services are best organised for marketing or management purposes as part of other services, or as "stand alone" services.

The main "external" influence on Unit structure is how best to define and manage services for marketing and contracting purposes. The related but "internal" consideration is how best to group services for financial and personnel management purposes. Resource management aims to delegate responsibility and authority for financial planning and control to Divisional and lower levels. Figure 4.3 summarises some approaches to decentralising financial responsibility since 1982.

1982 Unit Budgets
All finance allocated by Districts to Units. Some finance is for District services managed by the Unit. Some is finance for a Unit therapy service which is not part of a District service. Units allocate a budget to heads of different therapy services in the Unit.
Each Unit "has a budget" for "its" therapy services. That is, a Unit printout shows the salaries and other costs of therapy services in the Unit. Some of these services are part of District service, others are not. District heads have problems transferring finance from one Unit therapy service "budget" to another. Where they also provide a small service to another Unit it is unclear at what level of service the other Unit should tart to pay, or whether the service is financed as part of a District service.

1983 Management & Clinical Budgeting
Devolution of budgets in Units in "demonstration sites" so as to hold service managers accountable for effective use of resources under their control. One project defined three types of service managers: The first type, *Service (or functional) budget holders*, such as diagnostic support services sell their services to the second type, *User (or specialty) budget holders*, who are consultants or groups of consultants who are charged for most services & resources consumed as a result of their treatment decisions, and are charged by the third type, *Facility budgeet holders*, who are nurses in charge of wards, theatres, out patients etc, who also buy service from Service budget holders. Most projects classified therapies as Service budget holders.
Therapist's Objections:
- *Unit budgets restrict flexibility of District services,*
- *Consultants do not order or prescribe a defined amount of therapy - the amount is determined by the therapist,*
- *Therapists do work other than that ordered by Users, or done in Facilities,*
- *Therapy cannot be costed in standard Units like an X-ray,*
- *Therapists should not be Service budget holders, but User budget holders, ie clinical teams in their own right.*

1986 Resource Management
6 Acute and 13 Units developed decentralised budgeting, most using a directorate model. Status of therapies varied (Buxton et al (1989)).

1989 White paper proposes resource management in 260 Units by end of 1991. Pilots evaluated by Brunel HERG (Paxton et al (1991))

Figure 4.3   Financing Therapy Services- Unit Budgets to Resource Management

---

Where management structure is unclear, financial authority is usually defined, and can determine management control of personnel. The above discussion of Unit structure and financial arrangements sets the context for examining how therapy services are financed and managed as a result of the reforms.

4: FINANCING THERAPY SERVICES

The way a NHS therapy services is organised (Chapter 5) is related to the three different ways in which it can be financed.

Delegated Budget: The first method of finance is by a Divisional Manager who manages a Therapy Department allocating a budget to a Head of Department to pay for therapy services to the Division's clients, or to staff within the Division. An example is a Divisional manager of services to people with a learning disability funding a physiotherapy Department, which they also mange. The finance is to provide services to that client group, or to advise and teach other staff in the Division.

Delegated budget financing is also where a Unit general manager manages and finances a Therapy Department to provide services to the Unit's clients (ie those served by Divisions in the Unit). In both, the finance for therapists comes from larger contracts that the Division or Unit which manages therapists has agreed with purchasers. The Division or Unit decide to run and manage their own therapy service rather than to buy-in therapy.

Internal Contract: The second method is by finance from a Division which does not manage the therapist(s). The finance is paid as part of an "internal service agreement" or "internal contract".

External Contract: The third is by finance from a purchaser outside of the therapist's Unit. The finance is usually paid to the "parent" Unit as the accounting entity, and then allocated to the therapy service budget.

Although with each method of financing the therapy service "has a budget", the way the money gets to the therapy service account is different, and the autonomy of the head of service is different. In the first a manager finances and manages a Therapy Department for his/her service to his/her clients. They do not need to contract the service they manage, they decide where and to whom "their" therapy service is provided, and they decide whether the therapy head whom they manage to run their service agrees contracts with anyone else.

In the second, a manager buys-in therapy services which they do not manage. They can choose whether to or not, and can negotiate terms with the therapy manager. However, they can appeal to the UGM, who ultimately manages the therapy service in the same Unit, to direct the therapy service to provide services internally on certain terms. In the third the purchaser is outside of the therapy service's management Unit, and can only control therapists through contract.

The next chapter shows how these methods of financing therapy services are related to different organisational models. A service may have income from all three sources. We will see that the organisational model for the service can either facilitate or limit the proportion of finance from external contracts, and that in the future therapist's autonomy will come from contracts, not from delegated authority. Chapter 9 considers the nature of each type of "contract" or "service agreement" in more detail.

"Integral" or "Stand-Alone"?

The source and method of financing is in turn related to a decision about whether a therapy service is best marketed and managed as an integral part of other services, or as a "stand-alone" service (Fig. 4.4).

Some therapy services and therapy practitioners are an inseparable and integral part of other services, for example where a true multidisciplinary team service is essential. An example is an occupational therapy service to rehabilitate people with mental health problems. Occupational therapy is traditionally provided as part of a rehabilitation team service, rather than as a separate service to these clients. Another example is physiotherapists working as part of a stroke rehabilitation team.

In contrast, psychologists working in primary care operate as independent practitioners or as part of a mental health psychology service. Although cooperation with GPs and other community staff is important, psychologists are not an integral part of these services. They usually provide specialist secondary mental health services in a primary care setting, rather than primary care psychology (if it is the latter then the FHSA should pay).

"Integral"	‹--------CONTINUUM-------›	"Stand-Alone"
Part of other service eg "close knit" Multidisciplinary Team Links with profession "weak"	Some Teams	Uniprofessional Team eg Psychology service to adult Mental Health

In a service you know, where would you place each therapy service on the continuum at present?
How should you define each service in the future, so as to arrange:
- The best way of bringing skills and knowledge into contact with needs?
- The most attractive "package" for purchasers?
- The financing of therapist's time: contracts with whom, or managed and financed by a Division/Unit?

Figure 4.4   *"Integral" or "Stand-Alone" Continuum*

An "integral" service is one where the therapist needs to be in permanent close contact with others in one service to get work, or to continually liaise with them, or where others do not know when, or if a therapist is needed. A "stand-alone" service is one where therapy services are best provided as a distinct service because referrers or clients know when they need a therapist, or where continual close contact with one group is not necessary, and where a more flexible response is appropriate.

Many services fall somewhere between the two extremes. The issue is how are therapy services best marketed and managed, and this is a matter for debate. We will see in the next chapter that some organisational models preclude a choice.

These considerations influence decisions about which model of organisation is best for a therapy service. Therapists should not judge service management models only in terms of personnel management issues (eg only in terms of ease of organising cover, split posts for recruitment, professional support and development, and quality). How the therapists time is best fiananced and the service "packaged" for the market are also important considerations.

5: PUBLIC "MARKETS", NEEDS & FINANCE

The public "markets" of the reformed NHS and social services are neither free, nor much like the conventional image of a market. The main differences between current public markets and many commercial markets are,
- A purchaser buys therapy services for clients, rather than consumer-purchasers buying their own services,
- A complex range of considerations influence the main purchasing agencies' (DHA's) decisions about whether, and how much of a service to buy,
- Investment finance for providers is limited, not by the cost of capital, but by public policies and limits to the total amount of capital available,
- Many provider staff are managed and employed by the purchaser,
- Fixed pay rates (to date) and a competitive labour market for therapists, with high demand and low supply. Employers compete for labour more on conditions of work and career prospects than on pay.
- Most therapy services are purchased as part of other services, rather than purchased directly as "stand-alone" services,

An understanding of the purchasing and provider environment is necessary for therapists and others to decide which organisational arrangement is most suitable in an area. Three aspects of this environment need to be noted. The first is the nature of health needs and the concept of health gain. The second is purchasing power and sources of revenue. The third is sources of investment and the priorities of the Unit or Division which "hosts" the therapy service.

Needs: "Needs" do not exist waiting to be measured- needs are social contructs. There are different views about needs for therapy services which a therapy manager must bring together to form a general picture of the prevalence, amount and severity of needs: First, how many and how much clients and/or carers want the service. Second, for a service that relies on referrals, referrer's judgements of how many clients could benefit from the service. Third, therapist's judgement of need for the service. Forth, purchaser's judgement of the need for the service, relative to other needs they must purchase services to meet. Chapter 8 considers how to assess needs for therapy services as part of the process of formulating a service strategy.

Purchasers: Most therapy services in the UK are purchased by public purchasers, such as District health and local authorities, fund-holding GPs, and Unit Divisions such as Directorates. There may be evidence of need, but if there are no purchasers there is no market. The market is not just clients with a need, but includes actual and potential purchasers.

Investment Finance: Start-up or investment finance may be necessary before the service can be sold. If investment finance cannot be generated internally, a service has to persuade financiers (usually UGMs) that there are needs and purchasing power in future markets. In addition, that the service can develop the capacity to respond, and that this is a higher priority for the Unit than other investments. We will see in the next chapter that how the service is organised within (or outside) a Unit determines the availability of investment finance. If it is part of a Division, it is subordinate to the Division's development plan. If it is Division in its own right, it competes with other Divisions for the Unit's investment finance.

How therapists can respond to this new environment is the subject of the following chapters.

6: SUMMARY & CONCLUSION

The 1990 reforms and public markets had an immediate impact on the organisation and financing of therapy services, and will affect the professions in many ways. The history of therapist's organisation in the NHS showed an increase and then a decline in the management autonomy of these professions. Many therapists fear that the reforms will further erode their autonomy, but this depends on how they are organised and financed.

An understanding of the changes being made, and of the nature of public markets is necessary for therapists to decide a preferred model of organisation. This understanding also necessary to therapists influencing decision-makers to support a model which enables therapists to market and manage their own services. The different models which emerged from the 1990 reforms are described in the next chapter.

Chapter 5: Models of Organisation

With the merger of the two Units, the District Therapist was resigned to the break-up of the District service that she had spent eleven years building. For the past year she had been trying to uphold professional standards with no authority, and was concerned about how the purchasing authority would get professional advice. She and her staff were demoralised. People were already leaving, and she was reading books about pension rights and calculating her retirement options.

It was a surprise to get a letter from one of the UGMs asking her for the business plan for her service, and to come and discuss with him how a service spanning the proposed directorates could be organised. Apparently the new business manager had been putting an argument for making more of the reputation of the therapy services and for combining and marketing them. She decided she needed to find out about the 'Trading Agency' option, but realised that she only had two weeks to draw up her proposal. Then the phone rang. It was the District Chiropodist, whom she had not seen for over a year,...'Helen, do you know what a Trading Agency is?...Its just that the UGM........

1: INTRODUCTION

This chapter describes eight different types of organisation for therapy services. They range in size and "ownership" from the individual private practitioner model, through to supra-District NHS groupings. It discusses the criteria therapist's use to judge each model, as well as the advantages and disadvantages of each from the perspectives of different interest groups.

The aim is to help therapists and managers to make considered decisions about the best form of organisation for therapy services in a particular area. Arbitrary or pragmatic decisions with disastrous long term consequences are more likely when the alternatives are not known, and when the decision-criteria are not examined.

In the frequent reorganisations and mergers of the 1990's, it is likely that therapists will have to act quickly at certain times to secure their preferred organisation. They will need to be aware of the options and to keep them under review so as to be able to make the most of the opportunities as they arise.

2: MODELS OF ORGANISATION

Two considerations in deciding an appropriate model (Table 5.1), are,

- the size of the Unit relative to existing therapy departments (Figs 4.1 & 4.2 in chapter 4), and,
-the number of therapists in a Unit or District.

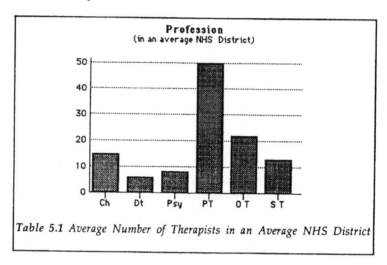

Profession
(in an average NHS District)

Table 5.1 Average Number of Therapists in an Average NHS District

Method for Representing Structure

The discussion of models of organisation below uses the terms and convention outlined in chapter 4 (Figures 4.1 & 4.2) to represent the position and nature of one or more therapy services in a provider Unit. Most therapy services in the UK and elsewhere are managed by, and from within Units. A therapy service may be a Division in its own right (eg some District Therapy Services), or the service may be within a Division (eg some Unit Therapy Departments).

The following starts with the independent private practitioner model, and then considers alternative "Unit-managed" models for increasing numbers of therapists, before finishing with the independent group practice model. Therapists can take part in multidisciplinary teams in all of these models, although model B is most appropriate for "close-knit" teams where therapy is integral to a service.

Model A: Individual Private Practitioner

In this model the practitioner is self-employed and has independence within the law and codes of conduct to decide their own working arrangements. They can decide who they accept as clients, the length and types of treatment, mix of cases and the proportion of consulting and other work, and how their practice is organised. To a large extent their decisions depend on demand and purchasing power in the local market. Where supply exceeds demand, individual private practitioners have less independence than employed practitioners, and are less powerful than practitioner collectives to shape markets or to compete.

A number of chiropodists and physiotherapists run their own private practices, and more members of the other four professions are taking up part- or full-time private practice. From the client's point of view there may be advantages to having a choice of therapists (if they can afford it), and competition may keep prices down and/or increase the quality of service. These advantages depend largely on there being a stable but competitive market, which is quite rare. It is likely that, in the UK, the numbers of therapists undertaking part-time private practice will increase, so long as practice insurance premiums and litigation remains relatively low. NHS services may sub-contract private practitioners.

Model B: Directorate or Locality-Managed

In this model therapists are employed by a provider Unit, such as a DMU, NHS-T or private hospital. Individual therapists or Therapy Departments are managed by Clinical Directorates, Localities, or other sub-Unit Divisions.

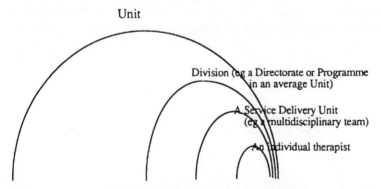

Unit

Division (eg a Directorate or Programme in an average Unit)

A Service Delivery Unit (eg a multidisciplinary team)

An individual therapist

Therapists manged by managers of Service Delivery Units, or Locality managers.

Model B: Directorate or Locality-Managed

Therapy services (individuals or Departments) are financed, managed and provided as part of these Divisional services, and from within Divisions. There may or may not be a senior therapist adviser inside, or outside of the Directorate - if the latter the question arises as to how their advisory time is to be financed.

This model, described as a "dispersed" option by some (Jones et al(1990)) or as "total fragmentation" by others, has disadvantages for therapists, and, in the long term, for general managers or clinical directors. There is the risk of professional isolation, and in many cases no senior therapist to assure professional quality or supervise junior staff. Some areas may not have a therapist, or even recognise the need for one. General managers or clinical directors may find it difficult to recruit or retain therapists, not least because they cannot offer a career structure or promotion prospects within the profession.

This model makes it more difficult to arrange and finance "stand alone" therapy services which are not an integral part of the Divisional service (eg those taking direct GP referrals). For this reason it is not suited to therapies, such as clinical psychology, with potential for "stand alone" service expansion in the new welfare markets. Some managers assume that this model is best suited to multidisciplinary team services. However, therapists can be full members of such teams but still managed from a separate therapy service, and working in the team under contract.

Model C 1 : Unit-Based Single-Therapy Division

In this model one therapy service is a separate Division in its own right within a Unit structure, rather than being part of another Division (as in model A). The therapy service is akin to a Directorate or Care Programme for planning and financial systems and for contracting purposes, and is managed by a Head Therapist.

Unit

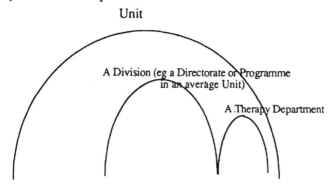

A Division (eg a Directorate or Programme in an average Unit)

A Therapy Department

Model C 1 : Unit-Based Single Therapy Division

In this model most therapists are contracted by the Head Therapist to work in the Unit's Directorates or Localities, and as part of these services. However, these therapists may also work part-time providing "stand-alone" Unit therapy services, which are not part of other services (eg Unit therapy service to budget-holding GPs, local employers or other purchasers). These services are contracted by the Unit Head Therapist to purchasers through the Unit's contracting system. They may be in competition with the same therapy services in other Units.

The critical issue is how much of the therapy service's finance is internal, coming from other directorates (where therapy services are sub-contracted by another Directorate), and how much is external, coming from other provider Units who sub-contract for therapy services, or directly from purchasers ("stand-alone" services). If large amounts are or could be external, and there are not many therapy services managed by other Units, then model D below is more appropriate.

The disadvantage of this option from the point of view of general managers in large Units is that most therapy services are "too small" to constitute a Division in their own right, with the possible exception of some physiotherapy Departments (eg at the Royal Free Hospital in Hamsptead London). From therapist's point of view, this model is better than model B because at least they are managed by "one of their own". There is less isolation, but therapists are tied to Unit objectives. Any investment is in terms of how the therapy service contributes to the Unit's overall strategy.

Model C2 : Unit-Based Combined-Therapies Division

In Units with a number of therapy services, the spectre of each therapy service with a set of contracts to a variety of external purchasers (as well as to "internal purchasers" such as directorates) leads Unit general managers to bring therapy services together in one Division or "Therapy Directorate". As in C1, each therapy service in the combined Division competes with therapy services in other Units.

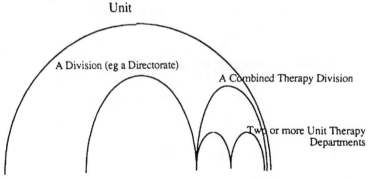

Model C2 : Unit-Based Combined Therapies Division

The advantages for general managers is that they only have to deal with one "Head of Therapies". Each therapy service has the same contracting framework and information and finance systems.

Each profession has to compete with others in the Therapy Division for investment finance. None have a direct line to the UGM, or a place on the top management team or Board, something which is possible with model C1 in a small Unit. The "Head of Therapies" may be part of the top management team, and does not have to be from one of the therapies. Alternatively they may be a head of one of the therapies in the Division, and have either a coordinating or a management role in relation to the other heads. Model D2 below is the District service version of this model, with a combined District Therapies Division.

Model D1 : Unit-Based District Therapy Service

Although in this model all therapists are still managed as a separate Division within a Unit, as in C1, there are two differences between this option and C1:
- All the therapists in the profession in the District (or Area) are managed from within the one Therapy Division in the "parent" base Unit, and ultimately by the District Therapist.
- There is a high proportion of therapy services contracted to purchasers external to the "parent" Unit, rather than to internal purchasers (eg Unit Directorates).

In this model contracts provide general managers and clinical directors in both "parent" and "non-parent" Units the control that they need. The advantages for therapists are those of C1, but more so. A range of therapy specialties are brought together and can be developed, and competition and possible duplication within the profession between specialities or Departments is minimised.

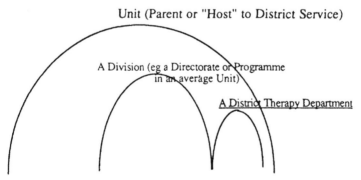

Model D1 : Unit-Based District Therapy Service

In principle the therapy service is free to develop and market services wherever it can find purchasers. But in reality the "parent" Unit influences how the service develops by being the channel, if not the source of investment finance. The Unit feels that it has first claim on services, even though internal contracts have the same status as external ones. Because the UGM manages the Head (or District) Therapist, it is difficult to separate the UGM's accountability for the overall service from their accountability for ensuring that their Unit gets the therapy services it needs, even with the clarification brought about by contracts.

It is for these and other reasons that a variation of this model is evolving which allows greater freedom for the therapy service - the therapy "Service Agency" described below as a variation of model "D". First we need to note one other common model.

Model D2: Unit-Based Combined District Therapies

This model is similar to C2, but in this case two or more District services are managed from the "parent" Unit, and combine to form a "District Services Division" in the parent Unit.

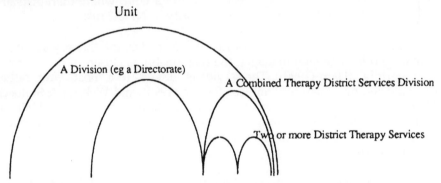

Model D2 : Unit-Based Combined District Therapies

In some Districts some therapies combine to form a Division in one Unit and some in another Unit. For example in one District, physiotherapy, occupational therapy, and dietetics are District services in one Division in the Acute Unit; and District Speech Therapy, and District Psychology are together in the Community and Priority Services Unit.

The disadvantages are similar to those in B2, but this model is popular with general managers, not least because of the income generation potential of District services for the Unit.

The Bath Therapy Agency:
"The departments of physiotherapy, occupational therapy, speech and hearing therapy, along with dietetics are now managed by a therapy manager who is also a district physiotherapist..... Such as merger has clear benefits. perhaps most obvious is that, united, the agency's therapy departments are now best placed to deal with the uncertainty governing the health service reforms. Should the government change hands, it is likely that we would remain accountable to the HA. Conversely is decentralisation forces ahead, the agency in its entirety would be incorporated into a neighbouring trust".
"Bath Capitalises on Merging Skills" - Therapy Weekly 12th Septemeber 1991

Basildon and Thurrock District Professional Services Division:
"A important reason for management being agreeable to this option was only having one head of services to relate to, and that our finacing and information systems could all be developed within the same framework. In fact we found doing this was easier than we thought it would be- in one day all six district heads met and thrashed out our shared contract specification format." Mark O'Callaghan, Director of District Professional Services.

Variation of D1 or D2: The Therapy "Service Agency"

How much independence is possible for a therapy service within models D1 or D2? The idea of a "Service Agency" tests the limits to the possible independence of a large therapy service within a Unit, where therapists are employed within the NHS by a health authority or NHS-Trust.

In the "Service Agency" variation of models D1 or D2, the therapy service is not managed by a general manager: the relationship is closer to "monitoring" or "loose-tight" (Ham (1990)). The service is "linked" to a "host" Unit, rather than managed by a "parent" Unit (see Paxton (1990), and Webster & Skilbeck (1991) for details). In the latter the service has to ask the "parent" Unit for permission to do different things, whereas in the former the "host" has less control over "the visitor" (the service agency) who is free to come and go within the house rules.

The terms illustrate some unclarity about the independence of the Agency and about working relationships of accountability and authority between the head therapist and general manager. The terms do reach for ways of describing a relationship which is different to management, and which is evolving (Webster & Skilbeck (1991)). However, there is no avoiding the accountability of the general manager for the financial performance of the Agency, for ensuring quality and safety to minimise negligence claims for which the Unit would be liable, and for the reputation of the Unit.

It follows from the accountability of general managers that they need authority to inquire into aspects of the management of the agency service, and to take action if necessary. "Monitoring" authority is not sufficient

(Jaques (ed)(1978)). It is for these reasons that the Service Agency is described here as a variation of model D, rather than a different model in it own right.

These and other issues need to be clarified before many general managers would be convinced that the "Service Agency" is better (or even different) to model D. The difference that they are most likely to see is that they can retain therapy surpluses in model D, but not in the "Service Agency" variation.

Model E : Independent Group Practice

In this model therapists form their own profit or not-for-profit group practice (discussed in Jones et al (1990)). One option is for some or all therapists in an area to leave employment by the NHS or NHS-Trusts and form a separate business or charity. To the author's knowledge no sizable group has done this in the UK, mainly because of uncertainty about getting large contracts from health authority or other purchasers to cover over 50% of the first years expenditure.

The more likely eventuality is that full or part-time private practitioners group together in different ways. These associations range from a loose referral and advice network, to a group practice business partnership. The author has not carried out any detailed field research with therapists into these variations of the model, mostly because there are few examples in the UK.

CLARIFYING THE CURRENT SERVICE MODEL

The following questions help to decide which of the models is closest to describing how a therapy service is organised.

1) In relation to practitioner management, does a therapy manager, or another manager have the final say about: the general duties of a practitioner post?; which therapist applicant to appoint to the job?; caseload?; changes to where sessions are worked?; upgrading?; performance appraisal?; training?; action over complaints?; disciplinary action?
If the answer is, mostly the other manager, then model B is in operation.

2) If the answer is a therapist manager, then does over 80% of the finance for the service come from inside the Unit, (from internal contracts negotiated by a therapist head with other heads of different Divisions ?) If so, model C is in operation.

3) May a the head therapist negotiate and manage a therapy services contract directly with a purchasing health authority? May they also carry-over budget surpluses or deficits into the next financial year? If so model D is in operation.

The above also helps to clarifies the authority of a therapy manager, which is related to the level of work which they can undertake (discussed further in chapter 7).

Summary of Models of Organisation for Therapy Services

Model A: Individual Private Practitioner
The practitioner is self-employed and has independence within the law and codes of conduct to decide their own working arrangements.

Model B: Directorate or Locality-Managed
In this model therapists are employed by a provider Unit, and are managed by clinical directorates, localities, or other sub-Unit Divisions. Therapy services (individuals or Departments) are financed and provided as part of these Divisional services, and from within Divisions.

Model C 1 : Unit-Based Single Therapy Division
One therapy service is a separate Division in its own right within a Unit structure, rather than being part of another Division.The therapy service is like a Directorate or care Programme for planning and financial systems and for contracting purposes, and is managed by a head therapist. Most therapists are contracted by the head therapist to work in the Unit's Directorates or Localities, and as part of these services.

Model C2 : Unit-Based Combined Therapies Division
Unit therapy services like C1 are grouped together in one Division or "Therapy Directorate".

Model D1 : Unit-Based District Therapy Service
All therapists in the District are managed as a separate Division within a "parent" Unit. A high proportion of therapy services are contracted to purchasers external to the "parent" Unit, rather than to internal purchasers (eg Unit Directorates).

Model D2 : Unit-Based Combined District Therapies
Similar to C2, but in this case two or more District services are managed from the "parent" Unit, and combine to form a "District Services Division" in the "parent" Unit.

Variation of Models D1 & D2: The Therapy "Service Agency"
A variation of model D1 or D2 in which the therapy service is not managed by a general manager. The service is "linked" to a "host" Unit, rather than managed by a "parent" Unit. One difference is that in D, UGMs can retain therapy surpluses, but not in the "Service Agency" variation.

Model E : Independent Group Practice
In this model therapists form their own profit or not-for-profit group practice

---

3: INFLUENCING STRUCTURE- Do Therapists Have a Choice of Model?

With the rapid changes in the NHS, and especially resource management (Packwood, Keen & Buxton (1991) and Directorates (Dixon (1989)), a concern of district heads was that District or Area services would be "Unitised"(Model B1). Worse, that therapists would be allocated to Directorates or "patch teams" and managed by clinical directors or general managers (model A).

District heads feared that therapists would not get the professional support which they needed, and standards would drop. That there would be not be a career structure within the profession, it would be less easy to rotate staff between specialities and arrange training, and recruitment and retention would be more difficult. District heads were concerned that they would be held responsible for "professional standards" but would have no authority.

There was little time to examine these issues with the tight timetables of the early 1990 NHS reforms. The scale and pace of change meant that, in most Districts, therapist's concerns were overlooked. Many felt that District services that had taken years to build were being swept away by managers who had little comprehension of the consequences. Therapists became resigned and demoralised.

However, provider Units continue to reorganise and merge, and therapists will have the chance to influence how they are organised. There is a choice, and the first step towards influencing events is to be clear about the alternatives and the arguments.

To do this therapists and managers need to examine the advantages and disadvantages of each option from the different perspectives of practitioners, clients, referrers, general managers, purchasers, and significant others (eg clinical directors). This helps to clarify which factors are most important (see below"Criteria for Choosing Between Options"), and to decide which model is the best balance between the ideal, and the feasible and achievable.

CRITERIA FOR CHOOSING BETWEEN OPTIONS

Considerations which influence the choice of organisation are highlighted by comparing the advantages and disadvantages of the different models. Each model should be judged from the perspectives of local clients, practitioners, general managers, referrers, purchasers, and therapist managers. Using this approach heads of service in workshops discovered that they were judging the models against the following criteria,
- continuity for clients between hospital and community services,
- choice of therapist, and ease of access to specialist therapists,
- ease of organising pre-qualification training (ease of arranging rotas)
- ease of staff recruitment (job attractiveness),
- staff retention (independence, professional development and challenge, career structure)
- supervision and support for newly-qualified staff,
- cover for sickness and leave,
- cost of providing the service, and effective use of time and skills (therapy services in areas where most needed/doing work which is most effective),
- maintaining and improving quality of service,
- ease of marketing and financing "stand-alone" therapy services,
- general management control, and directorate or medical control,
- number of points of contact for other managers/external bodies,
- duplication of systems and formats for contracts, information, etc..
- power.

Therapists who have rated their current organisation against the five most important criteria, and in comparison to alternative models, have found that this exercise makes it easier to be objective. In presenting the case for one option it is often more important to show that your objective appraisal recognises the disadvantages, and shows how they will be minimised, than to emphasise the advantages.

However, it is rare that decisions about organisation are made on a rational basis. Clarity and agreement about which model to try to achieve (or retain), and about the arguments for and against the model, is a necessary, but not a sufficient condition for achieving it. Therapists also need to consider the politics and timetables of formal and informal decision-making, and to influence allies, neutralise opposition, and "tip" "fence-sitters" who could help or hinder.

One factor which makes some models more viable is the ability of a Unit to deal with contracts. More sophisticated systems for accounting and managing contracts make it possible to handle a range of "small" therapy service contracts. In the first phases of the reforms contracts for "small" services such as therapy service were actively discouraged. However some therapy mangers struck "service agreements" to clarify their responsibilities, which were soon treated as "shadow contracts". In taking the initiative in this way this way, and in interpreting their roles as full-management roles they influenced the organisation towards C- and D-type models.

4: CONCLUSION

In the UK the 1990 NHS reforms led to a greater variety of organisational arrangements for therapy services. This chapter represented these as models of organisation, and considered some of the criteria used to assess the arrangements for an area.

Many therapists concluded that "Unitisation", general management, and finally resource management and Directorates would remove the autonomy which therapists had gained in the 1980s. However contracts and other changes open up opportunities for the therapy professions to develop services independently of medicine, and to set their own local direction. Contracts for therapy services make it possible for general managers and clinical directors to be sure of getting the therapy services that they require to provide their service. It relieves purchasers outside of a Unit of the responsibility for managing therapists and all that that entails (eg maintaining professional standards, recruitment, cover, etc). It makes it possible for them to have the control they need, but allows therapy-managers to maintain Unit or District Departments and to offer "stand-alone" services.

Therapists can influence, and perhaps determine the choice of model, especially during critical phases of market development and provider restructuring. They will need to do this to secure the type of organisation they need to take advantage of the opportunities which the reforms present for their professions.

Therapist heads can take the initiative by drawing up proposals and "shopping around" Units or directorates for the best home, negotiating the best future organisation for the service. The first step is to clarify with colleagues in other therapy services what arrangements they wish to establish. General managers have found it difficult to ignore a group of therapy heads working together to establish their preferred organisational arrangement.

> *"The lesson that has been learned is to persist if you feel the case to be made is valid....."*
>
> *"The District Department, which was originally managed by a District Psychologist holding the clinical psychology budget, was devolved to localities and managed by Assistant Unit General Managers. They advertised posts in an unco-ordinated way, resulting in an imbalance of services across the District. The District Psychologist post was lost and the Principle clinical psychologists were given a dual responsibility: primarily they were responsible for co-ordinating services within one of the five District localities and, in addition, they were expected to be Heads of clinical psychology specialisms.*
>
> *The loss of the District Clinical Psychology Department base, the budget, leadership, career structure, co-ordination and communication network had major consequences for service provision and staff morale. Over a period of months many staff left the District seeking posts elsewhere.*
>
> *Constant communication (by those left who formed a psychology advisory group) with the Unit General Manager and the District General Manager, including copies of letters of resignation, vacancy rates and accurate accounts of service mismanagement finally resulted in a reorganisation of clinical psychology services.*
>
> *In May 1990 a District Psychologist was appointed with a responsibility for managing the Clinical Psychology Department within the District. As a result of this appointment, the previously devolved budget has been centralised and is now held by the District Psychologist.....*
>
> *The implications of the centralised budget are far-reaching. The flexibility within the budget and the initiatives that can now be taken within the Department, have enabled the establishment to increase the range of services. New posts have been developed and funding is planned for further service developments. Most important, perhaps, the managerial accountability has been returned to the profession and managers use this accountability for advice and planning.."*
> (Strict & Bennun (1991))

Chapter 6: THERAPY PRACTICE AND PRACTITIONER AUTONOMY

1: INTRODUCTION

Therapists frequently complain that "bureaucratic" NHS management restricts the independence which they feel that they need to give the best service to an individual client, and to a population: that it defeats its own purpose of using their skills to the best effect. But is this "special pleading" different from the arguments presented by any workers for greater control and autonomy? Some NHS managers say that if it was not for the NHS there would be no therapy services in the area, and that, if left to their own devices, therapists would pursue their own special interests regardless of priority needs.

What exactly are the features of therapeutic work or of therapists as workers which need to be taken into account in their management and organisation? Do any preclude management by general managers? A discussion of the details of the organisation and management of therapists must begin with an understanding of the nature of the work, and of characteristics of the workers.

The chapter considers features of the work and of the workers and distinguishes between three levels of practitioner work, "Prescribed or Trainee Practice", "Basic Practice" and "Development Practice". It examines practitioner's accountability in private practice and in employment, and the different types of autonomy which are required by practitioners in different situations and at different career stages. The implications for managers and management structure are examined in the next chapter.

2 : FEATURES OF THERAPY PRACTICE

The approach taken in this book is that "professional" is a social construct, and that there is nothing in the nature of any work which is inherently "professional". Whether the same work or worker is termed "professional" varies between societies and within the same society at different times (Appendix 5).

However, in examining options for therapy organisation the research found that there were features of therapist's work which have implications for how they are best organised and managed. These features are:

1) *Flexibility*: In order to meet the needs of a client the therapist draws on both a body of knowledge and their experience to make a diagnosis and to formulate a treatment plan. Each case is different and requires a flexible response, which cannot be prescribed beforehand.

2) *Practice-based research & innovation*: The body of knowledge, skills and techniques are continually developed and evaluated by practitioners, and others. Those practitioners who are able to develop new knowledge, skills and techniques need to be encouraged to do so.

3) *Relationship with the client*: The practitioner-client relationship is central to the work, and the therapist needs to be able to establish and maintain appropriate "helping" relationships. This requires that they gain and retain the trust of the client, and are able to motivate and mobilise the client's own curative strengths.

The practitioner is involved in matters of intense personal concern to clients, and frequently needs to be able to delve into personal affairs and gain client's (and their carer's) full cooperation. The practitioner is placed in a position of responsibility, and they and their clients are sensitive to anything that interferes with the kind of helping relationship which is essential to a successful outcome.

4) *Evaluation of experienced practitioner's casework*: The professions believe that, above a certain level of training and experience, each practitioner's casework judgements are of equal value. Above this level a manager and other practitioners are not able to judge whether, for example, another intervention would have been better for a particular client. Much depends on the particular circumstances and relationship between the practitioner and client, on many intangibles and on the intuition of the practitioner, who draws as much on previous casework experience as on scientifically-established procedures. This is not to mean that the practitioner cannot improve, rather that peer review methods rather than management supervision are more appropriate at a certain level.

These features of therapy practice are not recognised by conceptualising therapist's work solely in terms of "skills", or even "competences". Education and supervision in terms of "skills transmission" alone is not an adequate preparation for therapeutic practice.

These features of the work are said by therapists to preclude conventional managerial hierarchies, and to call for certain types of management and organisational structure - in particular, for a form of management by members of their own profession. One argument for the latter is that a profession-manager understands the work and necessary conditions for therapeutic practice. We will consider the arguments shortly.

Individual level of work capacity

There is also a characteristic of therapists with implications for organisational structure. Any organisational structure is influenced by the abilities of the people employed, and to some extent structural changes are driven by their changing interests and abilities. One important characteristic is the ability of people to undertake work with higher or lower levels of responsibility.

There is evidence that this ability ("level of work capacity") increases with age, and develops at different rates in different people.(Jaques (1976), Stamp(1988)). The theory proposes that people seek to undertake work at a level consistent with their ability. As they develop their work and working relations change.

This can lead to a situation in which many practitioners are soon bored by "basic routine work" which was once a challenge, but which still needs to be done. One study of the work capacity of 12 clinical psychologists in one department concluded that, *"we are selecting individuals who, by the time they reach their late 30s will require greater work challenges than can be provided by most existing clinical responsibilities, or specialty and district head positions"* (Church (1990))).

This dynamic between changing ability, and the work which is called for, adds a complexity to designing professional organisation and managing professionals. Managing professionals is a continual balancing act between the work to be done and peoples changing ability to do it. If a service is to retain practitioners it must recognise and match individual's developing capacity to the work to be done. Arrangements to do this includes performance appraisals which lead to changes in level of responsibility, and frequent structural reviews to keep a match between different individual's work capacity and the work roles in the structure.

3: LEVELS OF THERAPY PRACTICE

The research used the theory of levels of work to examine therapy work and the work capacity characteristic of therapists (Rowbottom&Billis(1977)). The level of work undertaken by different practitioners has consequences for how they are best organised and managed. The theory of levels of work relates the work to be done to the level of responsibility of the therapist, and thence to how they should be managed and to organisational structure. Three types of therapy practice work may be distinguished, according to the level and type of response to need provided by the practitioner.

Prescribed or Trainee Practice

During training a student practitioner follows prescribed procedures and is closely supervised. The work they undertake can be described as "prescribed output work" (Rowbottom&Billis (1977)) where the expected outcome, the methods and time to be taken can be, and is usually specified in advance. The trainee practitioner works with a broad range of cases or situations, rather than with in-depth, long-term and complex work. This describes the type or work undertaken by most therapy helpers, assistants, aids, and therapy "technicians". The time scale for the longest task, or between reviews rarely exceeds 3 months.

One psychologist using this theory wrote that,*"Prescribed work was characteristic of clinical psychology when the predominant role was diagnostic testing. The doctor would define the problems prescribe the output he required and the psychologist, working as a highly skilled technician, would carry out the appropriate tests. This mode of working is enshrined in the Whitley system, where we are linked to those other diagnostic scientists, the biochemists and physicists"*. (Kat (1985))

Basic Practice

In at least two therapy professions, the work expected in "Basic Practice" in the NHS can be described as "situational response work". Rather than responding to presented demand according to closely prescribed procedures, the qualified practitioner is expected to assess the underlying needs of each client or situation by applying diagnostic techniques in a flexible way. They are expected to devise a plan of action tailored to the particular client or situation, which can be justified by reference to theory and past experience. The longest time over which the practitioner would undertake a treatment or project without external feedback that they were exercising their discretion appropriately would be 12 months.

This work differs from "Prescribed Practice" mainly in terms of the greater range and "depth" of response of the worker to the needs of a client, and in terms of the time scale over which the worker exercises discretion without managerial review or direct feedback from a client.

After an initial post-qualifying probationary period, the practitioner is expected to undertake the work without routine supervision. The type of work may be "generalist" or "specialist case work", or advice and support to carers and other professionals. Basic Practice is work at the same level ("level 2") as first-line management and supervisory work, and experienced Basic Practitioners frequently manage helpers and supervise students.

As the practitioner gains in experience and skills they are able to undertake increasingly complex case-work, and are better able to organise their time and prioritise their work to make the most effective use of their skills and knowledge. Typically, after about 10 years some practitioners are able to, and expected to undertake "Development Practice" work.

Development Practice

Development Practice work involves adapting and developing established theories and techniques to deal with new problems and situations. These new approaches are then used routinely by Basic Practitioners. It is higher level work than Basic Practice because the time scale is longer: between 1-2 years.

Usually the only recognised work at this level ("level 3") is management work, involving a responsibility for providing a systematic service to meet the needs of a flow of cases or situations. Private practitioners have to be able to undertake management work at this level to survive in private practice: simply responding to presenting cases and situations is not sufficient ("level 2" practice management). In the NHS, Development Practice is often combined with other management and planning work at the same level. However it is a particular type of level 3 work because the practioner draws on and develops theories and techniques associated with the profession and its practice.

The analysis of levels of work and of responsibility in therapy practice helps to understand and develop solutions to the following common problems,

1) Pressure towards specialisation

"Specialist"work is not necessarily high-level work with a high level of responsibility. "Specialist" work can be narrow, repetitive and involve short time-spans. Grade definitions, however assume that specialist work is higher level work, and managers find that they are only able to establish high level posts or promote a practitioner by arguing that the work is highly specialised, or involves supervising staff. There may be a greater need for high level generalists.

2) Different expectations of a practice role

Managers do not distinguish between Basic Practice and Development Practice when creating new posts or devising new structures, and can mislead job applicants. The concepts help to clarify the work which managers want done, and then to establish appropriate management arrangements.

3) Structures with no scope for therapist to develop in practice roles

Although managers recognise increasing skill, experience and self-sufficiency, they often do not recognise the developing level of work capacity of practitioners. When they do they are frequently not able to provide for higher-level practice roles in their structures, usually because they have not planned a structure to provide for clinical career progression. The theory of work capacity helps to predict individuals development needs and points of stress between individuals and structure, and to relate future structures to individuals abilities.

4) Single management structure for all therapy & "support" professions

Managers often expect all the professions to adopt the same type of structure, but each profession differs in terms of, a) the number of practitioners who are capable of undertaking Development Practice, b) expectations as to whether Basic Practice or Development Practice is the career level which all members should aspire to and be encouraged to attain (Chapter 10).

Figure 6.1Recognising Differences in Levels of Therapy Practice Explains Some Problems in Therapy Organisation

It is important to distinguish this work in order that employers can choose to establish development posts of this kind, and to recognise that practice posts at this level will need different management arrangements to those for Basic Practice posts. A manager will relate to a Development Practitioner in a different way to the way they relate to a Basic Practitioner.(Figure 6.1 shows how this analysis helps to understand and develop solutions to some common problems in therapy organisation).

The above considered features of therapeutic practice which therapists wanted to recognise in their organisation and management, and which are embodied in the concept of "practitioner autonomy". It also applied theories of level of work and of individual work capacity to clarify certain issues of organisation and management.

In the research these ideas led to concepts of two types of practitioner autonomy, "Case Autonomy", and "Practice Autonomy". These concepts proved useful in designing therapy organisation and in everyday therapy management. They are the conceptual link between therapy work and organisation.

Before discussing these concepts we need to consider another aspect of therapeutic practice: therapist's working relationships, and in particular their formal relations of accountability. This puts therapist's work in a social context and helps to understand the conflicts which occur for professionals employed by public services.

4: PRACTITIONER ACCOUNTABILITY

To understand therapy practice we also need to understand therapist's relations with clients and others. Here we will consider a therapist's formal relations of accountability.
The term "accountability" is sometimes used to refer to a person feeling responsible for something, whether or not they are formally accountable for meeting the responsibility they feel. There are many meanings to the term, some moral, some political, some religious (Day & Klien (1989)). The term is here used to describe an explicit social relationship, and is emphasised by the adjective "formal",

---

Formal Accountability
The person or body to whom you are answerable for meeting defined responsibilities, and for observing set rules and regulations.

With formal and explicit accountability the person entering the relationship agrees what they are prepared to answer for, and to whom. In so doing they agree that the person or body to whom they are answerable has authority to call them to account, and potentially to sanction them.

Therapists have formal relations of accountability with different bodies. There are potential conflicts between their different accountabilities.

A therapist in private practice is formally accountable to their customer for their actions and omissions. This accountability is not a felt moral obligation, but a defined relationship in law. When the therapist offers a service they do so under laws which regulate any commercial exchange. The customer can call them to account through a court of law, and the sanctions available to the customer are defined in the Sale of Goods and Services Act, and in other Acts.

This is the only relationship of formal accountability for therapists who are not members of a professional association, or regulated by the state in any way, apart from their accountability in law as a citizen (eg some psychotherapists).

When a therapist applies for membership of a professional association, they agree to be bound by the rules of membership, which usually includes codes of conduct and professional ethics. The are accountable to the association for observing these rules. Some of these rules define how members of the association should relate to clients.

Clients can appeal to the professional association for redress against the practitioner. Usually they only get a favourable response if other members of the association could be shown in a poor light by their complaint. The main sanction available to the professional association is to withdraw membership. If membership is a condition for state registration, then this sanction is stronger than it would otherwise be.

If the therapist applied for, and was granted state recognition (generally state registration), they are also accountable to the state regulating body (eg state registration council) for observing the conditions of practice set by this body. The sanctions available to this body are withdrawal of recognition, which may have a variety of consequences (see chapter 2).

A therapist may apply for an employment by a state employing authority, a private hospital, or a voluntary organisation. They decide whether or not to agree to the terms of employment, which in effect are to put their services at the disposal of the employer. The have a "contract of service" with their employer. Typically professionals do this because employment is not incompatible with their other accountabilities, and there is a commonality of purpose between them and their employer. Having agreed an employment contract they are accountable to their employer for meeting the responsibilities laid down in their contract, and for observing the employer's rules and regulations. The sanctions available to the employer are laid down in employment law.

In summary, the main formal relations of accountability for therapists practising in different contexts are to a court of law, to customers (in private practice), to a professional association, to a state regulating body, and to an employer. Two points need to be made which relate the above to organisation and management issues in the NHS.

The first is that if they are an employee a therapist has a different formal relation of accountability to their client to the relationship that they have if they are in private practice, although therapists would like to think of it as the same. As an employee they are not formally accountable to the client in the same way, and the client does not have the same redress against them as an individual private practitioner. The therapist is first and foremost accountable to their employer, so long as what the employer asks them to do does not conflict with their accountability to their professional association or state regulatory body.

In this situation it is the employer who is formally accountable to the client for the therapist's service. The employer is concerned about the quality of therapy services to an individual client, not least because they could be liable for negligence.

The second point is that state employing authorities have a responsibility to provide a service to populations, according to certain NHS priorities and policies. State authorities contract providers to do this and providers are accountable to the authorities through contract. Providers employ managers and therapists to help them meet their contracts.

Therapist's training, socialisation and professional culture, on the other hand, emphasises responsibility to an individual client, regardless of their formal accountability relations as employees. (This emphasis is not just because of a moral ethic of service, but because it is essential to the reputation and market position of the profession) Clearly services to populations are only provided through therapist's serving individuals, and, to date, the interests of the therapy professions and the NHS have largely coincided.

However conflicts occur because, at times, responsibility to an individual client conflicts with the state's responsibility to provide services to populations according to need and available resources. If therapists are not able to meet what they consider to be their primary responsibility to the individual client, then they must leave state employment and their "contract of service" and agree a "contract for service", as do GPs, or go into private practice.

These conflicts converge on therapy managers, and are played-out in terms of "professional autonomy", to which we now return.

The idea of "practitioner autonomy" embodies the independence practitioners feel they need. It links the features of therapy work described to the optimum organisational conditions for therapy practice. The concepts of "Case Autonomy" and "Practice Autonomy" makes it possible to balance this independence with manager's responsibility for providing services to populations.

5: PRACTITIONER AUTONOMY

Practitioner autonomy is defined by the limits which circumscribe the decisions and actions the therapist can take, and by the authority of their manager, if the therapist is employed.

Limits to autonomy

A practitioner in private practice is accountable for keeping within certain prescribed-limits to their practice. These are limits of the law. They may be called to account for their actions by courts of law and/or professional disciplinary bodies, and sanctioned in certain circumstances. Practitioners with employment contracts, in addition, are accountable for meeting their contracts, and for observing employer's policies.

Manager's authority

In addition to these established limits circumscribing the the therapist's practice, their manager sets policies and procedures. For example, policies to ensure safety and standards, that therapist's time is used to the best effect, and that they serve what is agreed to be priority clients.

Stronger therapy management and contracts means policies which impinge on areas which some therapist's view as issues for them to decide, such as case load, and closure criteria. Whilst such policies are helpful to inexperienced staff, they are viewed by senior staff as overly-restrictive, and as undermining their responsibility for their own practice management.

The area of greatest contention is whether manager's examine individual case work, and direct casework practice. Manager's accountability for safety and quality means that they need this authority. The research shows that the need for detailed case supervision varies between professions, and according to the level of experience of the practitioner (see the discussion of manager's accountability in the next chapter).

Case Autonomy

In examining the degree of freedom which practitioners require it proved necessary to distinguish two types of autonomy (Øvretveit 1984)).

Case Autonomy:
"The right to exercise discretion in assessing or treating a case without that discretion being reviewed or overridden by a higher authority, unless negligence is suspected or prescribed limits are infringed".

The professions vary in terms of how long a practitioner has to undertake Basic Practice before they are judged to be able safely to assume full responsibility for casework and to acquire Case Autonomy. In psychology the formal position is that just-qualified practitioners starting Basic Practice have Case Autonomy. However, careful managers review all cases, before they are satisfied that the practitioner can work independently. They also see this as a way of helping the practitioner to develop by "supporting" them through "supervision" of cases that the practitioner would otherwise find too complex.

The test of Case Autonomy is, what is done where there is a complaint? If the manager simply checks that standards were observed, and, if they were, does not direct the practitioner to alter their treatment, they are upholding the Case Autonomy of the practitioner. If the manager calls the practitioner to account in detail for their decisions, and judges the decisions to be poor, or instructs the practioner to revise their treatment, then they are, in effect, assuming responsibility for the case, and removing that responsibility from the practitioner (most social workers do not have Case Autonomy).

If managers do not undertake routine supervision and case reviews, how can they and their employers assure quality? Is it sufficient to assess a person's credentials for a role with Case Autonomy, and then "leave them to it" unless there is a complaint?

Managers certainly need to monitor such practitioner's aherance to policies. They also need to establish quality assurance processes such as peer review to ensure and improve the quality of the practitioners work (chapter 9). These are methods for holding practitioners to account for the responsibility and authority that they have been given, without undermining that responsibility. Regular supervision can undermine a practitioners sense of responsibility, and cross-cut their working relations with clients. However it does not follow that without supervision they will be more responsible.

Although many Basic Practitioners have formal or *de facto* Case Autonomy, they still need to be managed. As we will see in the next chapter, their manager needs authority over non-casework activities if they are to meet their responsibilities.

Practice Autonomy

A second type of autonomy is where the practitioner's autonomy extends beyond individual case decisions to decisions about how they organise their practice.

> *Practice Autonomy*
> *"The freedom to exercise discretion in the immediate management of a practice, specialty or department, without that discretion being reviewed or overridden by a higher authority, unless budgetary or other limits and procedure are infringed".*

Some experienced Basic Practitioners have Practice Autonomy to decide how they use their time within their speciality. Most Development Practitioners and some heads of department have Practice Autonomy, and are managed through general managers, directors or district heads setting the limits to the practice.

The argument is that experienced practitioners, suitably trained and working within parameters such as those defined by contract, can make the best decisions about how they use their time and run their practice. Close direction of their practice management is not only frustrating but prevents them from assuming responsibility for work management. However, assigning them responsibility and autonomy over these matters does not assure the practice is run well: there has to be guidance about priorities and arrangement for holding them to account for their decisions without destroying autonomy.

If we recognise the developing level of work capacity of practitioners, as well as the effects of supervision on the client-practitioner relationship, we can understand the arguments for Case and Practice Autonomy, and the frustration or abdication of responsibility of practitioners who are "closely managed". Managers should exercise their work-reviewing authority and delegate work with regard to the amount of experience and the level of work capacity of the practitioner.

Managers undertaking case reviews of just-qualified staff report that a time comes when they do not find it necessary to review every case, but only the more complex cases. Basic Practitioners often experience reviews of simple cases or of short-term work as intrusive, but they find it helpful and a relief to discuss complex or long-term work.

One explanation for this observation is that the practitioner not only accumulates experience, skills and confidence in the practice situation, but also grows in their capacity to carry higher levels of work. This is indicated by their ability to actively progress casework over longer periods of time without reassurance from a professional superior that they are exercising their discretion appropriately.

6: SUMMARY & CONCLUSION

Therapists frequently argue that they need more independence in their work and that management structures undermine professional autonomy. Sometimes they leave the service for private practice for this reason alone, only to find other restrictions. To retain staff and make the best use of their abilities, employers can create conditions which allow appropriate degrees of freedom, and at the same time assure quality, and that therapists time is used to the best effect. The chapter presented research which described the different organisational conditions practitioners need at different stages of their career.

It summarised these conditions in two concepts: Case Autonomy, which defined the degree of freedom appropriate to a case responsible Basic Practitioner role; and Practice Autonomy, a wider degree of freedom for more experienced practitioners who are able to make local and day-to-day decisions about how they use their time to the best effect.

Chapter 7: MANAGING PRACTITIONERS

1: INTRODUCTION

Therapists in the NHS carry-out many different types of work with different client groups. But who decides whether to employ a therapist, what their role will be, and how they will spend their time every day?

This chapter examines what managing therapists means in theory and in practice. In the NHS stronger therapy management is needed to meet the challenges of the 1990s - to make better use of scarce resources and to ensure and improve quality. It considers the arguments for and against general management or profession-management of therapists, and how either can provide the independence practitioners need, and also meet their responsibilities. The chapter addresses the following questions,
- *What is the role of a therapy manager in the reformed NHS ?*
- *Are therapists better managed by someone from within their profession (a"profession-manager") ?*
- *Are managers accountable for all, or only some of the decisions of the therapists whom they manage? Who is to blame if something goes wrong ?*
- *How can a manager ensure that therapists' skills and knowledge are used to the best effect ?*

The next chapter discusses high-level therapy management roles, and business strategy and structure. This chapter concentrates on operational management and accountability.

2: MANAGEMENT WORK

First we need to consider *what* management work needs to be done, and then *who* should do this work.

General Principles of Management

Management is often described as a set of tasks, or skills that managers need, such as personnel management, budget control, planning, etc. This can obscure the main purpose of all management work, as well as the differences between types of management work. The purpose of management is to use resources in the most effective and efficient way to meet needs. The aim of management is to get the best match between needs and resources, over the short, medium and long term.

Part of the work is to find out about the extent, type and severity of needs. Another part is to understand what type of responses to needs are possible with current resources. The difficult and creative part is to decide how best to respond to meet needs, and how much time or resource to allocate to different areas. What does this mean in practice?

Individual Practice Management

Some of the most expert "short-timescale managers" are experienced practitioners managing their time under the pressure of demand, whether they are self-employed or employed in the NHS. Their management work involves:
- assessing hourly, daily and weekly the incoming demands, and the needs for their skills and knowledge,
- prioritising demands, deciding how to respond and how much time to spend on each thing, guided by policies,
- keeping an eye on how they are using their time, and ensuring that they are using their time and skills to the best effect.

In some professions this management work is done entirely by practitioners, in others, managers do most of this work, and either set detailed policies or direct practitioners. How much of this management work a practitioner does depends on what policies are set for them, and how much discretion these parameters allow to make management decisions. It also depends on how well they have been trained to undertake practice management, and their abilities to carry-out practice management, as distinct from casework.

Experienced practitioners are often the best people to decide how their time and skills are used to the best effect, so long as they are working within appropriate policies, have training in time-management, and are held to account for their decisions. Success in private practice depends on practice management abilities. But, in the NHS, who sets the policies and holds therapists to account for how they use their time?

Team Service Management

In many services, work management policies are decided at the level of the group or team, and by a profession-manager. For example an occupational therapy department has a policy that "x type" of cases are top priority, and should account for 40% of the departments casework time. This sets one of the parameters within which practitioners manage their time every day.

Management at this level is using collective time and skills to the best effect to meet needs. The work involves:
- assessing the weekly and monthly incoming demands for the group's skills and knowledge,

- prioritising demands, deciding who will respond, and how much time should be allocated,
- keeping an eye on the overall distribution of the time of the group to different areas and projects, and adjusting how people spend their time in line with policy, or changing policy.

In occupational therapy one manager will do this work, in consultation with staff. In clinical psychology sometimes a group carries-out this work, with a group coordinator (eg a child and families specialty).

Comprehensive Service Management

Where there are a number of groups combined in a larger service, for example a cross-Unit or District service, resources are matched to needs in different way, and over a longer term. Management work at this level is deciding what type of groups or teams (eg "specialties") to establish, the parameters of their service, and how much resources to put into each so as to meet the most pressing needs over a three to five year timescale.

This management work is done within parameters set by higher levels, for example in Unit plans in models C & D in the chapter 5. The next chapter considers this strategic management work in more detail. In the past this management work was usually done by district therapists.

MANAGEMENT

Management is the work of getting the best match between needs and resources, over the short, medium and long term. To make the most effective use of scarce therapy resources, management is needed at the level of,
- the individual practitioner
(using their time and skills in the best way to meet priority needs)
- the group/team (where therapist are managed together)
(using the collective time and skills in the best way to meet needs)
- the services as a whole
(planning and positioning different groups in the best way to meet needs)

It involves, assessing needs, assessing how therapists can respond, and deploying them to respond to priority needs in the most effective way. It also involves getting and using feedback on the impact of these management decisions (service quality and evaluation).

This gives an idea of what is central to all management work, and the different types of management work to be done. In the past the work was not always done or done well. The following now turns to how to ensure that it is done, and who should do the work.

3: MANAGEMENT RESPONSIBILITY & ROLES

If management work at any level is not done a service is not cost-effective. To make sure that this work is done, health service organisations must have a management structure which,
- clearly assigns responsibility for the work (usually to a manager, or to a group or to individual practitioners),
- assign the necessary authority to do the work (eg over staff, finance, to get information etc),
- hold those responsible to account for how well they have done the work.

Who should be responsible for the work? A general manager, or a profession-manager, or both? What authority do they need, and how are the held to account for the work? Can groups do the work effectively, without a manager with authority to make final decisions? Exactly what management work should practitioners do?

To answer these questions we need to be more precise about the different types of management work, and about what we mean by accountability, especially "professional" and "managerial" accountability. The following builds on the discussion above to define the different types of management work. It also considers who could do this work, and then discusses the accountability of managers. This discussion provides the buiding blocks for defining the details of a therapy service management structure, the outlines of which were sketched in the models in chapter 5.

Levels of Management Work

The theory of levels of work (Rowbottom & Billis (1977), Jaques (1989)) helps to further define and distinguish different levels of management work. It helps to consider what management work should be undertaken by practitioners, what parameters should be set for them, and by whom.

Situational Management

This work is matching resources to demands in the short-term, by responding to situations as they occur, and within policies set by higher levels. For example, whilst treating a client, a practitioner gets a phone call from a referrer with an "emergency" case. The practitioner decides to continue treating the client because she judges this to be higher priority than the "emergency". Another example is a helper telephoning-in "off sick", and the therapy manager deciding to reallocate one helper for that day.

Responsibility: There is an argument that an experienced practitioner should carry-out this management work- we will discuss presently how they could be held to account for how well they did it. To make the best use of resources, trainees and helpers need "situational management", and this is usually done by a member of the profession with the skill and experience to do it.

Operational Management:

This is matching the resources of a team (eg 2-12 people) to demands over the medium term (6-18 months), within policies set by higher management (discussed above as "Team Service Management"). Management work at this level is to set policies and procedures for handling situations as as they arise, so as to make the best use of resources and to ensure quality and safety. It often involves means changing practitioner's sessions to allocate more time to priority areas.

Policies about, for example waiting lists, priority cases, and treatment methods set the parameters within which situations are dealt with and casework is undertaken. Judgement is needed to set policies sufficiently open to allow therapists flexibility, but not so open as to give no guidance about priorities.

Responsibility: Many therapists argue that a general managers do not know enough about possible treatments and ways of responding to be able to set policies which use resources to the best effect. They also argue that practitioners need "support" of different kinds which requires an experienced member of the same profession. Some general managers argue that they should have some involvement in operational management, and feel that agreeing a contract for services may not be sufficient.

In some areas psychologists establish groups to do this work, making decisions on a "democratic" basis, like medical specialty management groups, with a coordinator as "head of department"(Bexley Department (1980)). The available evidence (Appendix 3) is that these groups do not confront and carry through the difficult resource allocation decisions, mainly because most members of the group consider themselves to have "Practice Autonomy". For example, one review of a large psychology service found that, *"It appears to managers that clinical psychologists can largely pick and choose and define their jobs and they are invariably not in the areas of greatest need"* (Piper & Webb (1990)).

Comprehensive Service Management:

Management work at this level is matching needs to resources by deciding what teams to form, their size and what services they will offer to which clients. Management decisions at this level set the parameters within which operational management decisions are made. This strategic management work is discussed in the next chapter.

Responsibility: In many Units and Districts there are departments and therapists in different areas. The issue of whether they should be managed as one comprehensive service was considered in chapter 5, and will be discussed in the next chapter, as will the question of whether a general manager could carry-out management work at this level.

BETTER MANAGEMENT OF THERAPY SERVICES

For therapy services to remain self-managed in the post-1990 NHS, therapists need more effective management structures and processes to be able to sell their services and deliver on contracts. They need information and procedures to ensure, and prove to purchasers that resources are matched to needs. In practice this means agreeing policies or guidelines on:
- *priorities between direct client/patient work and other categories of work*
(ie how resources are used-should be informed by research)
- *priorities between types of clients (propose what should be in contracts) and converting this into practical guidelines about eg,*
- *publicity,*
- *receiving referrals,*
- *accepting for assessment,*
- *waiting lists,*
- *accepting for treatment/intervention*
- *reviewing work,*
- *closure,*
- *recording and reviewing effectiveness,*
and most importantly, implementing and reviewing these policies.
Some therapists fear closer scrutiny of, and less independence in their work. Some welcome more guidance about their role and priorities.

In summary, management, is getting the best match between needs and resources, and this work needed to be done at the individual, team and service levels. The above further defined the different work to be done at each of these levels. It began to consider who could be responsible for doing management work at each level, and noted that their work produced parameters which set the context and boundaries for work at lower levels.

One conclusion of the above is that the arguments for profession-management are less persuasive the further one moves from therapeutic practice: the argument is strongest for managing just-qualified staff and helpers.

The chapter now turns to consider therapy management structure and the simplest arrangement for ensuring the management work at each level is done: the managerial hierarchy. It considers whether any type of managerial hierarchy is compatible with the independence which therapists say they need (discussed in the previous chapter).

Some practitioners argue that they do not need a manager and are trained and able to undertake their work without supervision, as they would in private practice. However, the last chapter argued that providing therapy services as an employee is different to working as a private practitioner. Employed therapists are not formally accountable to the client in the same way as a therapist in private practice.

A public service employer is potentially liable for claims against a practitioner, and carries accountability for the quality of the therapy service which they offer. At a minimum, a public employer of therapists have a duty to ensure safe practice, both because the public expects a basic standard, and because the employer can loose public money in a claim against it. On the more positive side, appropriate management support can both improve the quality of a practitioner's work, help in their career development, and raise morale. What then is "appropriate support" for practitioners doing different work, with different degrees of experience and at different career points?

The main questions we will address are, what management arrangements should employers establish to,
- make the most cost-effective use of therapists skills and knowledge to provide a service to a population? (which means knowing when the therapist is in the best position to decide, and defining their scope to do so),
- ensure the safety and quality of therapist's work with individual clients?
- improve the quality of therapy services?

4: ACCOUNTABILITY & AUTHORITY OF THERAPY MANAGERS

The last chapter considered the formal accountability of practitioners to their clients, their profession, the state, and employers. This chapter considered managers responsibilities and now considers the nature of their accountability and the authority they need.

The following examines manager's responsibilities and accountability for the quality of therapist's casework decisions in relation to an individual client, and then in relation to services to populations. In particular, a) the parameters managers need to set to therapist's practice to ensure the effective use of resources, yet leave scope for the practitioner to detailed decisions about how they spend their time, and, b) how managers and therapists are held to account for their work-management, as opposed to case-work decisions.

Manger's Accountability

'Is a general or profession-manager accountable for a therapist's mistake?'
'Am I accountable for the quality of therapist's casework decisions?'
'What does it mean to be 'accountable for the effective use of resources'?'

In NHS in the past people were only called to account when something went wrong. The aim was to apportion blame and/or try to stop what happened happening again. This kind of accountability is to determine culpability.

More positive "preventative" accountability is for someone with authority to check a person is following policies and procedures. In addition, to assess the quality of their work within the parameters which are set for them, and to give them feedback about their performance. We note that this makes people more answerable for their performance in meeting their responsibilities, and that peer review is one process for more positive accountability (chapter 9).

Work Responsibilities: The work a person is contracted to do. Includes ongoing duties and tasks assigned by higher management.

Accountability: Individual or body to whom a person is answerable. Implies that the individual or body is authorised to call the person to account for their actions or inactions within an area (eg work responsibilities), and is authorised to exercise sanctions under certain conditions.

Authority: The rights and powers assigned to an organisational role by an employer (usually through higher managers) which a person working in that role needs to meet their work responsibilities.

Some general managers find it curious that therapy managers are unclear about their management responsibilities and their accountability. Surely therapy managers are managers in the full sense, being accountable for their own work and the work which they delegate to their staff ? They manage therapists, and as managers they are accountable for the actions or inactions of their staff, and have the authority to set whatever policies and they need to.

We saw in chapter 3 that, in the NHS, this was true in the past. In the 'seventies therapy managers were accountable for the case decisions of staff, and had authority to regularly review casework and direct treatment if they thought it necessary. Some therapy managers were also accountable for deploying staff in the best way to meet demands, and had authority to move staff, and to decide referrals. The management structure was a managagerial hierachy, in essence the same as for nursing.

Accountability for Casework Decisions

With the increasing skill and expertise of senior therapists, managers did not need to monitor casework so closely, and often did not have the expertise to do so. The convention evolved that senior therapists were responsible for their own case-work, and managers would not, and could not review case decisions. This was described as "Case Autonomy" in the previous chapter.

In many situations senior staff also assumed responsibility for deciding their caseload and siting of work, that is, for making "operational management" decisions. They assumed "Practice Autonomy". The situation was different for just-qualified and some basic grade practitioners, where managers felt that it was important for both training and safety purposes to review case-work.

However at present the accountability of heads of department for the casework decisions of practitioners differs between professions, and is frequently unclear. Their responsibilities and authority in relation to practitioner's casework is also unclear. Two critical questions are, what does the manager do if there is a complaint about a practitioner's case decision, and does the manager routinely review casework?

The current situation appears to be as follows. Psychologist's professional association states that a qualified psychologist is personally responsible for their own case-work. This implies that a psychologist head of department cannot be held accountable for another psychologist's casework decision, so long as the psychologist observed established policies and standards. The head of department assures quality by ensuring that there are agreed and observed quality policies, and by establishing peer review processes.

In practice some psychology managers regularly supervise the casework of just-qualified staff, and feel that they carry some responsibility for the casework decisions of these staff, until the practitioner has proved their competence on the job. Managers thus allow increasing degrees of autonomy as the practitioner demonstrates their competence, safety and decreased need for supervision. The situation is similar in speech therapy and dietetics, and chiropody.

In physiotherapy and occupational therapy it is recognised that the basic grade is a training grade, with supervision and without Case Autonomy. The point at which practitioners assume Case Autonomy varies between the two professions and between departments, but usually coincides with grading as a senior.

In all the therapy professions it is generally accepted that a practitioner in a senior grade carries full case responsibility and Case Autonomy. A manager only has authority to review their cases if a complaint is made, and then only to satisfy themselves that established policies and standards were observed. The area of uncertainty appears to lie between the first years in practice and the later experienced practioner: during this period the manager will decide whether a practitioner carries full-case responsibility and has Case Autonomy, depending on their judgement of the needs and abilities of the practitioner. Often it is pressure of work and travelling distances which decides.

Types of "Supervision" and "Review"

To ensure minimum standards and to develop staff, different types of "supervision" are appropriate for therapists at different stages of their career.

Managerial Review (and accountability)
Routine Managerial Review: A profession-manager examines each and every case and can direct action.
Manger Decides Review: Profession-manager asks practitioner to bring selected cases for review, often sets date for review of complex cases when allocating them.
Practitioner Requests Manager to Review: Profession-manager makes clear to practitioner that practitioner can and should request review with manager if necessary.

Peer Support
Practitioner Requests Advice from Peer: Practitioner asks colleague for "advice", or chance to "talk-through" a case to get a different perspective. Practitioner remains responsible and accountable for their casework.
Collective Peer Review: Case presentation or audit to colleagues for learning and quality improvement.

The accountability/support dilemma: If the accountability of a manager for a practitioner's work is not clear this can discourage the practitioner from seeking "support": they and their manager do not know if their manager has to direct them if they take a different view about treatment, or whether the manager is not accountable and can take a different view without directing them (ie the manager is not a "full-manager").

The management issues are therefore,
a) Whether to formally recognise Case Autonomy, or whether manager's accountability for quality and provider liability means that managers, or others, should regularly scrutinise the casework decisions of practitioners.
b) If Case Autonomy is recognised, how to recognise when a practitioner is sufficiently experienced to work in a position with Case Autonomy, and decide what quality assurance arrangements are necessary instead of case review (chapter 9)

A different set of issues arises in relation to manager's responsibilities for services to populations and for work-management as opposed to case-management decisions. We now consider what authority they need to be held to account for this work.

Accountability for effective use of resources

Again it is useful to start by considering the accountability and authority of managers in the past in a traditional managerial hierachy. Chapter 3 showed that heads of department would have received all referrals to a department, and allocated referrals to practitioners according to their skills, experience and current caseloads. They had authority to redeploy staff to other sites and to review caseloads to decide which cases should be closed to make room for more urgent cases waiting to be seen.

With this authority therapy managers could be held to account for the effective use of resources and for providing a service: they had authority to implement their judgements and were held accountable for their decisions.

With the increasing specialisation of senior staff, and more working in the community, arrangements evolved where it was accepted that senior staff were better able to decide such details as how they used their time, from whom they took referrals, and size of caseload. The role of managers in relation to these practitioners became one of setting and monitoring the broad parameters to their practice. It was a situation where managers retained the authority which they had in the past, but rarely exercised it.

Over time, custom and convention became formalised so that a point was reached where it was accepted that the previous authority of managers was no longer appropriate, and that senior practitioners had the *right* to make decisions about the management of their practice. Chapter 6 described this as Practice Autonomy.

The current situation is one where managers are being held to account for the effective use of resources when they do not feel they have the authority to redirect senior staff. One of the purposes of employing more senior therapists is because they are more able to respond flexibly to the needs in a particular area: their experience enables them to decide how to use their skill to the best effect. A manager closely directing senior therapists causes dissatisfaction, and people leave the service. To meet their responsibilities, however, managers need authority to negotiate and monitor the parameters of the senior therapist's practice, and to undertake reviews of work in an appropriate way. In the NHS at present therapy managers are exploring the scope of the authority they need, and what parameters are necessary.

Summary

Therapy service management structures evolved away from full-management structures to ones which allow practitioners autonomy over casework decisions, and over practice management decisions. In these ways therapy management structures differ from both nursing and medical management structures. This type of structure and type of management are often not understood by general managers and others, especially when managing multidisciplinary teams (Øvretveit (1987)). There are arguments for formally recognising roles with Case and Practice Autonomy, and for deciding what stage of their career a therapist would be able to fulfil such roles. More attention to quality and effective use of resources will test the limits to both types of autonomy. Establishing therapy management structures of this type ensures that the necessary management work is undertaken. We now turn to a more complex option for managing therapists, the co-management option.

5: CO-MANAGEMENT ARRANGEMENTS

'A man cannot serve two masters'
Portugese proverb.
'Co-management has only worked because most therapists are women, and more diplomatic than men'
A Birmingham therapist.

Co-management was a compromise solution to the question of general or profession-management, and much used in the 1980s. These arrangements can be established for managing therapists, and for managing profession-managers such as heads of department.

Co-management of Therapy Practitioners

This is a common arrangement for managing therapists in multidisciplinary teams, or where the therapy manager is some distance away. Typically the practitioner is described as being "professionally accountable" to a profession-manager, and "managerially accountable" to a team coordinator, locality manager, or general manager.

The arrangement can work if the two managers have a good working relationship, and if the details of who is responsible for what, and the authority they have in relation to the therapist is agreed and defined (Appendix 4 gives a check-list for defining these matters). Often neither happens and the therapist gets the worst of both worlds: they lack professional support and are "over-directed" by the local manager, or both managers give directions which conflict.

In my experience this arrangement is the least attractive of the options for managing therapists. It takes time to agree the responsibilities of each manager, and time to sort out the misunderstandings or manipulation which can still happen, and which are latent in any three-party relationship. General managers or team coordinators find it complicated to allow different degrees of autonomy for different practitioners - it may mean different formal agreements for each person in a team.

For these reasons one of the following two options is to be preferred, each of which gives clear management with one manager responsible:

a) *A therapy manager* manages the therapist, and the therapist works under contract in the team or locality. The contract is negotiated and agreed with the local manger, and the contract can define the day-to-day control that the local manager needs. The contract provides the control and accountability general managers need, but releases them from the personnel work of recruiting, covering for sickness, and other management work to assure quality. This option is suitable for therapists in models C and D (chapter 5).

b) *A general manager* manages the therapist, and they make arrangements for themselves and the therapist to get advice on a range of matters from a more experienced therapist. The general manager is responsible for managing the therapist and for the quality of their work, and can call upon the more experienced therapist to advise them about how to manage the therapist (model B in chapter 5). The senior therapist is not accountable for the quality of the therapist's work, or for such things as arranging cover. If she is, a co-management arrangement exists, and her responsibilities and authority would need to be defined.

Co-management of Therapy Managers

The second co-management arrangement is where a therapy manager, such as a head of department, is "managerially accountable" to a general manager and "professionally accountable" to a more senior member of the profession (or in some cases a doctor). This arrangement is half-way between models B and C in chapter 4.

Again there are frequently problems where the responsibilities and authority of the general manager and the senior member of the profession (eg a district therapist) are unclear. Often there is conflict between the general manager, who wishes to maximise control over therapy services to their area, and the senior member of the profession who believe they are responsible for providing a cross-Unit service.

Again it is best to decide one way or the other. Rather than managing the department, the general manger can contract the service. The alternative is for the general manager to manage the department (model B2 or C1 in Chapter 4) and call for advice about the management of the department from elsewhere. The latter precludes a fully-managed District or cross-Unit therapy service.

Co-management of Cross-Unit Therapy Managers

In the past therapy managers who managed services across Units (eg a district therapist) were sometimes accountable to their "host" unit general manger and "professionally accountable" to a director of public medicine or other at district level. This arrangement, which had little meaning in most places, lapsed with the separation of purchaser and providers, and led to a new question: how is a District Health Authority or other purchaser to get authoritative advice about where therapy services are needed?

The options are, a district therapist from the same or another District, a therapist from a Regional or surpra-District "advisory" committee, or a therapist from a national advisory organisation. At the time of writing no research into these options was available.

6: CONCLUSION

Where therapists are employed, employers need to make arrangements for,
- ensuring that services to many clients are available, according to severity of need and ability to benefit from therapy, and that therapists time is used to the best effect to serve populations,
- ensuring that the therapy which is provided to a priority client is of the highest quality, and that the employer's liabilities are minimised,
- improving quality by developing staff and making use of quality methods.

Whether a profession-manager or a general manager is responsible for management work depends in part on the level of management work to be done. The chapter concentrated on situational and operational management, and looked at what a manager would need to do to ensure that staff time was used effectively, and that inexperienced staff got the supervision and support which they needed.

The chapter proposed that senior practitioners needed to be managed in a different way to junior and just-qualified practitioners. It distinguished between case work decisions and decisions about practice management, and considered practitioner and manger accountability for each. It proposed that management would be improved if Case Autonomy and Practice Autonomy were recognised, if the parameters to therapists work were more clearly defined, and if therapists with Practice Autonomy were trained in how to manage their practice.

Therapy management in the 1990s is likely to place more constraints on therapists work than they have been used to, and put it under closer scrutiny. There is an argument that profession-managers, suitably trained, are the best for the job. They have the expertise to supervise and develop newly qualified staff, decide the best use of their time, decide the practice parameters to the work of more experienced staff, and have the credibility to lead quality assurance.

Defining responsibilities alone does not ensure that the work is done. To carry out this management work, and to be accountable for it, a person needs authority. It is fashionable to emphasise management style as the way of "getting things done", rather than clearly assigning authority and having an effective accountability and review process. Where "formal structure" is not defined, all managers have to depend on is style and persuasion. This may not be sufficient, and often leads to unnecessary power struggles and manipulation.

Chapter 8:   STRATEGIC MANAGEMENT

'Unless we can get sufficient clinical psychologists in the right place at the right time, and working in settings which facilitate their effectiveness rather than conflict with it, then we might as well not exist.' (Kat (1985)).

1:   INTRODUCTION

- *When does a therapy services need strategic management ?*
- *How should a therapy manager formulate a strategy and a business plan?*
- *How should therapists decide which therapy services to provide and how to finance them?*

This chapter considers the strategic management role of profession-managers of services which are organised according to models C, D or E in chapter 5. It presents concepts for analysing a "public market" to decide the strategy and structure of a therapy service. It outlines a series of steps for involving therapists in formulating a strategy.

In the past in the NHS many district therapists were responsible for strategic management, and some district posts still retain this responsibility. The chapter does not examine the arguments for and against a District service or a district therapist. These issues are discussed in detail in documents issued by professional associations and in other literature (Kinston et al (1982)). Some of the arguments were discussed in chapter 5.

2:   THE NEED FOR STRATEGIC MANAGEMENT

The question of whether a therapy service needs strategic management, and whether a therapy manager should be responsible for this work depends on a number of factors.

The first is how the service is currently organised. In chapter 5 we saw that where therapists are managed by divisional general managers (model B) it is not possible to plan and organise therapy services as a whole over the longer term. There is no distinct therapy service strategy because there is no distinct therapy service beyond individual therapists.

In this model each divisional general manager plans their service, and decides how many of which type of therapists they will employ and how they will be organised. Plans for therapy services are part of, and subordinate to the division's plan. If there is a therapy adviser, possibly outside of the Unit, who may even have the term "District" in her title, she is not responsible for, and does not have the authority to carry-out strategic management.

In contrast, strategic management is not just possible but essential for services organised as cross-Unit, District, supra-District, or as independent group practices (models D and E (and some model C services)). Here therapists are organised together as a distinct management division.

The reason for organising on this basis is not only to make operational management easier, but to make the most of the opportunities to expand therapy services. A decision to establish therapy managers with authority and management training in these models is the practical expression of a Unit wish to ensure that therapy services are developed.

In combined therapy models (C2 and D2) the final decision about strategy is taken by a head of therapies, who may be a general manager.

Sometimes the situation is unclear, for example when a Unit is restructuring, or where services are organised as in model C. In this model most of the therapy service is provided to one directorate or other Unit divisions, and financed by them. Some strategic management is called for to plan and negotiate therapy services with directors or general managers in the "parent" unit, but the choices in this "internal market" may be limited. There may, however be scope and Unit support to market therapy services to purchasers external to the Unit.

A second factor in whether strategic management is called for is the potential for service expansion. We will see that this depends on needs, service capability, purchaser finance, and investment finance. The irony is that it needs a strategic analysis to decide whether there is scope for strategic management.

A third factor is whether a "parent" provider Unit is restructuring. In these situations therapists who develop a sound strategic plan, which gives evidence of market opportunities, may be able to influence decision-makers to form a distinct therapy service when they would not otherwise do so.

In summary, whether strategic management for therapy service is undertaken depends not on the number of therapists in a service but on,
- how the service is currently organised within a Unit (which model),
- the potential needs and market for therapy services, especially "outside" the unit,
- the percentage of service already provided and financed separately as "stand alone" services (ie not part of other Unit services (chapter 4)),

- the ability and willingness of the "parent" Unit to invest in therapy service expansion, as opposed to expanding other Unit services.
- the abilities and determination of a therapy head of service.

The last factor is important because it takes vision to see the potential, and ability to advance a persuasive case. With determination and some support therapy heads can overcome some of the limitations of Model C, and develop their service. It also takes ability to recognise where there is no chance of a Unit supporting therapy service expansion and no way of carrying through a longer-term plan.

3: STRATEGIC MANAGEMENT ROLES

There are four common types of role, each with different proportions of strategic management work.

Operational Manager and Coordinator

The last chapter described operational management roles (eg a head occupational therapist, a superintendent physiotherapist). Some operational managers also have responsibility for coordinating therapists across divisions and Units (eg district superintendent physiotherapists). A therapy coordinator combines the operational management of their own staff with the coordination of therapists managed elsewhere by other therapists or general managers. The therapy coordinator liaises with them to arrange such things as training, rotas, cover, and quality programmes.

Therapy heads who are ready for a strategic role not only see gaps in the service, but start to explore possible finance and how to set up or expand a service. Here the therapist's management role is not intended to be a strategic one, but by virtue of their position and abilities, the therapist may try to do strategic management work. They may be continually frustrated in trying to carry through their plans, or they may be able to acquire the authority they need to fulfil their assumed responsibilities.

Operational Manager and Strategic Adviser

Some heads of service have responsibilities for advising their general manager about how their therapy service may be developed over a two- to five-year period. Alternatively, a head of service may be called upon to give advice about how the therapy services in the District many be developed as a whole over this timescale.

In both situations the head is not a strategic manager: the general manager not only decides whether to develop the therapy service, but also the details of the plan, and carries out the negotiations with purchasers and other managers. Sometimes it suits general managers not to clarify whether the head is in an advisory or strategic management role, for example where the general manager likes the advice, and wants a more detailed business plan before commiting themselves.

Strategic Manager

A "strategic manager" role in therapy services involves responsibilities for,
- setting up a strategy planning process, involving all of the therapists they manage,
- planning strategy and producing the annual strategic plan,
- carrying out strategy, for example by promoting the service, negotiating contracts, and delegating budgets to heads of service to carry-out plans by recruiting staff to priority areas.
They have the financial and personnel authority to do this, as well as skills in marketing, market research, finance, and business planning.

Strategy Coordinator

In some psychology services each sub-service head is responsible for their own strategic planning and management. To coordinate plans, one of the group undertakes the work of ensuring the plans of each sub-service are compatible. The role does not involve authority to override the plans of any sub-service, and the person coordinating is not accountable for the success or otherwise of individual sub-service plans.

The strategic management role of a therapy head depends on how the service is currently organised, the authority delegated to them, and their abilities.

4: STRATEGY- GENERAL POINTS

How then should a profession-manager (or a general manager) formulate a strategy for a therapy service? The following explains what a strategy is, why therapists organised as a distinct service need one, and how a strategy is formulated. The last part of the chapter considers how to decide the sub-structure of a therapy service to best market and manage the different services.

One of the arguments for District services and district therapists was to get a better balance of therapy services across a district, thus making the most of a scarce resource. With Units, and then general management, district therapists found that this was not always easy, but that it was still possible to manage a therapy service strategically. Some therapists fear that the reforms will make it even more difficult to provide their services to people whom that therapists think could most benefit from it.

Strategic management is impossible if a therapists do not understand the 1990 reforms and how the "market" works, and do not pay sufficient attention to what purchasers want and how they may be persuaded to finance the service. In this sense strategic management of therapy services is similar service management in any sector.

Why do therapy services need a strategy?

- The 1990 NHS reforms changed the environment in which therapists work, especially in relation to income and competition.
- Where distinct therapy services are retained, therapists have to secure income from purchasers, who may be able to choose to contract other therapists, substitutes, or nothing.
- Looking forward can ease predictable (and unpredictable) problems in the future: it is better than fire-fighting,
- It provides some assurance to potential investors by showing exactly how the finance will be used: there is no chance of investment finance from general managers or others without a thought-through rationale.
- It describes and justifies to staff the reasoning behind changes, increases their commitment to the changes, and raises management credibility,
- Provides a yardstick for control of income and expenditure.

A strategy is a 5-year plan describing, of all the possible alternatives, the aims for the service, the plans for achieving the aims, and the values which support the means and the ends to be achieved. It provides a vision of the position the service wishes to occupy in the health "marketplace" and unifies, orientates and motivates staff towards a common purpose.

The elements of a strategic plan are,
- An analysis of the business environment for each sub-service and the service as a whole,
- A rationale for reducing, maintaining, or developing different activities,
- The resources needed (people, capital and revenue),
- The end points to be reached (strategic objectives),
- A Business plan, giving details of cash-flow projections and investment finance requirements.

A business plan is different from, and part of a strategic plan. It is a detailed 2-year statement of the actions and resources needed to sustain and develop a defined area of business activity, and the financial projections and details. A business plan,
- Predicts future problems and prepares solutions to overcome them.
- Provides the financial and marketing details and rationale for the strategy.
- Demonstrate how a service will use resources to take advantage of the opportunities in the market.

- Answers investors questions about whether the organisation can deliver the services successfully with the resources available.

The Strategy Planning Process

As important as the content of the strategy is the way in which therapists formulate it and review it annually. The strategy planning process should involve all therapists in gathering and analysing information and in debating the strategic direction. A strategy is no use if therapists are not working together to make it happen. A structured planning process may take time to set up and use, but it is the best way of winning their commitment to and understanding of a strategy which is finally produced.

The process is also important because of rapid change. Long term planning is still necessary but plans become out of date more quickly. Therapists cannot produce better plans by predicting the future better, but they can improve their processes for revising strategy, and for recognising and responding to significant changes. An effective strategy planning process and frequent revision of strategic plans is essential.

5: STRATEGY: CONCEPTS & PRINCIPLES

The basis of service strategy is the needs-response model, already used in earlier chapters to explain principles of management. How does it apply at the strategic level? First consider how a commercial service decides whether to offer a service:

NEEDS   +   RESPONSE

What customers want   +   What service we can provide = Profit or Loss
/Price they will pay for it   /Cost to us to provide it

Relative to competition

Commercial services do market research to find out if there is a demand for a service. Demand is where people want the service and they will spend money to buy it: where there is a need and purchasing power. The other "response" part of the equation is what service can be provided and the cost of doing so.

If there are customers who want a service which can be provided, and the price they are prepared to pay is higher than the cost of providing the service, then a commercial service will consider offering the service.

Therapy services do similar calculations for private markets for their services, but the "needs" part of the equation is more complex. In the UK there are two main types of private markets for therapy services, both of which are growing.

The first is where individuals are both clients and purchasers of the service ("customers"). Private therapy services differ to many commercial service in that where there is a difference between what clients want and what therapists think that they need, therapist's ethics are supposed to prevent them from providing services which may make a profit, but may not be in the client's long-term interests.

The second is where an insurance company or an employer is the purchaser, and they decide the price paid for the service. They also have a view about the client needs that they are prepared to pay therapists to meet.

A strategic decision for some NHS therapy services is whether to enter private markets. Their decision is influenced by policy, therapist's values, and by calculating the profit potential after assessing each part of the equation for the local market.

Most therapy services are concerned with public purchasers such as District health and local authorities, fund-holding GPs, and Unit divisions such as directorates. To decide whether to offer a service in a "public market", a therapy service analyses and calculates as follows:

NEEDS $\quad + \quad$ *RESPONSE*

What is wanted by, $\quad +$ What service we can provide $=$ Survival
- clients (& carers), and,   /Cost to us to provide it   or profit
thought to be needed for clients by,
- referrers,
- therapists
- purchasers,
/Price purchasers will pay

If we refer to the discussion of the nature of the "public market" in chapter 4, we can see that the two parts of the equation are different for a therapy service in a public market.

NEEDS

In comparison to commercial markets the assessment of needs is more complex, in part because there are more perceptions to take account of. The term "needs" here refers to a number of factors which a therapy service must assess. First how many and how much clients and/or carers want the service. Second, for a service that relies on referrals, referrer's judgements of how many clients could benefit from the service. Third, therapist's judgement of need for the service. Forth, purchaser's judgement of the need for the service, relative to other needs they must purchase services to meet.

It may be clear from assessing all these perceptions that there is a need for the service. However it is financial suicide to offer a service without calculating the other parts of the equation. The "needs" part is completed by assessing the price that purchasers are prepared to pay for the quality of service which therapists are prepared to offer (the "cost-quantity-quality balance" is discussed in Chapter 9). This involves looking at competitor's prices and "sounding-out" purchasers.

RESPONSE

The "responses" part involves assessing what type of responses would satisfy needs, as perceived by each party, and assessing what skills are available or can be recruited to respond in this way. Then the cost of this response is calculated.

Where new staff have to be recruited and money spent to get a service to a point where it can be purchased (improvement or "start-up" costs) public therapy services also have to assess whether they can get investment finance. How the service is organised within a Unit will determine the availability of investment finance: it is more likely to be forthcoming in model D than in models C.

After assessing all these elements, therapists can calculate whether a particular service is financially viable. Shortly we will look at how therapists can assess their sub-services to decide which to expand or contract.

These then are the principles of service strategy in public markets, but how would a therapy manager go about formulating a service strategy? In practice, how can therapists analyse their services and decide which to expand and which to contract?

6: PRACTICAL STEPS FOR FORMULATING A STRATEGY

The following outlines a series of steps used by therapy services to formulate a service strategy. Appendix 5 gives further details of each step, and Figure 8.1 below gives a summary.

Step	1	Service Mission
Step	2	Aims & Objectives
Step	3	Current Services

Step 1   *Service Mission*
Step 2   *Aims & Objectives*
Step 3   *Current Services*
          Sub-services(deliver one or more "products")
          Competitors, Comparitors.

Step 4   *Market & Capability Analysis*
          for each sub-service
4a Data   Assessing current and future demand, market shares.
4b gathering Our current & future capability to respond, costs.
             Current and future competitors
4c Analysis SWOT for each sub-service.

Step 5   *Strategic Decisions*
          Understanding sub-service interdependence/synergy.
          (eg could a sub-service be fully-independent?)
          Combining analyses of each sub-service to decide
          which to expand or contract

Step 6   *Change Strategy*
          & Business Plan
          Details, justification, and basis for control/reassessment,
          for markets, capability and finance.

Step 7   *Implementation*
          Timetables, landmarks and responsibilities
Step 8   *Review-Return to "Aims & Objectives"*

Figure 8.1   FORMULATING STRATEGY - Steps in the Process

Step 1: Service Mission

The first step is to formulate a service mission statement which encapsulates the overall purpose and values of the service. The mission is why the service exists and what it is for.
eg *"Our mission is to improve peoples' psychological health and relieve psychological suffering from illness at the lowest cost and to the highest quality"*

The mission is a "banner" motif or motto which embodies the essence of the service- it's identity. The debate about mission and the arguments about priorities are in many ways more important than the final statement. It must be owned, understood, and an inspiration to all who work in the service. One approach is to ask therapists to propose mission statements, circulate the proposed statements and hold a meeting to discuss and debate each.

Step 2: Aims & Objectives

The statement of aims of the service are general, but begin to define what is necessary to fulfil the mission. The aims give "compass direction", and help to choose the best "routes". Aims must support the mission, and should not divert attention or energy from core purpose, or be too many.

eg   "- *to be responsive to individuals and carers needs,*
         - *provide a satisfying work environment,*
         - *develop centres of excellence and innovative therapies,*
         - *continually reduce costs consistent with other aims".*

Objectives are related to aims and mission, but are more specific, achievable, measurable, and have time-targets. Objectives are corporate and apply to all sub-services and are reflected in all staff objectives. They prioritise key parts of the service's aims. Too many objectives suggest that the the service has not worked out its priorities - the more objectives the more likely that they will conflict and will not be achievable.

One of the dilemmas of formulating service strategy is that it is not possible to decide objectives until the analysis of each sub-service is done, as described in the next steps (Appendix 5 refers to this as the "chicken and egg" of strategy "). When first drawing up a strategy, objectives are not defined until the process is complete, and after step 7.

Step 3: Current Services

In this step a decision has to be made about how to define the different therapy services so as to perform a business analyses for each sub-service in the next step. The simplest way is to define the sub-services in terms of the existing management divisions. Heads of service can then lead the business analyses for their sub-services, and report back in Step 5 below.

The last part of this chapter considers service structuring. Note that a strategic analysis does not have to be done in terms of existing management divisions. They might not be structured in relation to a coherent market, but structured for convenient management of staff who happen to be based in one area. One of the later steps is to question whether current sub-service definition and structuring is the best way of packaging responses to need in the future. For example there may be specialties within services which should be developed as services in their own right, or some specialties may be better as parts of other services.

Step 4: Sub-Service Business Analysis

This is the most detailed and lengthy step. The "needs-response" model discussed above is the basis for each sub-service to gather data and analyse

their market and their capability to respond. The first part is a market analysis for each sub-service. The aim is to,
- gather data for each sub-service about different perceptions of needs, for the past, and extrapolating into the future,
- assess what proportion of the total needs the sub-service currently meets (market share),
- assess what proportion is met by other services/competitors, and is unmet,
- assess the purchasing power of the market for the sub-service, and what needs purchasers will pay to be met, and decide how to influence them.
(A format for collecting data and for analysis is provided in Appendix 5).

These are all judgements, based on whatever evidence is available from a variety of sources. Assessing needs is difficult and complex. The aim is not an "objective definition" of needs (there is no such thing), but to make better-informed judgements supported by evidence, and to avoid misleading conclusions.

Figure 8.2 contrasts the information which is required, with the information which is usually available. For strategic planning, better management information is needed for more accurate judgements to be made about the top-right hand corner.

	Last Year	Next Year	Five-Years Time
1) What is need for therapy service?	?	?	?
2) Of need what % presents as demand?	?	?	?
3) Of demand what % do we respond to?	Accurate information	?	?
4) Of those we respond to what % do we serve effectively	?	?	?

Figure 8.2:   Information for Strategy: What information is available vs what is needed

The market analysis for each sub-service builds a picture of needs, and picture of who might pay for needs to be met. The market potential is summarised by placing the sub-service on the following grid:

MARKET ASSESSMENT		
Good	*Service to develop high risk from competition*	*High volume service with strong position*
Market Growth		
Poor	*Poor growth potential Low share*	*High volume service low growth potential*
	Low **Market Share** High	

The market is both needs and the finance available to buy services. Thus "market share" refers to both the proportion of needs met by the sub-service, and to the proportion of the total purchasing power which is income for the service. "Market growth" refers to both the forecast rise or decrease in needs, and to the forecast rise or decrease in purchasing power. A market has little potential if the share of demands currently met is low, the growth of demand is high, but the purchasing power is declining or static.

Step 4b: Capacity to respond

This part of Step 4 is to assess the sub-service's capacity to respond, and its costs in comparison to competitors. The market may have high potential and be attractive, but the service's capacity to respond may be weak (eg costs too high to compete, or cannot recruit staff). The data which is collected is summarised by listing strengths and weaknesses of the sub-service in comparison to competitors.

Step 4c: Overall Business Analysis for a Sub-Service

High		
	Seek new markets	*Expansion*
Capability (from strengths & weaknesses summary)		
Low	*Reduce service*	*Improve*
	Low	High
Market Attractiveness/Potential (From market summary: needs & income potential)		

This part of step 4 summarises the above sub-service's analysis of needs, and its ability to respond. By placing the sub-service on the above grid, this part relates market potential to capabilities and strengths, considering the risks and weaknesses :

Step 5: Strategic Decisions & Overall Analysis

In this step the business analyses for each sub-service are brought together to decide the overall strategy. The aim is to decide which sub-services to develop, consolidate, close, or contract, and to reassess the structuring of sub-services. Therapists compare the prospects for each sub-service by comparing and discussing the summary grids produced by each sub-service in step 4c. Step 5 also involves considering any interdependences and synergy between sub-services, so that reducing one does not undermine another which is to be expanded.

Steps 6-8

Having decided the overall service direction, the final steps are to gather the details for a business plan, and to work out the change strategy for the service - primarily how to change attitudes and working relationships.

Using this approach therapists can set up a strategic planning process to work through these steps and to produce a service strategy with,
- a statement of the aims of the service in terms of the type of clients and their needs to be met in the future, and the type of sub-service which will be provided because it meets needs at the lowest comparative cost,
- a statement of the distinctive features of service to be developed, which are known to valued by clients, referrers and purchasers,
- a general statement of the service package, design of the service, and plan for developing it.

We now return to the question of how to structure or group services into "sub-services".

7: THERAPY SERVICE STRUCTURE

This part of the chapter considers how a therapy service should be sub-divided into sub-services (the primary divisions of the service), and what type of primary divisions should be created for managing arrangements therapists in these divisions.

Ideally, the structure of a therapy service into sub-services reflects an understanding of where the most pressing needs are and how therapists are best assigned to meet these needs. In the past the type and amount of therapy services provided to different areas was decided more by personalities, historical accidents, windfall finance, and opportunism, than by rational planning. District services and district therapists were supposed to change this, and in some areas they did achieve a better match between therapy services and population needs.

Strategic management relates therapy responses to needs over a 2-5 year time scale. It does this by deciding how much time of which therapy posts to allocate to different sub-services, and by deciding the type of sub-services to establish. The strategy planning process above showed how a therapy manager in a strategic role would lead a review of an inherited structure to decide a strategy and structure for public markets.

Chapters 6 and 7 considered the "vertical dimension" of structure: the different levels of work carried out by practitioners and managers. Here we are interested in the "horizontal dimension": how a service is divided into fields or areas of work. An example is a physiotherapy service divided into four divisions: two acute physiotherapy services (each a department in the two major acute hospitals in the District); a service to people with a learning disability; and a community physiotherapy service.

Therapy Service Divisions: How best to group therapists?

In principle a therapy service can be sub-divided in many different ways:
- in terms of different types of client group (where people's needs are similar, and different to other people's needs)
- in terms of therapy techniques, methods, or areas of knowledge,
- in terms of geography, either population areas or where therapists are based,
- in terms of unit structure.
Management-divisions should group therapists together in relation to the markets for their services.

Strategy-Driven Primary Divisions (or Sub-Services)

Should the service be divided into teams of therapists each serving different client groups? Is a better basis for division in terms of where therapists are located - to group therapists in the same area or site under the management of one head? Should therapists be grouped in terms of which Unit or which Unit division they serve? Or should the primary divisions be groupings of therapists whose skills and techniques are similar, and different from other therapists in the same profession?

Frequently the decision is complicated by unclarity about who manages which therapists, and whether sessions or posts can be changed. Even if a head of service has authority to decide therapy service structure, their decision is not easy and they must weigh the importance of a number of factors.

If a therapy service is to develop, the decision about which divisions to establish and how much resources to put into each must be driven by a service strategy. The discussion above showed how to analyse market potential, and the capability of existing therapy sub-services to respond. A strategic analysis of this type starts by clarifying the current range of therapy sub-services, considers the potential of each, and leads to an analysis of which to expand.

Clearly if the market (ie needs & purchasers) for a sub-service shows little potential relative to other sub-services, it does not make business sense to invest scarce resources in the sub-service. Alternatively, there may be needs and purchasers, but the sub-service may be weak in relation to the competition (eg comparative cost or quality), or it may be difficult to expand (eg difficult to recruit staff). The strategic analyses help to decide which sub-service to invest in.

Basing future service structure on past sub-services usually leads to incremental restructuring by gradually expanding and contracting existing divisions. The disadvantage of this approach is that if existing groupings undertake the strategic analyses, although they are the experts they are also biased: they tend to propose developments within their own field when this may not be justified relative to other fields. Sometimes a service head's promotion or current grade depends on retaining or expanding the sub-service.

It is important that gaps in the service are recognised and market analyses undertaken for new services. It takes a strong service head to carry through radical change, and forge a consensus amongst a group of established and experienced heads, who may prefer to align with Units or directorates.

If the strategy steps are followed, with a collective and objective appraisal in Step 5, the end result will give clear indications about how to structure the service to make the most of the opportunities in the market.

Nature of the Sub-Service or Division

Apart from defining services in relation to markets, the other key consideration in deciding structure is the best operational management of therapits. In management terms there are three types of division.

1) *A Profession-Managed Division:* This is typically a group of about 2 to 20 therapists, managed by a head of service carrying out an operational management role.

2) *A Co-Managed Specialty Division*: This is the same as above, but the head of service is not in a managerial role, but 'co-manages' with a general manager or director the therapists who work in the same field.

3) *A Specialty Division of Development Practitioners*: This type of division was common in clinical psychology. Here development practitioners working in the same field have practice autonomy to decide their own work management, but are coordinated by a specialty head. Basic practitioners in the division are either managed by the specialty head or a development practitioner.

Note that a therapy "specialty" may, or may not be a management division.

Management Divisions and Specialties

"Service groupings" often evolve in an unplanned way and frequently do not operate as true management divisions. They are often titled "specialties", with a nominal "head", and simply describe the fact that practitioners deal with certain clients or share specialist knowledge/skills.

A management division is a group of people accountable for providing a defined service to a client group: it is a self-regulating service entity which continually matches the available resources of the group to the needs of the client group. A "speciality" thus may be a management division, or it can be the name given to a specialist field of work undertaken part- or whole-time by one or more practitioners. Heads of specialty may be managers of a division, or simply the most highly graded practitioner in the field, and without a clear management role.

The approach proposed here is that not only should divisions be defined in terms of the markets for therapy services, but that they should also be management divisions, with a head of each division.

The level of work and authority of heads of different divisions may be different. Some may only be responsible for situational management (discussed in chapter 7). Some may be operational managers and some may be responsible for strategic management of the division. Where the top therapy manager has authority, they can decide to establish a high-level management post to head one or more divisions to ensure that the division is developed.

Thus therapy service divisions are structured not just to cover a defined area or field of work, but to be able to carry out different levels of work. Some divisions can be structured to develop, and some to respond to demand without major changes, depending on the level of work of the head of division. Whether a therapy manager makes these decisions depends on how the therapy service is organised - heads of Model D or E type services clearly have such a strategic role.

A Simple Service Structure Review

Many services do not have the time or resources to carry out the type of strategic analysis described in this chapter, but still need to restructure to respond to changes in the market and Unit organisation. The following describes a simple review process to assess the balance of services in different areas and to decide future primary divisions. A more detailed review would examine the management arrangements within each division.

Step 1: The first part of a service review clarifies the existing primary divisions or sub-services. Therapists contribute information to build up a profile of how their time is spent on work for different client groups, and on different activities. The format below uses clinical psychology as an example:

Name	Job Title	Grade	Session	Description &Location	Service Grouping
Rick	*Head of Department*	*Principle*	*5 sessions* *2 "* *3 "*	*Psych. Hosp.* *LocalUnit .* *G.P. Surgery.*	*Adult Mental Illness.*
Anna	*Child Psychologist*	*Senior*	*6 sessions* *2 "* *2 "* *etc.*	*Children's Hosp.* *Out Patients .* *G.P. Surgery.*	*Children &Families.*

Step 2: A "pie chart" is then made to shows how the overall resources of the service are used. This shows the real priorities of the service. After becoming aware of how time is spent, therapists are forced to make a conscious decision to continue or to change priorities. Therapists are often surprised by the proportion of time spent on particular client groups and activities. By questioning the surprise it is possible to make explicit the assumed priorities, and this lays the basis for formulating objectives for the future service plan.

Step 3: In this step therapists discuss where the gaps in service are and what would be a better matching of needs and resources. They produce another "pie chart", this time based on the ideal proportions of time in three years. Questions should be raised about whether it is sufficient to readjust proportions or whether new service divisions are necessary.

Step 4: Therapists can then consider where the finance might come from to pay for the ideal distribution. They also consider any barriers to changing service allocations and structure. This also helps to clarify how to market the service, and what information is lacking about needs and how time is used.

In formulating a proposed strategy and structure it is important to understand how the existing distribution of posts, groupings, and sessions arose, and who will loose and gain by the proposed structure.

8: SUMMARY & CONCLUSION

Strategic management is necessary for a therapy service to thrive in private and public markets. Heads of therapy services which are organised as distinct services have a strategic management role. The proportion of time they will be able to devote to this work will depend on a number of factors, such as the position of the service within a Unit, how much responsibility they have for operational management of one of the therapy sub-services, and how much the service depends on external finance.

Where management arrangements are unclear, a therapy manager and their staff can formulate a strategy to prove that there is a market for their services, and that distinct therapy organisation is the best way to organise the service. Whether a therapy service needs strategic management does not depend on the number of therapists and how they are currently organised. It depends on the potential for expansion and the "parent" or "host" unit interest in expanding the service. Accurate information about needs, current staffing, the labour market, and purchaser priorities is essential.

SERVICE STRATEGY

A service strategy involves,
- Identifying client segments, and their wants, needs and expectations,
- Research into purchaser's and referrer's expectations,
- Estimating what service can be provided, and costs,
- Deciding which clients and services to concentrate on, by building on service strengths to exceed expectations and cover costs. Identifying what will differentiate the service from the competition,
- Developing a unique "service package" for competitive advantage,
- Making sure that all staff, clients, purchasers and referrers are aware of what is distinctive about the service and its aims, ideally through involving them in formulating a strategy.

A successful strategy is not just based on evidence of need, but based also on a realistic appraisal of possible purchasers. It must also objectively assess the strengths and weaknesses of each sub-service's ability to respond to needs, in comparison to competitors. A strategy takes time to formulate, but the time is well spent if it ensures that therapists understand, are commited to and own the strategy. An effective process also ensures that the strategy is regularly updated.

The successful services will not be those that provide services which they think clients need. It will be services providing what clients, purchasers and

GPs say they want, and that use their information about needs to convince purchasers to place contracts. An understanding of these views is essential to formulating a service strategy.

The strategy should also decide the broad structure of the service, in terms of how the primary divisions are defined, and the number and level of posts in each division. Two other issues of concern to strategic managers are contracts and quality, the subjects of the next chapter.

Chapter 9: CONTRACTS & QUALITY

===

'Do we need contracts for all our services?'
'What do you do if general managers say you have to provide a service to them, and that there is no need for a contract?'
'How detailed should a contract be and what should it cover?'
'What happens if you can't meet the contract?'
'How can you raise quality when the pressures are to cut costs and increase the number of people served?'
'How do you get therapists to examine and improve the quality of their service?'

1: INTRODUCTION

Two important skills for therapy managers are to be able to negotiate and manage contracts, and to apply new quality methods. Contracts and quality methods are management "tools": devices to help managers achieve their objectives of making the best use of resources to meet needs. They are the means by which therapy managers carry-out their business and marketing strategies.

This chapter, shows why contract and quality management is important to the future of therapy services in public markets and to their "business autonomy". It gives an introduction to the concepts underlying contracts and quality assurance, and shows how managers can start to negotiate contracts and introduce quality methods.

2: "BUSINESS AUTONOMY" & FINANCING THERAPY SERVICES THROUGH CONTRACTS

Although many therapists feel that contracts restrict their flexibility, contracts are the main way in which therapy services secure their independence and future. General managers, directors, GPs and others will employ and manage their own therapists, unless it is more attractive for them to buy-in the therapy they need to provide their service.

In most other sectors, organisations buy-in services rather than manage their own if they do not have the expertise, or if managing it distracts attention from the core business. Buying-in is also a better option if suppliers can provide a less expensive service of the same or higher quality, or can better respond to high demand or fluctuations in demand.

Therapy managers can show general managers that they can get an assured service without the personnel management problems if they buy-in therapists under contract. In so doing therapy managers can influence moves to break-up District or Unit departments, and retain the management of their service. They are more convincing when they already have experience of contract preparation, negotiation and management, for example with external purchasers. Therapy managers not only need skills to negotiate contracts, but need to improve their personnel management, and information and financial management systems to plan and manage contracts.

Independence for therapists also comes from having a variety of purchasers. Many therapy departments or District services are likely to be financed mostly by their "parent" Directorate or Unit. More external contracts means greater independence, although the "parent" Directorate or Unit which manages the service may oppose this.

Before looking at the details of how to prepare and negotiate a contract, we need to consider who the potential purchasers or contractors are, and the main elements of a contract.

Contracts for What and with Whom?

A contract is a framework within which two parties reach, and then monitor an agreement about what each will provide. It makes explicit and formalises a relationship of exchange. We are concerned here with service-for-finance contracts, where one party provides a defined service in return for finance.

| | "Position" of Contractor | |
	External to *"parent" District, Unit, or Division*	Internal to *District, Unit, or Division*
Level of Contractor		
Statutory Purchasing Authority	Other District or Local Authority	Own District or Local Authority
Unit	eg Non-"parent" UGM	"Parent" UGM (manager)
Division/Directorate/Programme	eg Director	eg Director in Unit or own Directorate (manager)
Others		
GPs	Outside District	Own District
Insurance	"	"
Employers	"	"
Private patients	"	"

The more external large contracts (top left hand corner), the greater the business autonomy.

Table 1   POTENTIAL CONTRACTORS FOR THERAPY SERVICES

In its ideal form a contract is freely entered-into by both parties, and although this ideal is rare in practice, too great a power imbalance turns a contract into a directive. Therapy managers do sometimes reach "service agreements", where no finance is exchanged. Sometimes they are not free to refuse to accept the terms of managers in their own unit, and they cannot "contract" to their own manager. Given these qualifications, and the general definition of a contract, Table 9.1 (above) outlines the potential contractors and purchasers of therapy services.

In considering contracts we need to remember the three main ways in which therapy services are financed (chapter 4):
Delegated Budget: By a block allocation or "budget" by a divisional manager (eg general manager) to the therapy service they manage to pay for services to clients of that division (models B2 or C1 in chapter 5). For example by block allocation from a Director to a therapy department managed by the Directorate to provide therapy services within the Directorate and to the Directorate's clients.
Internal Contract: By finance from another Directorate or budget-holder within the Unit (Termed "internal service agreement" where no finance is exchanged)
External Contract: By finance from a purchaser outside the Unit. The finance is usually paid to the "parent" Unit as the accounting entity, and then allocated to the therapy service budget.

The nature of the contract is different in each case, and is a more freely-entered into exchange by two independent parties in the third. Two other factors have a bearing on the source of therapy service finance: the way in which Units and Districts handle contracts, and the Unit's accounting system:

Unit Contracts

Units are continually reorganising to be able to better "package" services to sell to purchasers, and to manage contracts. Their management structures increasingly mirror their main contracts.

In the early 1990s it is unlikely that purchasing health authorities will form separate contracts for therapy services: they are not able to handle the number of contracts this would lead to. Consequently most therapy services will be financed as part of other contracts which the Unit agrees, and the Directorates will either manage or "sub-contract" therapists.

Problems then arise financing therapy services that are not "part of" other Unit contracts or Directorates. In theory, therapy services should be "sub-contracted" (or managed) by a Directorate if therapy is integral to (or complimentary to) the Directorate's service, and externally contracted if it is a "stand-alone" service(Chapter 4).

Accounting Systems

In practice in the early nineties only a few Units had sufficiently sophisticated financial systems to carry out internal financial transfers, or even external NHS transfers from neighbouring districts. In the early 1990s Unit managers actively discouraged therapy heads from trying to establish contracts, mainly because their time was taken-up dealing with large-scale contracts with purchasers.

During this time astute therapy service managers were more concerned to reach "service agreements", mainly to assert their managerial control of the therapy service, and to clarify their responsibility for providing the service. For· these purposes the question of who pays and how finance is actually transferred is less important. However, when a Unit introduces resource management, it is essential that the accounting systems correspond to the desired management arrangement rather than subvert them (see Figure 4.3). It is the same astute therapy managers who work closely with finance staff to ensure systems can handle external and then internal therapy service contracts.

3: THE MAIN ELEMENTS OF A CONTRACT

The three key elements to specify in a contract are price, quantity (sometimes called "volume"), and quality. Each is related to the other two (Figure 9.1).

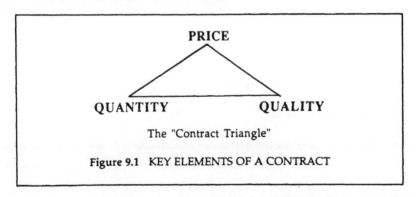

PRICE

QUANTITY   QUALITY

The "Contract Triangle"

Figure 9.1 KEY ELEMENTS OF A CONTRACT

We can illustrate the relationship between the three "corners" of the "contract triangle" if we use simple ways to specify quantity (therapist's time), and quality (grade of therapist). Consider a purchaser who has a fixed budget to buy the therapy service. For this they can buy "x" amount (eg 2-days a week therapist time), at "y" quality (eg a qualified therapist). If they want a higher quantity (4 days time), for the same price, the quality must be lower (eg an assistant or trainee therapist). If they want a higher quality service (eg a senior therapist) for the same price, then the quantity must be less (1-days time). Fixing one corner of the triangle means that if another goes up, the other must come done (the exception to this is discussed below).

Contract negotiation is a bargaining process: Purchasers try to get the most quantity and quality they can for the price, just like therapists do at the supermarket. Providers then threaten to withdraw from negotiations at a point where they know they cannot deliver (so as to protect their reputation), or at point where they know that the purchaser has no alternative. All three corners of the triangle must be specified to carry-out meaningful negotiations, and to protect the contracting parties' interests:

Quantity.

The quantity of service is the easiest to specify and monitor, either in terms of the resources supplied ("input"), for example the therapist's time, or in terms of the "amount" of service delivered ("output"), for example the number of cases treated or assessed.

Price: The price is what the purchaser is charged. The cost is what it costs to provide the service. If the service is to build-up a surplus, it must charge a price higher than cost. The difference is "margin", or profit. Table 9.1 shows a simple way to calculate cost, and then price.

---

1) TOTAL COST OF SERVICE
    Practitioner's Salaries (inc NI, Superannuation, etc.)...........£
    Secretaries and managers salaries.......................................£
    Training...£
    Equipment (clinical, admin.)...£
    Consumables (clinical, admin.)..£
    Telephones, post, any office rental charges.......................£
    Travel..£
    Reserves for contingencies and development fund(min 5%)...£
    Unit or "host" additional overheads ....£

                                                    Total cost..   £_____
    (Add % margin or profit to decide final ideal production cost-price, then consider the market to decide how to price)

2) DECIDE UNIT OF SERVICE TO SUPPLY UNDER CONTRACT
    For example,
    - by time (hour, or half day sessions) (work out how many chargable days avalable (220-240 a year)
    - by quantity of cases assessed/treated (weigh cases)
    (Different service may be sold as different Units off service (eg time for consultancy, or case episodes)

3) CALCULATE UNIT PRICE
    From total cost and according to Unit of service which is supplied. Always be able to quote an "off the record" average price.

    Table 9.1   Calculating the Cost and Price of a Therapy Service

---

Therapy managers decide the type of "unit of quantity" in which to sell different therapy services (eg a basic "unit" is one half-day or hour therapy session). From this they calculate an average price in order to give potential purchasers some idea of the price of a therapy service. To begin with the price and quantity are based on records of last years service, plus a percentage for reserves and contingencies. This is "production costing", but "market pricing" is emerging, based on an estimate of what the market will bear, usually determined by purchaser demand relative to supply.

Many therapists underestimate the true cost of their service, and fear that their price is too high. It is only through getting out the records and doing these calculations that managers can monitor their costs and judge the effects of any changes on their unit costs. Clearly accurate management information of the right kind is essential, not just to be able to invoice purchasers, but to be able to offer the most competitive price in contract proposals.

Quality

This is the most difficult of the three elements to specify, yet failure to do so exposes both purchaser and provider to possible exploitation by the other party. Quality can be specified in terms of the quality of resource supplied (eg grading the quality of the therapist), or the quality of the work carried out (eg that what is done is done in a way that meets certain standards), or in terms of the quality of outcomes (eg change in health status of the client).

The incentive to specify quality is not just to be able to complete a contract specification and monitor what is done against it. Rather, specifying and measuring quality is part of the process of improving quality, and is essential for a therapy service to enter a market and improve its competitive position. This chapter considers below how to specify quality as part of a service's quality assurance programme.

From the purchaser's point of view there are two approaches to specifying quality. First to specify quality in detail, second to specify that the provider uses an approved quality system. The latter approach is preferable for both purchaser and provider. It reinforces the provider's responsibility for quality, and purchasers do not have the expertise to decide what details to specify, or the capacity to monitor a detailed specification. A good quality system ensures that those things that are essential to quality are specified and that performance is documented. The purchaser then monitors the system- they are becoming increasingly knowledgeable about which are the better quality systems.

4: PREPARING AND NEGOTIATING A CONTRACT

The following describes one approach to preparing, negotiating and managing a contract (Figure 9.2). Other methods appropriate to therapy services are described in Heywood (1990) and Morgan & Marchment (1990). DoH general guidance may be found in DoH (1990d).

---

1. Collect Historical Data
To ascertain what services were provided, and were needed:
Quantity   a) Demand (Numbers, Type of cases)
           b) Responses (Time provided or numbers of clients seen (different case weightings))
Cost   Calculate Unit cost per session, or case episode (see Table 9.1)
Quality   Define the quality of service provided in the past, in relation to you therapy service policies or
           other criteria.

2. Plan Proposal
    For service(s) you propose to provide (this should follow Service Strategy (Ch 8):
    Estimate what you will provide and quantity, define quality, decide price (and method of invoicing and
    payment), and work out alternative cost-quantity-quality options.
    Clarify what you need from the purchaser and others (eg facilities, equipment, information, other services)
    Clarify the value to the purchaser and clients and others of the service (Ch 8)

3. Call asking if you can send a proposal, then send draft proposal to purchaser and ask for a meeting to discuss.

4. Meet with Purchaser and discuss.

5. Revise and prepare contract.

6. Formally agree and "sign" the contract.

7. Monitor and document what is provided at what quality. Purchaser monitors.

8. Review performance with purchaser, and discuss what changes would be necessary to secure a new contract.

Figure 9.2   Preparing, Negotiating and Managing a Therapy Service Contract

---

Accurate records are essential for preparing and monitoring contracts. Therapy managers revise their record systems to manage contracts and to help prepare contract proposals. Korner information, supplemented with discussion with staff and other records, gives sufficient data to get started.

Implications for management Information

Contracts and markets mean that accurate and appropriate management information is essential for survival, and gives a competitive advantage by allowing precise pricing, better prediction and early-warning. Therapists need more detailed information about numbers and types of cases, categorised in terms of the time and level of skill required, sources of referral, as well as information about the type and amount of non-casework activities. Prices should be available for purchasing by time, or by "type" of case treated, or for block contracts.

It is also important to quantify services which are an integral part of other services/teams, and those which are "free standing" (eg work not initiated by consultant referrals) which purchasers may wish to finance directly. A service that can show that it has, or could have a large proportion of work which is of this "free-standing" variety has a stronger case for retaining its own distinct Unit or District organisation.

Figure 9.3 below gives a format and headings for preparing a draft contract.

---

1. Client Group (Who is the service for?)

2. Purpose of Service (Results to be achieved)

3 Service Description
   General description of service to be offered, where offered, how often, and details of:
   Quantity
   Quality
   Price per unit purchased (plus invoicing arrangements)
4 Monitoring & Review
   Information you will provide to the person monitoring the contract.
   How reviews will be conducted with the monitor.
5. Support Services
   Services you need from the purchaser and others.
6. Hazards
   Steps you will take to predict and prevent problems, and steps you will take if you percieve difficulties in
   meeting the contract.
7. Appendices: Specific details and items common to all contracts (eg Quality Assurance System)

Fig 9.3   Example Headings for a Therapy Service Contract

5: QUALITY

How do we prove to potential purchasers that we will give them a high quality therapy service?
How should quality be specified in a contract, especially the outcomes of therapy?
How should a therapy service manager and a purchaser monitor quality?

Quality-Why Now?

Therapists and their professional associations have long been involved in assuring and improving the quality of therapist's practice. Recently they have taken a more systematic approach to quality, and begun to pay attention to what would convince others of the quality of their services. The motive to do so has often been external pressure from general managers and purchasers, who want quality specified and some proof of quality assurance activities.

But quality is much more than agreeing contract specifications. Quality is a set of proven methods, a philosophy, and an organisational revolution that has hardly begun in health services. I have argued that new quality methods, adapted to the special circumstances of different health services, are essential to respond to the challenges of the 1990s (Øvretveit (1990)&(1992)). Therapists will need to understand and apply these new quality methods, and relate their approach to quality to that of their Unit and to purchaser's conceptions of quality.

The purpose of this part of the chapter is not just to consider how to specify quality in contracts, but to give an introduction to quality methods for therapy services and to look at what therapists can do to apply these methods.

Quality, Quantity and Costs

Before going any further we need to answer a question asked by many therapists, and which, if not answered, makes further discussion of quality of little interest: how can therapists improve the quality of their service when the pressures are to increase the quantity of service and to reduce costs? In discussing contracts we saw an association between the three corners of the "contract triangle": surely raising quality means higher prices, or fewer clients?

To some extent it does, and this means that therapists have to agree with purchasers what standard of quality of service they are prepared to provide, and how many people they can serve for the cost of giving this level of quality. In contract negotiations therapists need to be clear about the minimum standards of quality, below which they are not prepared to drop.

However, the whole point of using quality methods is to raise quality *and* lower costs at the same time. I will argue that the real question is not whether to improve quality, but how much to invest in quality improvements, at what rate, and which are the most important things to invest in at a particular time. To show how quality costs less (in the long run), not more, the following considers quality concepts and principles before looking at quality methods.

What is "Therapy Service Quality" ?

Some define health service and therapy service quality in relation to the six areas of accessibility, relevance to need, equity, social acceptability, efficiency, and effectiveness (Maxwell (1984), West Midlands Regional District Chiropodists (1990)). Although such pre-set "feature" definitions of quality do reach towards important aspects of public health services, they ignore the concept of quality as being what "users" want.
Some definitions go to the other extreme and define quality only in terms of "customer satisfaction". Apart from the fact that there are different "customers" for therapy services (ie clients, purchasers, referrers, carers), an

important dimension of therapy service quality is what professionals define the quality of service to be. A client may want a treatment that is downright harmful, and may judge the quality of a service to be poor if it does not give them the treatment. Even if they do get symptom relief, most clients are not be able to judge the professional quality of a treatment.

But quality is not just providing what "customers" want, or what professionals assess them to need. A service could provide both, but it might do so in a wasteful way, and thus be available to fewer people. One dimension of the quality of a therapy service often ignored is the efficiency and the productivity of the service: that it uses resources efficiently and without waste, mistakes and errors - that it is low-cost. These points underlie the following definition of quality as,

---

Therapy Service Quality
"Meeting the needs of those in most need of the service, at the lowest cost, and within directives and limits set by purchasers and higher authorities"

In Øvretveit (1990) & (1992) I argue that there are three dimensions to the quality of a health service:

Client-Quality:
What clients and carers want from the service (individuals and populations);

Professional-Quality:
Whether the service meets the professionally-assessed needs of its client, and,
Whether it correctly carries out techniques and procedures which therapists believe to be necessary to meet client needs;

Management-Quality:
The most efficient and productive use of resources,
within limits and directives set by higher authorities/purchasers.

Quality methods are systematic ways to improve each dimension of the quality of a service simultaneously. Before considering how this is done we need to look at the Professional-Quality dimension in more detail.

The "Professional Quality" of Therapy Services

The Professional-Quality dimension of a therapy service has two aspects. The first,"*Whether the service meets the professionally-assessed needs of its clients*", is judged mainly by assessing outcome. There are many ways to measure the effects of a therapy service on clients. They range from a battery of measures in an evaluation study, to one or more professional's judgments of the effects of the service. (The client's and carer's judgements of outcome are at least as important, but they are part of the "Client-Quality" dimension).

The simplest measure is a rating by both therapist and professional referrer of the change in the client's presenting condition that can be ascribed to the intervention made by the therapy service. For example a GP or a surgeon and a therapist rate the change in the client's presenting condition. This is perfectly adequate to get started- new techniques for routinely assessing outcome will soon be developed.

The second "process" aspect of the definition is concerned with how well professionals carry-out assessments, treatments, and other procedures, and with the effectiveness of these interventions. *"Techniques and procedures which therapists believe meet the needs of clients,"* refers to the fact that many therapy interventions are based on clinical experience and tradition and have not been scientifically-evaluated. One of the biggest quality costs in therapy services is due to therapists continuing to use discredited or outdated treatments.

This part of the definition recognises that there is no point in carefully following procedures and setting standards for interventions that are of unproven benefit. It recognises that therapy service quality would be significantly improved by a more rigourous evaluation of techniques, and by developing treatments on a more scientific basis.

Most therapy services can do little to change "believed by" to "proven" because they cannot afford scientific evaluations. But they can ensure that therapists are up-to-date with recent research and regularly review and change the methods they use in the light of research. Where there are techniques and treatments which are proven and effective then Professional-Quality depends on how well therapists select and use them.

Assuring Professional-Quality thus means ensuring that staff are knowledgeable and skilled in the range of techniques necessary to assess and treat the type of clients served. It means that there are professional procedures and policies, ensuring that staff use these techniques properly, and that there is supervision or colleague support to give guidance.

Improving Professional Quality

Therapists improve the Professional-Quality of their service by professional audit, and by managers helping to make changes to the service arising from audit. There are many types of audit, but all have in common a systematic approach to identifying quality problems, and to making and evaluating changes.

There are two drawbacks to most audit approaches. Whilst audit is systematic, it is often partial. The focus is therapists' clinical practice, but the most serious service quality problems are often between professions and departments (eg communication and coordination). Another limitation is that audit rarely considers Client-Quality or Management-Quality (Fig 9.4). Professional audit alone is not sufficient to assure the overall quality of a therapy service.

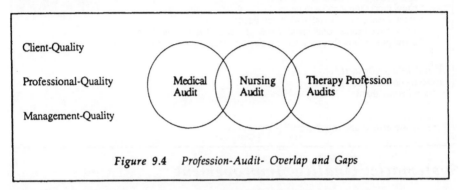

Client-Quality

Professional-Quality

Management-Quality

Medical Audit

Nursing Audit

Therapy Profession Audits

Figure 9.4   *Profession-Audit- Overlap and Gaps*

The culture and organisation of health services is such that there are good reasons to encourage each profession to develop their own audit arrangements in the early stages of a quality programme. However at some point a multidisciplinary service has to consider how to relate these audit activities to other activities for improving the Client- and Management-Quality dimensions of the service.

6: IMPROVING THERAPY SERVICE QUALITY

The above gave a broad definition of quality covering three dimensions. It did not define a set of quality standards. To do so would be to undermine what is essential for a therapy service to improve quality. This is, for the service to establish a process for formulating and revising quality standards. This ensures that the standards are appropriate, but more importantly, that staff are involved in the process and "own" and understand the quality standards.

Many services have quality standards, and some measure performance in relation to these standards. A few even take action where performance is poor. It is rare, however that therapists take a systematic and sustained approach to solve, once-and-for all, common quality problems, and to continually raise their quality performance. Most therapy services say that their main quality problems are caused by factors outside of their control. This is not true - the main barrier to raising quality is the attitude that uses reasons like this to justify not doing something about quality.

Why Therapists Need to Take a Systematic Approach to Raising Quality

- Therapists do things every day to maintain and improve quality, but their efforts would be more effective if they used quality methods within a structured framework,
- Learning how to use quality methods will be essential in the future,
- A better quality service is a better place to work,
- Need to give evidence of quality to purchasers and referrers:
    * show clients views of the service,
    * show target those most in need
    * show meet professionally-assessed needs
    * show have professional standards & procedures & follow them
    * show purchasers that they are not paying for duplication, mistakes, delays, and waste.

What to do about it?
Extend current initiatives by,
- coordinating them
- using more quality methods
- establishing a quality system to ensure a comprehensive and methodical approach
- recognise efforts and involve staff.

Systematic Quality Improvement

A systematic approach to quality takes time, but is the only way to ensure that significant improvments are made and maintained. The key elements of a systematic approach are as follows:

Set Standards: Part of proving and improving the quality of a therapy service is to set standards for features of quality on each of the three dimensions, and measure performance in relation to these standards. The standards may be of inputs (ie "structure"), of process, but ideally of outcome for each dimension. The decision about which standards to set and how to set them is critical: too many early-on and staff loose interest; the wrong ones and people focus on things which are not essential to market performance; pre-set standards imposed from above are not "owned" by staff.

Measure Performance: Once quality is defined as standards, then the quality of the service can be measured. Different methods are used to measure and document what is happening and to compare this against what is intended. The principle is to select a few standards to measure routinely, and to have a broader set for annual reviews.

Take Action: Either congratulatory or corrective. Where quality performance is poor pick a subject for corrective action. Some quality problems can be solved easily. The more complex ones need a systemtic and sustained approach if the problem is to be solved once and for all, using the "Quality Correction Cycle" (Fig 8.6 below).

The Quality Management and Quality Correction Cycles

All systematic approaches to quality assurance use a version of the quality cycles (Fig 8.6)

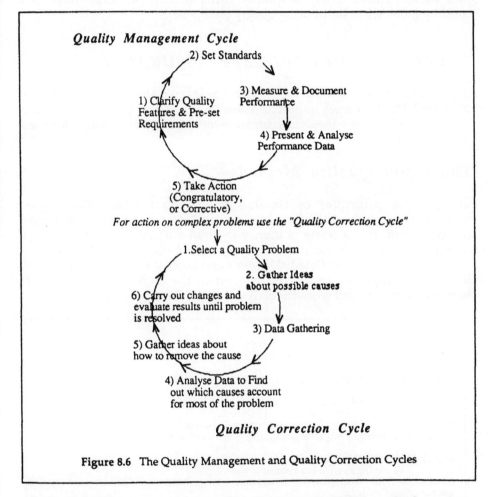

Figure 8.6 The Quality Management and Quality Correction Cycles

These cycles give a framework within which to use quality methods, such as methods for setting standards or for measuring quality performance. The idea is to ensure that staff in a service carry-out each of the steps above. Sometimes a service gets stuck at the standard-setting stage: there are too many standards to measure, even annually. Sometimes a service does measure and document quality performance, but does not take any action.

Sometimes all the steps are carried out but the service does not revise its standards.

More details about quality methods for therapy services can be found from the Kings Fund Quality Abstracts service and from (Øvretveit (1990)). The last part of this introduction to quality turns to the two most important considerations when introducing quality assurance.

7: INTRODUCING QUALITY ASSURANCE

In practice how would a therapy service manager go about introducing these methods? The two most important considerations are "phasing-in" quality methods, and winning therapists commitment to quality and motivating them to use the methods.

Phasing-in Quality Methods

The general principles of phasing are to start where the biggest improvements can be made for a low cost, and to go at a pace which people can cope with. It is a waste of money to build a detailed quality system if responsibilities are not clear and if people cannot understand the system or give the time to work it. Detailed systems and sophisticated techniques come later when people are ready for them, when the foundations are there to support the system and when the early easy gains have been made.

Phasing-in Quality

PHASE 1: CLARIFYING OBJECTIVES AND RESPONSIBILITIES
(Getting Organised)
Ensure the foundations of organisation are established before using quality methods.

PHASE 2: OVERCOMING OUTSTANDING QUALITY PROBLEMS
(Making fewer mistakes)
Not just by trying harder, but by using methods to find out and remove the root causes of problems in a systematic way through a Quality Correction Cycle.

PHASE 3: DEVELOPING QUALITY MANAGEMENT
(Covering all areas in a systematic way)
Establish the Quality Management Cycle and build a comprehensive set of standards and measure and control performance.

PHASE 4: PREVENTING QUALITY PROBLEMS BY ASSURANCE
(Process control and controlling critical variables)
Use statistical process control methodology to control critical variables.

Phasing-in quality methods may not be possible when purchasers require a therapy service to adopt a detailed set of quality standards. Purchasers sometimes prescribe in too much detail and undermine the therapy service' responsibility for developing and appropriate set of standards, which includes some required by purchasers. Purchasers should be concerned about the progress therapists are making to establish a quality system, and with assessing this system, rather than with the detailed standards. In addition to phasing-in methods, it is important to link quality to staff concerns and values. Quality is as much about attitudes and relationships as it is about quality methods and systems.

Motivation to Work at Improving Quality

One of the biggest problems in introducing quality assurance is a service culture which gives "lip-service" to quality, but which is defensive and unwilling to change. The main way to change a service culture is to inspire staff with an idea that is consistent with values that they hold, and which helps them to make meaningful changes. A quality service culture is instilled when therapists find that quality not only fits with their values and helps to crystalise their desires for the future, but when they find that quality methods work.

Quality is, and can be presented as a way in which therapists can uphold professional and service standards. Cynicism after all is often the only socially-acceptable way to express despair. Quality provides staff with a weapon against the decline and a way of ensuring that clients do not suffer from the reforms. It gives staff a way of testing what management are saying about changes being made to improve patient care, and gives them control over some changes.

Tangible benefits-what is in it for us?

But the motive to defend and improve services to clients is not sufficient to power a quality strategy. For a strategy to work there has to be something in it for staff and managers that is tangible. Quality assurance has to be presented to make these benefits clear - it has to be "sold" to therapists.

Most therapists do not work in health services just for the money. Although in some areas health is the only employer, there are usually jobs with better pay and conditions. The intrinsic satisfactions of the job motivate people, and can motivate them to do better, or at least to come back to work the next day.

SHOW HOW QUALITY UPHOLDS STAFF VALUES
-AND   PROVIDES TANGIBLE BENEFITS

> The most valuable things in the service are the professionalism and commitment of staff, which have been eroded and need to be nurtured. Quality reverses the downward spiral. A quality approach can be introduced in a way that connects with staff values and concerns and offers a realistic and worth-while way forward.
>
> But quality methods should not be presented only as a way of defending a service, or as something which resonates with and advances core values. It also has to be shown to provide something tangible for staff, as something that will help them protect their jobs and acquire necessary skills in competitive markets. As something which will save time in the long run and remove the headaches and common complaints at work.

If introduced in the right way a quality approach taps into this pride and motivation. It makes it possible for therapist to keep improving their service and to show that they are doing so. Quality should be presented in a way that shows staff how it will make their work more intrinsically satisfying. This can be done by showing how staff can use quality methods to overcome the headaches and time-wasting that stands between them and a good job and that can make working life such a chore.

Just as important is the satisfaction of helping a client, and the client's recognition of a staff member's proficiency. It is a proficiency that is possible because of the quality of the service process and organisation. A major source of job dissatisfaction is being criticised by clients for poor treatment that a staff member knows was poor, but which they could not have given any better because of the system, the rules and other people's indifference.

Besides recognition and valuation by clients a further motivator is recognition by superiors and peers. All too often therapists time improving the service and their effort or the results are not recognised. A quality approach first ensures that time and effort is spent on the right things and gets results, and second it makes the effort visible through specification and measurement.

Quality in Contracts

How then to specify quality in a contract? The above argument was that therapists need to specify standards of quality as a first step towards improving quality. The fact that doing so produces standards for a contract is a fortunate by-product of a process which is essential to the competitiveness of the service.

Therapists taking a systematic approach to quality first find out from purchasers and others what features of quality are critical to them. They also define the quality features which they as therapists think are important. They then formulate a comprehensive set of standards which are available for contracts, and measure quality performance to help them improve quality.

These measurements are then available to purchasers as evidence of quality, but they are far more valuable to the therapy service's programme of improving quality to remain competitive.

QUALITY: WHAT IS "IN IT" FOR THERAPISTS?

- A way in which therapists can uphold professional and service standards.
- Raises work satisfaction and the sense of achievement and pride that comes from doing the job well.
- Makes it possible for people to make continual improvements and to measure their progress.
- Overcomes the headaches and time-wasting that stands between them and a good job and that can make working life such a chore.
- The satisfaction of helping a client, and the client's recognition of a therapist's proficiency.
- Fewer dissatisfied and irate clients.
- Makes the effort visible through specification and measurement.
- Colleagues' and managers' recognition and valuation of a person's achievements.
- Ensures that time and effort is spent on the right things and gets results - can do more with less effort.
- New quality skills and experience are increasingly necessary in the job market.

8: CONCLUSION

Most therapy managers were ill-prepared for the public markets which emerged in the 1990s. They did not recognise that in the new environment professional autonomy depended on business autonomy, and that this depended on their ability to negotiate and manage contracts and apply quality methods. The work of preparing and negotiating contracts and of introducing quality assurance for services illustrates the major change in therapist's management role, if they are to respond to the challenge of the public markets. Understanding what is involved helps therapists to decide whether they are prepared for, or ready to take-up the responsibilities involved.

Every minute of therapists time has to be paid for. One of the tasks of high-level managers of therapy services is to find finance for the service. It is easier to look to the "parent" division or Unit for finance, but this puts restrictions on the service. Therapists who have taken the initiative and negotiated "service agreements" or "contracts" have influenced structure towards a profession-managed service. They found that the initial work of preparing and negotiating contracts made it easier to manage services, and that therapists were clearer about their role in the areas which they were contracted to.

Quality assurance is increasingly important for selling therapy services and for reducing costs. Quality methods make work less frustrating for therapists, gives them more control and makes recruitment and retention easier in competitive labour markets. It defuses client dissatisfaction by negotiating expectations, and avoids negligence claims.

Chapter 10: GRADES, PAY & CAREER
PROGRESSION

---

1 : INTRODUCTION

Of all the subjects of concern to therapists employed by the NHS, level of pay, grade systems and career structure have raised the strongest feelings. Grades confer status as well as pay, they are viewed as an indicator of the value of a person's work, and upgrading and promotion are ways in which people judge their " rate of progress" at work and assess their career development.

Although pay determination methods and grading systems are the source of widespread ill-feeling and dissatisfaction, they have yielded the least to attempts at improvement. Pay flexibility to take account of local labour markets may add further confusion and dissent. The impact of grade definitions and pay systems on professions are rarely thought-through.

This chapter clarifies the purposes of grade systems, separates grades from organisational structure, and considers ways of assessing level of responsibility and work in professional practice. It then considers grade systems in relation to career structure and individual career progress.

2 : PROBLEMS

Practitioners and their managers have raised variety of problems in discussion about grades and structure (Øvretveit et al(1982)), as have professional associations in trying to influence national negotiations. These included:
- The low levels of pay for therapists employed by the NHS, and unsatisfactory arrangements for negotiating pay increases. Some therapists say that the most capable and skilled members of the profession leave the NHS because pay and opportunities are better elsewhere;
- Some practitioners think that grade systems encourage specialisation too early in their careers;
- Most feel that grade systems do not encourage a career in clinical practice and do not recognise and reward "clinical ability and experience". There is a clinical career "ceiling" which many reach at an early age, after which they feel that they are "standing still" with no recognition for their developing practice skills. Pay incentives encourage able clinicians to take on managerial roles leaving them less time to develop theories and techniques in clinical practice, which is to the disadvantage of the profession and to patients;

- Grades frequently do not correspond to people's felt level of responsibility. The traditional grading criteria (eg,"Specialist skills and experience", "Head of specialism", number of staff "supervised", or population served), are quick and easy to apply, but are poor indicators of felt level of responsibility, or of level of work;
- Grade definitions which do exist are ambiguous and abused by managers trying to recruit staff to unpopular areas. In different places, posts with the same responsibilities may be graded differently (e.g. considered "specialist work" in one place but not in another), or posts with different responsibilities may have the same grade, causing bad feeling and resentment;
- Grade definitions tied to "head-count" lead to distortions in service structure and organisation, and encourage hierarchy and empire building: the easiest way to get a pay rise is to gain staff to "supervise". Staff resistance to restructuring is increased by imagined or actual lowering of their grade if they loose staff to "supervise".
Finally, a problem of service structure which is related to grades,
- Service structures frequently make no provision for career progression, and able staff become frustrated or leave. At the other extreme service structures can be entirely driven by individuals' interests and career plans. Managers frequently do not recognise potential, or provide opportunities for staff development which are compatible with service objectives.

The Purpose of Grades

Most of the problems and dissatisfactions arise because grade systems are used for the wrong purposes, or are called upon to serve a number of purposes. The purpose of a grade definition is to describe work and responsibilities in order that a manager can decide the pay to allocate to a particular post. A decision about the work to be done and about the responsibilities of the post should be made before then deciding the grading (ie. the pay) of the post.

This view is based on the premise that pay should be for the work a person does, rather than for characteristics of the person such as skill, experience, or for their past achievements. Because these characteristics are more easy to assess than the work itself, they are frequently used as a proxy measure of the work that the person will do. This is not to say that professional excellence, skills, and achievements (which may be manifest in work output) should not be recognised and valued. Rather that this recognition and valuation is a different question to the question of how to assess work to decide fair payment.

In the reformed NHS, pay also needs to be related to the local job market and to the supply and demand for labour. The argument below is that, once the work to be done and the grade are decided, managers then need flexibility to offer enhanced pay if necessary to attract and retain therapists.

3: CONFUSION OF GRADE LEVELS AND MANAGEMENT LEVELS

A common mistake is to confuse a grade title and definition (eg Principal or Senior) with the title of an organisational post and the responsibilities of the post (eg Head of Department or Specialty). Some organisational charts name the posts on the chart by the grade of the post. Staff assume that a highly graded post on the chart automatically has authority over, and accountability for, staff in a post with a lower grade. In fact grades do not carry with them any definitions of the authority and accountability of a post - these are matters which need to be carefully defined for each post.

Although grades may, and should be ambiguous about detailed local management arrangements, these matters are particularly important when establishing and reviewing organisation. One example is management of just-qualified basic grades: are they fully-responsible for their casework? If so, routine management review of all cases undermines that responsibility. If they are responsible for their cases but "supervised", what type of "supervision" is appropriate, and what exactly are the responsibilities of their supervisor if something went wrong? These are questions to be addressed through specifying organisation, not through grade definitions (chapters 6&7).

One reason why confusion between grade definitions and job descriptions has occurred is because an easy way of trying to describe work and level of responsibility is to list the number of staff "supervised", or for whom the post-holder is "responsible". The consequences are that it provides an incentive for staff to gain other staff to supervise, producing extra and unnecessary levels of management. It rules out certain options in restructuring where staff would drop a grade because they "loose staff", and it makes it more difficult to establish high-level practice-only posts.

The discussion below considers ways of improving grading systems, or of devising new types of payment system which do not rely on head-count and which more closely relate to level of work and responsibility, especially in clinical practice.

Career Structure

There is a difference between a grading system and a career structure. A set of grade definitions attempt to, a) cover the range of types of post and work to be done, b) provide differential reward according to the value to the service of the different work done, c) correspond to people's feelings about the different level of responsibility or "weight" of different work. It is a lot to expect from short descriptions, but in addition, grade systems are also expected to serve as a career structure for a profession.

A grading system is not of itself a career structure. The career structure and career opportunities in a profession will depend on whether local employers decide to establish certain posts for certain work. A grade system, however, does directly affect career opportunities if it does not make provision for certain work to to be graded at a certain level of pay (notably high-level practice or research work), and if it only recognises and rewards management work as high-level work.

Professions want employers to establish posts which further the interests of the profession. Professions want a set of definitions which cover a range of types and levels of work which are important to the profession, so that employers are at least not prevented from establishing posts because there are no appropriate grades or ways of deciding the pay of the post.

4: DISTINGUISHING AND DEFINING HIGH-LEVEL PRACTICE WORK

One of the main dissatisfactions of therapists, and a problem of concern to therapy professions, is that there are few, if any, highly-paid practice-only posts in the NHS. Many take the medical profession as an example of a profession which has both a grade system and posts which provide a career structure which encourages members to remain in, and excel in clinical practice.

In fact consultant posts involve a high proportion of management work, and doctors only qualify for consultant posts after a long training under the management of another consultant, during which time the consultant carries full case responsibility. One of the characteristics of the therapies is that practitioners assume full case responsibility at an early stage in their careers. The medical structure and grade system is a poor model for professions wishing to retain Case Autonomy, and to establish high-level practitioner roles with minimal management responsibilities.

Part of the problem is the difficulty of devising a pay system which distinguishes between basic and high-level practice work, and relates the latter to similar level management work. Such a system would not of itself ensure that high-level practice roles were established because employers would still need to be persuaded that they should spend more on high-level practice posts.

However, clarification of the differences between basic and high-level practice work in terms of work output would also clarify the advantages for managers and the public of establishing high-level practice roles. It would help to decide whether such posts were needed, and whether they were worth the extra cost.

In the light of the above the important questions become,
- what is the difference between basic and high-level practice in terms of the work undertaken by the practitioner?, and,
- is there a simple, cheap, universally-applicable and fair method for assessing the level of practitioner work, in order to decide the pay to allocate to a post?

At present the usual way in which practice posts and work are distinguished for pay purposes is in terms of grade definitions. These define higher-level practice grades as ones involving "specialist" work skills or expertise, as not requiring supervision, and/or requiring a set number of years experience. Although this method is cheap and simple, it does not describe the work, only characteristics of the person. The definitions are ambiguous and are abused, and specialist work is not necessarily higher-level work.

A second method is through peer assessment. Again this typically does not describe the work but rather assesses the past achievements of the person. Even if the criteria were applied to the work and were clear and agreed, the method is subject to intra-professional biases and prejudices. This is a drawback as the high-level posts to be assessed involve developing new techniques, treatments and theories.

Although the author's research has not developed a satisfactory solution, some progress has been made by applying the "Time-Span of Discretion" measure to analyse tasks undertaken in high-level practice posts. Previous research found that the Time-Span of Discretion gives an accurate measure of the level of work of a post, and is related to a person's felt weight of responsibility of a task, as well as their view of felt-fair pay (Jaques(1977), Stamp (1988)). At present the measure is not a suitable method for a national pay assessment system.

However, time-span measures have helped to identify tasks which are distinctive of high-level practice and which involve longer time spans: tasks which, significantly, newly-qualified or basic grade practitioners do not undertake. These tasks include complex casework where active intervention is carried out over one or more years before there are objective signs that the interventions were appropriate or not.

Other casework may involve shorter time-spans, but what emerges is that the cases are the more complex or difficult cases which junior practitioners are not able to deal with. Further, that the problems presented are new to the profession, or there are no established techniques, and the work undertaken by the practitioner is to develop approaches and theories through their casework practice which are then routinely used by less experienced practitioners.

It is this type of work which requires years of experience and particular abilities (including high level of work capacity), and which is so important to advances in the profession. When members argue that the profession should nurture its "clinical roots" the argument is not just that most members should stay in practice, but that practice-based developments should be encouraged. Professional advances do not come only from basic scientific research, but often from experienced practitioners being confronted by problems for which there are no established solutions and developing new approaches in practice. Given the importance of this development work to the professions and society, it is remarkable that so little support and encouragement is given to practitioners - they do it in spite of the conditions, and often in their own time.

There is a need is to clarify the different work which would be undertaken in a high-level practice post, in order to fairly discriminate high-level from basic practice, and to make it possible to judge whether such a post is needed, or worth the extra cost.

The Time-Span measure has helped to identify higher-level practice tasks, and makes it possible to develop definitions for high-level practice grades which correspond to higher levels of work and felt levels of responsibility. The conclusions of this work so far are that high-level posts would be established where practitioners were needed to work unsupervised on complex cases, or on cases where there were no established theories or techniques. Such posts would be needed to set up new services, and would involve a proportion of teaching work.

Other advantages of such posts include, providing junior staff with expert supervision, enabling them to successfully undertake more complex casework than would otherwise be possible. This experience and supervision helps to recruit staff, and such posts provide career opportunities, which also helps to attract and retain staff.

5: CAREER PROGRESSION : "Standing Still" with "Nowhere to Go"

In discussions about the lack of career opportunities in practice roles, therapists frequently described feeling that they had "reached the top", had "nowhere to go", and were "standing still". There was certainly much practice work to be done, but it was viewed as routine work which did not "stretch" them.

Part of the problem appeared to be that time was not available for development practice (routine work was priority), and partially that there was no extra pay and recognition for the higher-level practice work. At first sight it appeared that staff simply wanted more increments on a pay scale, or higher grading for number of years in service. The only justification for this was that it might counter the feeling of "standing still".

Further discussions showed that pay was not the only or even the main issue. The general dissatisfaction with low overall levels of pay was masking the fact that many staff used pay as an external referent for judging career progress. Increments in pay and upgrading were used by individuals to judge career progress in relation to their level of aspiration.

If grade systems are also to help judge career progress, the "width" of different payment bands has to relate to individual development in a way that provides a sense of progress. However, what was also missing from the discussions, from the grading system, and from reviews of service structure was an understanding of individual development at work.

The feeling of "nowhere to go" was perhaps a realistic feeling that one's practice skills and abilities had developed but that there was little opportunity to use them in practice work, that there was no recognition in payment terms for doing so, and that there were no posts in the NHS to go to, apart from management posts. Some had moved into management posts, not simply because it was the only way to increase pay, but to be able to use abilities and gain work satisfaction for which the was no scope in practice-only roles. This phenomenon was not confined to practitioners: managers described lack of career opportunities because no higher level posts were open to them.

Individual Development at Work

The theory of individual work capacity helps to understand people's development at work, career progression, and the dynamic between individual development and service structure (Jaques (1977)).

Individual development at work is often viewed as learning and applying new skills. Career progress is viewed as being able to successfully take on more complex and challenging work. Research at BIOSS has found that skills and experience are secondary to the critical factors of the level of work of a post, and the ability of an individual to successfully undertake a particular level of work - their "level of work capacity" (Stamp (1989)). Further, that an individual's level of work capacity develops with age at a predictable rate, and that they will actively seek-out work at a level which is consistent with their capacity.

There is evidence that problems arise when there is not an equilibrium between the level of work an individual undertakes, their level of work capacity, and level of payment for the post. If the level of work is lower than the person's level of work capacity, the result is often boredom or frustration, even though the amount of work may be high. If the level of work is higher than their work capacity the person will feel overwhelmed and persecuted by the difficulty and magnitude of the task. People also have a strong sense of fair payment for the work, which is closely associated with the level of work.

As regards career progression, the hypothesis is that people judge upward or downward movements in their pay in relation to an inner idea of progress, which is closely related to their sense of their work capacity, as well as to the level of work of a post. That, is that people use pay level, and rate of pay increase as an index of career progression. The underlying and important issues are the rate of development of the person's work capacity, and the opportunities available for work in posts at appropriate levels of work and with appropriate types of work (eg practice or management work).

The implications of this theory for managers is that they need to recognise that different therapists have different level of work capacity, which will also develop at different rates over time. Therapists will seek not only variety in work but, over time, will naturally take on higher-level work.

In delegating work, managers need to continually assess not only the person's skills, but their level of work capacity. Managers develop individuals by delegating tasks which comfortably stretch their skills, with review dates at time periods which are consistent with their level of work capacity.

In attempting to match level of work to level of capacity, and to level of pay, managers need to be aware of three types of career progression. The first is a rise in pay within a grade, which has been termed "merit progression", and which has traditionally been through annual increments. "Upgrading" is a movement upwards into a higher grade, but within the same level of work bracket, and not necessarily involving a change of manager. "Promotion", however involves a change of grade into a higher level of work, a new manager, and a significant career transition for the individual.

Over the longer term, reviews of service structure need to take account of people's developing work capacity, and make provision for work or posts for people to move into if they are to remain in the service. The level of work of a post is largely a function of structure. The job description and authority of the post set the level, and management or supervision arrangements also influence the level of work: frequent short term supervision reduces the level of work.

Reviews of service structure thus need to balance the work to be done with the level of work capacity of staff, and be based on an understanding of the likely level of work capacity development of different staff.

6: REQUIREMENTS OF A PAY ASSESSMENT SYSTEM

Although this chapter does not have clear solutions to the problems described, it is possible to list criteria which can be used to judge any proposed improvement to current pay systems. A system should,
- Be easy and simple to use, unambiguous, and universally applicable.
- The system should clearly distinguish levels of work. Decisions about the pay for a post should not be open to a variety of interpretations of the meaning of terms such as "specialist";
- Cover the full range of levels and types of work which may be required;
- Provide differential reward according to, a) the value to the service of the work to be done, and b) the types of work which the profession wishes to recognise and value;

At present it seems that the most likely pay system for the future will be a set of grade definitions, possibly supplemented with a peer assessment method for assessing high-level posts. To minimise problems arising from such an arrangement there would need to be :
- Pay increments within grades, and pay differentials between grades which corresponded to people's feelings about the different weight of responsibility of different work;
- Grade definitions specific to each profession;
- A distinction between grade titles/definitions, and post titles/job descriptions;
- Clear criteria to be agreed for use by peers in assessing posts;
- Scope for flexibility in relation to the labour market - ways of offering more pay which recognises that the "enhanced" pay is because of supply shortages in the area.

7: CONCLUSION

The main purpose of grade definitions is to describe work in order that managers can decide the pay for a post. A decision about the work to be done and the responsibilities of a post should be made before then deciding the grading of the post.

A good grade structure should enable managers to decide the pay for posts they wish to establish to do certain work, should incorporate the profession's views about work which it wishes to encourage and recognise, and should correspond to practitioner's feelings about different levels of responsibility. There then should be flexibility to respond to the local labour market.

Professions wishes to encourage certain work because it is important to the future of the profession (eg practice-based research and development). Hence the profession requires that there are grade definitions which can be used to pay posts established to do this work. The availability of such grades represents a recognition by national government that such work should be undertaken.

A set of grade definitions is a grade system. It is not itself a career structure - this will depend on how local employers use the grades, and whether they establish posts at different levels which provide career opportunities.

The problem of lack of career opportunities in practice work arises partially because of a lack of appropriate pay systems for high-level practice, and partially because employers do not want, or can not afford high-level practice-only posts. A solution to the first problem (a way of distinguishing high-level practice), could provide a solution to the second problem in clearly describing the different type of work undertaken in high-level practice, and thus why managers and the public should pay extra for such work to be done.

Pay level and rate of pay progression are important ways in which people judge career progress, compare themselves to others, and feel that their work and abilities are recognised. Managers need to recognise and understand the implications of a person's developing level of work capacity. The difficulty for managers is to match people's level of work capacity and career development needs to the needs of the service (ie. clients) and to the service structure. An understanding of the developing work capacity of staff makes it easier to predict points of strain, to select the right staff for the work, and to delegate work to staff which develops their capacity.

Chapter 11: CONCLUSIONS & THE FUTURE

'All the therapy professions in the UK were children of the medical profession and the NHS. They are upset and confused that one of their parents appears indifferent to their plight. Are any strong enough to forge their own futures?

To onlookers, speech therapist's strategy appears to be to one of market expansion as 'communications therapists'. Dieticians are riding high on public preoccupations, but cannot find buyers for their health promotion and prevention roles. Chiropodists recognise that the public service demand is to keep elderly people on their feet, and are unsure whether the future lies in their strong private base.

Clinical psychologists are their own worse enemies when it comes to collective strategies and organisation. There has never been a grater need for their innovation and research, but the finance for this is and training is uncertain. Physiotherapists are reluctant to sever their medical connections, but have an understandable product and effective local and national organisation. Some are talking again about merging with occupational therapists, the other twin of the family. O.T.'s have a more diffuse product, but may be able to use this to their advantage to adapt to the new markets and to Case Management.

Their diversity kept them apart, and was exaggerated by their own efforts to mark-out their differences from each other and from medicine. Adversity could bring them together'.

1: INTRODUCTION

This chapter summarises the theoretical arguments of the book and considers the future for the therapy professions, inside and outside of the reformed NHS. It shows that research into organisation can contribute to social scientific knowledge about professions, and to solving practical problems in organisation and management.

2: PROFESSIONAL AUTONOMY

The theoretical issues addressed arise from a perspective within the sociology of professions, originating in the works of Freidson (1970) and Johnson (1972). In contrast to earlier studies, Freidson proposed that,
- the oft-noted social and economic characteristics of professions, which are said to distinguish them from other occupations, derive from their autonomy,

- there is a difference between a dominant profession such as medicine and others: only the medical profession is "truly autonomous",
- the autonomy of medicine is sustained by the dominance of its expertise in the health division of labour,
- autonomy is more likely if a profession has a "legal privilege" such as state licensing which gives the profession "ownership" of an area of work, and prevents other occupations from carrying out that work.

To test Freidson's theory Chapter 2 considered "legal privileges" in the UK, which Freidson proposed as creating a protected market and the basis for professional autonomy. It described the structures and processes which exist in the UK at the national level to regulate the medical and therapy professions, and considered exactly what control and autonomy these provided for each profession.

The evidence showed that state regulation through licensing in the UK alone does not assure professional autonomy and a protected market in the absolute way which Freidson suggested. In addition, rather than joining with professions to support their interests, the state only acts to regulate in this limited way when parliament is persuaded by the public that practice by incompetent practitioners (defined as "unqualified") is a danger to the public.

Professional "control" at the national level is a complex set of influences and is indirect, mostly through the professional association influencing training and qualification requirements. The evidence from the UK does not support Freidson's theory.

How then do we account for the division of labour which undoubtedly exists in heath services, and for the power of the medical profession in comparison to that of the therapy professions? Chapter 3 proposed that we could learn about more about the nature of professional autonomy by looking at organisation at the local level. It presented the specifications of management structures produced in research with physiotherapists and clinical psychologists since 1968. The research showed that,

1) During the 1970's health professions were grouped into professional hierarchies headed by a profession-manager ("Profession-Management Autonomy").

2) Different types of autonomy and control were recommended by the state and institutionalised in management structures: "Profession-Management Autonomy"; positions for heads of profession on top management teams, with voting or veto rights; and at the practitioner level, "Clinical Autonomy" and "Practice Autonomy".

3) By distinguishing different types of autonomy it is possible to compare the autonomy of different professions, and to document changes over time.

4) In the 1970's the state supported profession-management autonomy through health circulars and other central government recommendations,

5) The state withdrew support for profession-mangement autonomy in the 1980's, and therapy hierarchies were divided into smaller divisions. All forms of autonomy then depended on existing profession-managers competence and their political and diplomatic skills.

6) Medical dominance over therapy professions declined at management and practice levels, and was replaced by general management controls.

3: THEORETICAL CONCLUSIONS

Two theoretical conclusions of relevance to the theory of professions can be drawn from the research reported in Chapters 2 and 3.

The significance of expert knowledge.

Freidson and other theorists proposed that expertise is the basis of autonomy. Without expertise, they argued, it is impossible for others to evaluate or effectively manage practitioners.

The research found that clinical expertise was only necessary for first-level management and supervision, and then only up to a certain career grade. Above a certain level, professionals themselves argued that even other members of the profession could not and should not fully evaluate each others work. Managers above this level did not need to be, and confessed that they were not expert in the details of a specialty.

The arguments for profession-management for some operational, and all strategic management roles were rather that practitioners were more willing to follow the leadership and directives of one of their own profession than those of another profession or a general manager. It was a question of loyalty and confidence that someone from the same "background" would protect their interests. Profession-managers on management teams "represented" the profession. Clinical expertise was not the basis of autonomy in management structures above first-level management. If the profession-manager did not have management skills their position and credibility was tenuous.

At the national level expertise becomes significant if the state can be persuaded that the public cannot tell expert from inexpert practitioners, and that inexpert practitioners are a danger to the public. This in itself does not lead to autonomy through state regulation, because the state then has to be persuaded that there is an effective way of discriminating expert from inexpert, and that the profession should have a role in doing so.

Even then, the usual form of state regulation - state registration - does not create a "protected market" in the absolute way Freidson suggested. The profession only decides competence at entry, and after only acts in cases of blatant negligence.

Finally, Freidson proposed that medical dominance arises because the medical profession is able to convince others that medical expertise encompasses the expertise of other professions. If we are more specific about what we mean by "medical dominance" and look at the evidence of different types of medical control, we see that this argument only applies at the practice level. There are a variety of reasons for medical influence over therapy professions and over the health service as a whole. Of interest is how "rational" arguments are advanced by the medical profession in the process of organisational change, and why they are accepted, not least by therapists themselves.

By focusing on the social structures and processes which regulate professions and on their organisation, it is not necessary to assume that particular occupations do or do not have particular knowledge or skills. Claimed expertise is one of a number of considerations in the decision to grant authority to an occupation or an individual over a particular function. The areas of interest become how claims to expertise are advanced and perceived, and the nature and consequences of the structures which are created.

Authority not Autonomy

The second theoretical conclusion is that authority is a more useful concept than autonomy for understanding the nature of professions and the differences between them. If we consider the different types of professional autonomy we can see that these are in fact forms of authority.

The state and the public do not decide to "institutionalise the autonomy" of an occupation. Rather the state empowers members of the occupation to carry out certain functions on its behalf - to assess competence, and to manage practitioners to provide a public service within public policies. It authorises members of the occupation to carry out these functions, and as a result the occupation acquires a certain "independence".

To talk of autonomy is to take the perspective of the profession and of the practitioner. Autonomy, as Freidson noted, is independence from direction, or degree of freedom. Of greater theoretical and practical significance is delegated authority to act and to direct others, and the process through which authority is achieved.

A focus on authority rather than autonomy brings into view the processes and relationships through which individuals and the public empower professionals. A focus on autonomy and "rights" to self-determination, looses sight of the relationship and way in which those "rights" are granted. The positions attained by professionals are because clients and the public put them in these positions, even though the processes and structures through which they do so are complex.

Bringing these conclusions together we see that the authority of the individual practitioner in relation to clients does not derive from expertise alone, but in addition from their social position granted by their professional association and/or their state regulatory body which recognises their initial competence to practice.

Where practitioners are employed by state welfare authorities, practitioners also derive authority from their position as employees of the authority. Clients comply with therapists advice and instructions in part because they are assured that the employing organisation has judged competence to practice, and that the employing organisation is liable for incompetence. Client coercion through monopoly of services is less important than the willing compliance of clients through their accepting the authority of the practitioner as a result of the practitioner's social position.

4: MANAGEMENT EXPERTISE AND PROFESSIONAL POWER

These conclusions and research into the organisation of the therapy professions help us to understand some of the current issues facing the therapy professions.

The research showed that the state significantly influenced the shape and size of these professions, and that local management structures had a greater effect on these professions than is recognised. In the 1970s the state upheld professions claims to expertise to the extent that it accepted that profession-management was necessary. In the 1980s professional expertise as a justification for self-management became questioned.

At a national level there was a growing awareness that professions were poor at self-regulation: medical or therapy practitioners who were clearly incompetent, if not negligent, were not disciplined by professional associations, and did not loose their registration. The quality of profession-management, and organisation by profession was criticised: neither appeared to be able to respond to rising health care costs and new demands. Poorly-trained profession-managers did not know about, and were not making use of new managerial techniques.

Chapter 4 outlined the 1990 government reforms and described the new public markets. These reforms derive from government ideologies and preoccupations with cost control and service quality. Chapter 5 describe the new forms of therapy organisation emerging from the reforms. If, in the past, the state delegated authority to professions on the basis of their professional expertise, in the future their authority and autonomy will come from proven competence in management. The alternative is general or medical management. Chapters 6, 7, 8 and 9 discussed some of the management and organisation concepts that profession-managers who decide to take up the challenge will need.

In summary, a study of the organisation and authority of professions shows that,
- the independence enjoyed by different professions arises from authority bestowed by the state,
- the state will authorise professions to regulate themselves if they are persuaded that only members of the profession have the expertise to judge competence, and that incompetent practitioners are a danger to the public,
- such regulation provides a profession with a limited control over the division of labour,
- professions manage themselves in state employing authorities if managers in these services are persuaded that profession-management is more cost-effective than the alternatives, and that there are profession-managers with the managerial expertise and competence to do so,
- the future shape and size of the therapy professions will be influenced more by profession-manager's management skills and business competence than any other single factor.

5: THE FUTURE: PROFESSIONAL AUTONOMY THROUGH BUSINESS AUTONOMY

'Our weaknesses stem from historical professional rivalry between therapy professions. This, unless curtailed, could seriously damage our long-term viability'
(Evans (1991)).

The following risks some speculations about the future, based on current research with the therapy professions, and on the history of their organisation to date. It is likely that the shape and size of each of the professions will be affected by how they respond at the local and national levels to the following issues:

Unqualified Assistants

The 1990s will see an expansion in the numbers of assistants as a result of three trends:
- pressure to cut costs and to use qualified and more experienced therapists more selectively (highlighted by contract costings),
- a shortage of qualified practitioners due to limited training capacity, and loss of therapists to the NHS and the professions,
- more degree-level qualified practitioners, who are less willing to spend their whole career undertaking basic level practice.

It is possible that shortages might lead to "horizontal substitution"of therapists by nurses. It is more likely that each profession will promote "vertical substitution" and seek to control the training and management of assistants, and hence the labour market and pay rates for their members. This will put an extra demand on existing therapist to train and supervise assistants and students, and they will need new management skills, not least to assure quality.

A related issue is the question of generic therapy assistants, and generic therapists. Rehabilitation and stroke services are considering the latter.

Provider-Determined Training & Finance

In the future the number of therapists trained will be determined largely by provider's estimates of the numbers they need, and by Regions placing training contracts. One implication is that therapists will need to ensure that providers know what therapists can do to help fulfil the provider's strategy. They will need to put in favourable estimates, based on evidence of demand and purchasing power, and the future contributions of therapists to health strategies (DoH (1991))

"Advice" to Purchasers

Purchasing authorities are developing more sophisticated pictures of needs. They are prepared to consider different types of service responses, including new types of health promotion and prevention. To avoid being overlooked, the therapies need to organise to provide informed "advice" about needs for therapy services. Purchasers will also need independent advice about the quality and costs of a service which they are considering contracting, and then independent reviews of services. The options are for local therapists to do this, or to organise Regional or National sources of "advice".

Developments in Theory and Practice

In the past new theories and techniques depended on links between educational institutions and the NHS. Increasing emphasis within the NHS on "turnover", "face to face" contacts, and short-term market considerations restricts therapists from developing the new approaches which are essential to their futures. At national and local levels each profession will need to seek a variety of sources to finance research and development work. Research into routine outcome measures and evaluation research are both priorities.

Multidisciplinary Teams- The Emperor's Clothes?

The number of multidisciplinary community teams grew rapidly in the 1980s especially in mental health services, and in services for people with a learning difficulty and for the elderly. Therapy managers put in "bids" for new posts tied to these teams, without thinking-through how therapists would practice in the teams. Some therapists found their autonomy limited to the degree that they were not using their skills to the best effect. A variety of problems resulted from poorly-organised teams (Øvretveit (1986)), but teams are still popular with general managers.

The time has come for a reassessment of teams and closer evaluation of different types of teamwork and team management. Where therapists are in teams under contract, contract specification will help clarify some issues, as will case management.

Quality

People are beginning to expect as least as good service from health care professionals as they do from services in the high street. Many therapists have a complacent or defensive attitude to quality. Professional associations will need to do more to help assure quality than vet training courses and initial competence to practice. They need to play a greater role in changing attitudes, in adapting new quality methods, and in promoting quality, especially through treatment and service evaluation

Therapist's attention to professional quality must be more systematic, and their concerns widened to the Client-Quality and Management-Quality dimensions of their services. Managers need to lead the changes at the local level by introducing new approaches, and by paying attention to proof of quality.

Management & Organisation

Much of this book pointed to the organisational choices now open to therapists. It considered the new management and business skills needed by profession-managers, and many practitioners. Whether they take up the challenge depends in part on the availability of suitable management training, and on regional and national support within, and outside each profession.

These changes highlight the critical role that professional associations have to play in the coming years to help secure a future for each profession. One of their tasks must be to ensure that therapist's understand and are able to respond to the opportunities of the new public markets.

6: CONCLUSION

Needs for therapy services will increase in the 1990s, as will the variety of employers and ways of organising therapists. Having "grown-up" in the NHS, many therapists still feel that their future lies with the service. That to explore alternatives is to turn their backs on the values which inspired the creation of the NHS: of equal access according to need, not according to ability to pay.

But it is a changed service and will change even more. Access may have been free, but it was not always fair. It may be that forms of organisation outside of provider Units, and different sources of finance are the best ways of making therapy services widely available. It is certainly true that to survive and develop with a distinct identity, therapists will need to pay more attention to organisation and be less ambivalent about acquiring, adapting and using modern management skills.

I hope that this book put some of the current changes in an historical context, and helped therapists to see ways to create a future which meets their needs, and the increasing needs of the community for their services.

John Øvretveit   Seven Springs, Natural Bridge, Virginia, August 1991.

Appendix 1:THE SOCIAL-ANALYTIC METHOD FOR ORGANISATIONAL RESEARCH

Social analysis is a method for the collaborative analysis of organisational problems and possible solutions. The purpose of the method is both to help to devise and test improvements to organisation and to develop scientific knowledge about organisational structure and processes which can be generalised to other situations. This combination of practical and theoretical aims situates social analysis as one of a number of action research approaches, which aim both to solve practical problems and to develop social scientific knowledge, and which holds to the view that, "To understand a social system and how it works, one must study how to change it". [Lewin (1947)]. The following describes the distinctive features of the method,and builds on the earlier descriptions of Jaques (1947), (1951), (1965), (1976) &(1982), Rowbottom (1977), and Øvretveit (1984).

Definition

Social analysis can broadly be defined as:
(1) a collaborative, problem-focused method for
(2) making explicit the current and future social context of individual behaviour, and,
(3) developing a scientific understanding of the relationship between social structures and individual behaviour and characteristics.

The main features of the method are :

1:   Client Invitation
A prerequisite for collaborative working is that there is a "client" within the organisation who invites the researcher to investigate one or more organisational issues of concern to the client. Usually the researcher works directly with the client (an individual or group) who asks for help, and for as long as the client finds the researcher help useful. Under certain conditions the researcher will work with people nominated by the client, as long as they perceive there to be a problem which they wish to explore further. (The client does not always finance the research).

2:   Client Problems
The starting point and the touchstone of the method is the organisational problem(s) of concern to the client. The researcher only works on problems which the client wishes to explore and to find some solution to, rather than on problems which are of concern to others or of research interest. It is this, and client invitation which assures, as far as is possible, that the client will be motivated to work towards describing and specifying organisation.

3:   Client Confidentiality
It is a condition of the research that the researcher maintains strict client confidentiality. Discussions with and reports to clients are confidential. However, when material has been worked through with clients, it is usual that they give permission for it to be passed to others, or even published.   Even when such "clearance" is given it is usually not necessary to identify individuals, and the researcher aims to report general principles and concepts which are of relevance elsewhere.   Projects are never undertaken unless the principle of client

confidentiality is recognised and accepted by sponsors, and no covert verbal or written reports are made.

4:   Client Responsibility

The method aims to affirm and strengthen clients' responsibility for owning and resolving their own problems. The researcher has no executive power to propose or introduce changes, and any future action has to be taken by the client. The researcher does not make recommendations or give advice.   The aim is to help the client to clarify the nature of the problem and its possible causes, to conceptualise future possible forms of organisation, and to explore the advantages and disadvantages of each alternative.

5:   Researcher Independence

A basic condition for the researcher to be able to provide help is to maintain an emotional and practical independence from the problems and the organisation. The researcher has nothing to gain or lose by any particular outcome, is able to put the problem in perspective, and is often more able to perceive the logical and rational features of the situation and future possibilities.

6:   Analysis and Conceptualisation

An important feature of the method is that the researcher helps the clients by enabling them to achieve a better conceptualisation of the problem and possible solutions. The researcher helps the client to focus on central features of the problem (sometimes using existing concepts and/or theories), to conceptualise key features of current organisation, and to conceptualise alternative forms of organisation. By making organisation explicit and by providing concepts to allow discussion of certain features, the researcher and client are able consciously to review and explore different possibilities.

In this aspect of raising awareness of social organisation to enable conscious development the method shares features of a tradition of social research and criticism. This analytic and conceptual explication not only helps one person to understand and explore possibilities, but also forms a basis for developing a common language and understanding amongst a group of people, who are then better able to explore and agree new forms of organisation.

7:   Theory and Concepts of Social Structure

The method is based on assumptions about social structure and about the nature of individual's and of organisational problems. The assumptions are that certain common organisational problems arise because of uncertainty and lack of agreement amongst staff concerning key aspects of social structure and process (responsibilities, authority, etc). The assumptions are that improvements to organisation can be achieved by clarifying and agreeing these key aspects of structure and process.

In addition to these assumptions there is now a body of knowledge developed through research in many organisations which can be drawn on by the researcher where relevant [Rowbottom et al (1973) Jaques (1976) and Jaques, ed (1978)]. Thus a feature of the method is that the researcher is able to draw on already established concepts and theories, where these are relevant, to help clients to understand problems and develop new arrangements.

8:   Social Process for Refining and Agreeing Future Organisation
A further feature of the method is a process through which individuals, after clarifying their views, discuss and agree possibilities with each other, and group reports are produced. The researcher will sometimes act as a "broker" in this process to clarify, in increasingly larger groups, the possible forms of organisation to be adopted. At each stage it is the group which agrees and decides further action, but the analyst often facilitates and accelerates this process.

9:   Evaluation and Testing
Where new forms of organisation are agreed and adopted it is possible to test in practice the ideas which were developed, to discover subsequent problems which occur and to find out if the new organisation does indeed overcome the problems. Because the researcher produces a clear specification of new organisation it is possible to evaluate the change by finding out to what extent the change was introduced, and by noting divergencies from the original specification.

Not all social analytic projects follow the full sequence from individual discussion to group agreements and then official implementation and evaluation. As a result ideas and concepts produced in one project may have a lower validity and reliability than those produced in another project where the ideas have been fully refined and tested and put through the full process.

The following describes the full social-analytic process before then considering the reliability and validity of the different types of research material produced in social-analytic research.

The Social-Analytic Process

The process starts with organisational members' perceptions of a problem or a series of problems. Typically the situation is best described as a "mess", or as disorganised, and the various problems are presented as exemplifying or illustrating the breakdown on organisation.

Usually it is more senior members of the organisation who recognise core problems, or are in some way responsible for dealing with the situation, and who initially define the problem. However, the first stage of the process involves the researcher in helping various members to clarify their perception of the problem, and to formulate a joint analysis of causes and possible solutions, usually in discussion with individuals.

Reports are fed back to individuals and groups for revision to check that the researcher's formulation accords with clients' views, and to help the client to develop their ideas further. It is usually at this stage that key concepts need to be defined and agreed.

The second stage is when individuals' definitions and analyses of the problem are brought together, and a group meeting is held to develop shared conceptions and to examine alternative models. Further revisions may be carried out before the third stage of the process, which usually involves workshops attended by individuals from other organisations and sites with an interest in the problem and alternative models. This enables further revision of concepts and models and makes it possible to identify the conditions under which certain concepts and models are usable or representative. Larger workshops thus help to identify the situations where the concepts and models can be applied, and the extent to which they may be generalised to other organisations.

Once the new organisation has been subjected to thorough and widespread discussion-testing, criticism and revision, it can be submitted by the relevant group to a higher authority which is empowered to introduce the change. The changes are then officially implemented and the researcher is available to help with problems of implemention or which arise subsequently.

The practical test of validity of a concept or model, using the idea of "validity" which underlies the process, is whether the original problems are resolved and the new form of organisation is effective over a number of years. It is not always possible, however, to follow through the full process to implementation and review. Higher authorities sometimes do not agree to implementation, and the researcher is not always invited back to review the operation of new organisation, especially if it is successful in resolving the initial problems. The following table summarises some of the differences between traditional interview methods and the social-analytic method.

	Traditional Interview Method	Social-Analytic Research Method
Research initiative:	Researcher requests interview.	Client invitation.
Focus of interview:	Researcher's questions andinterests, directed by theoretical issues or gaps in knowledge.	Client's problem & possible solutions.
Purpose of interview:	For the researcher to gather information.	Joint analysis and conceptualisation: For the client to clarify organisational problems and solutions and the researcher to gather descriptions of organisation and processes.
Discussion of concepts and theory:	Rarely. Concepts and theory developed by researcher from data, usually by induction.	Concepts and theory offered by researcher where relevant to help joint analysis.
Independence:	Complete researcher independence.	A "disinterested concern" to help to improve organisation.
Cross-checking interview information with other sources:	Always.	Rarely systematically under-taken outside of the social-analytic process.

Dimensions for Comparing Social-Analytic and Traditional Interview Methods

Research Limitations and Advantages

From a social scientific research perspective there are limitations as well as advantages to the method when compared with other methods for researching social organisation. The above description of the types of data produced by the method and of the overall process is a development of earlier descriptions. This development is necessary to establish how data produced by the method can be drawn on to contribute to social scientific knowledge, and to show the appropriateness of the method for investigating the subject of the thesis.

Validity

One limitation of the method is that the descriptions rely on reports by staff members about situations or of ways of working: the researcher does not typically directly observe actions or situations as in participant observation. Although the researcher is frequently involved in the everyday life of the organisation in meetings and visits, the method focuses on staff perceptions and interpretations. Descriptions built up from direct observation are of higher validity in one respect, but the researcher would need to be present for long periods of time, leaving less time for comparisons between sites.

The method produces descriptions of existing organisation and of future organisation.The latter descriptions are intentional statements or "social contracts" adopted by members and sanctioned by their employing organisation: they are agreements which members have been concerned to establish, and have invested their time and energy in specifying correctly, and have chosen to be bound by. The way in which members are involved in creating these descriptions through the social-analytic process results in data of a different nature to direct observation data, or interview or questionnaire response data.

The validity of the explanatory theories developed in parallel with these descriptions is a separate matter, and the methods for generating and testing such theories are here the same as for any social scientific theory [Øvretveit (1984)]. Thus the researcher may develop insights, hunches and finally formulate hypotheses as a result of being involved in the process, but the process itself rarely allows for the rigorous and systematic testing of explanatory theory. An example is the explanatory theory of pyramidal hierarchical organisation structure [Jaques (1976)] which was developed over a series of research projects. At a simple level the method of discussion-testing and other aspects of the process do not make it possible to seek out disconforming instances, but these methods are not designed to test the explanatory theory.

The validity of descriptions of organisation is therefore judged according to:
-whether all who take part in, or who follow the organisational procedures and policies described are involved in formulating the descriptions;
-the way in which they are involved, i.e. that they invite the researcher to help them to describe the organisation, in confidence, individually and then in groups, and during the latter stages using concepts common to the group as a whole;
-the extent and nature of discussion-testing, using examples to test whether the concepts are being used in a common and consistent way, and whether staff do, or will do, what they said;
-direct observation (rarely systematically undertaken in social-analytic research);
-cross-checking with disinterested observers.

One criticism of the validity of the description is that it is not clear whether, or how, the researcher influences the way specifications are made of existing and future organisation [Whittington and Bellaby (1977)]. In previous reports (e.g.Jaques, ed. (1978) some descriptions have been reported in a way in which others are not able to tell whether the description is of existing organisation or of a future model. Where organisation is implemented this is clear, but a further criticism is then that the researcher has introduced prescriptive theories (e.g. levels of work, individual work capacity) which have influenced members to adopt a particular form of organisation.

One of the purposes of collaborative research is for the researcher to help the client, and this inevitably and intentionally involves influencing the client. The question is how the researcher influences the client, and how previously developed concepts and theories are used in defining organisation. The guiding principles are, (a) the researcher only introduces such concepts and theories where they are directly relevant and likely to help to clarify the situation, and, (b) the client decides whether the concepts and theories are relevant and helpful.

The client and the problem-centred approach also leads to certain research limitations which have already been mentioned. The researcher cannot choose the subject of investigation, and is not able to direct the investigation towards their areas of research interest.   This disadvantage counterbalances some of the advantages of access to, and within the organisation, and staff motivation and involvement in accurate specification.

A further criticism is that problems are often defined and chosen by higher management, or that a one-sided managerial description and perspective about the organisation can be developed.   However, a requirement of research is for free access to the researcher by all members for confidential discussions. The researcher assumes a responsibility for making themselves available to all members of the organisation, and for explaining the kind of help that they can provide. In addition, changes in organisation are discussed and agreed by all concerned before implementation.

Access
One advantage of the method is that the researcher is able to gain easy access to members of the organisation. The problem-focused and confidential approach can result in greater cooperation and trust than with other methods This makes it possible not only to gain descriptions of organisation, but also to gain members' views about the "real" motives and factors behind certain forms of organisation, and to be part of the free discussions amongst members about the advantages to them of adopting certain arrangements (e.g. if a professional group chooses 'x' model, they are more likely to gain an extra post in 'y' site and avoid coming under the management of 'z'). This is data of a different order to description, and was data used by the author to develop explanatory hypotheses.

Confidentiality
The accuracy and the richness of the data gained because of easy access, is limited by the principle of client confidentiality. A criticism of the method is that only the descriptions and matters mentioned in confidential discussions, which members then agree to being widely reported ("cleared"), can be used in research publications.

Confidentiality is a necessary condition for the research, and there are cases where members have refused to allow publication. However, the main research experience is that refusals usually arise because there are flaws in the descriptions, and that alterations and changes to ensure anonymity make it possible to publish descriptions. It is less easy, however, to report motives and political strategies which are discussed and which can be used as evidence to support explanatory hypotheses.

Summary

The research method of social analysis provides a way of both directly contributing to resolving practical organisational problems and of developing knowledge which can be generalised to other sites. The distinctive features of the method are: a focus on client's organisational problems, at the client's invitation and in a confidential setting; that analysis and conceptualisation are provided to help clients to clarify the nature of their problem and future possible organisation; that a conceptual framework can be drawn on where it is relevant to assist the analysis, and that the analyst facilitates an organisational process for clarifying, agreeing and implementing changes.

The method produces different types of research data with different validity and reliability :
(1) a public statement of existing organisation;
(2) an individual's perception of organisation;
(3) an individual's and researcher's joint description;
(4) a description of organisation agreed by a group, and
(5) data on new organisation which was implemented and reviewed.

The outline abovediffers from earlier descriptions in, (a) acknowledging the theoretical assumptions underlying the method; (b) recognising the way in which researchers using the method draw on both concepts and explanatory theory, and (c) distinguishing the different reliability and validity of different types of research data gained by using the method. Such developments in the methodology of the method are necessary to meet legitimate criticisms [Whittington and Bellaby (1977)] and to establish the ways in which both social-analytic and action research can contribute to social science theory [Øvretveit (1984)].

Appendix 2: Main Field Research

The following lists the main research projects and research sources.

Psychology Organisation Research 1984-87
A)Project Title:Northumberland Psychology District Service Organisation
B)Dates: March 1984 (3 days)
A)Project Title:North Manchester Psychology District Service Organisation
B)Dates: January 1985(3 days),
A)Project Title:Eastbourne Psychology District Service Organisation
B)Dates: February 1985(3 days),
A)Project Title:Macclesfield Psychology District Service Organisation
B)Dates: March 1986(3 days),
A)Project Title:Dudley Psychology District Service Organisation
B)Dates: March 1986(3 days),
A)Project Title:Oxford Psychology District Service Organisation
B)Dates: July 1986(2 days),
A)Project Title:St. Helens and Knowsley District Service Organisation
B)Dates: October 1986(3 days),
A)Project Title:Gwynedd Psychology District Service Organisation
B)Dates: Jan 1987 (3 days),
A)Project Title:Nottingham 1982 Trail Project.Psychology organisation sub-project.
B)Dates:November1981,
Regional Workshops
(Sept 1984), West Midlands Region Workshop,22 attended .
(June 1986), Northern Region Workshop ,19 attended.
(March 1987), West Midlands Region Workshop ,23 attended.
Brunel Workshops
23/24 Nov 1983, 18 attended,13/14 Feb 1984,16 attended,23/24 Feb1984,19 attended,13/14 Sept 1984 15 attended,27/28 Sept 1984,16 attended,30/31 Oct 1984 ,14 attended,31 Jan/1 Feb 1985,16 attended,13/14 Feb 1985 ,13 attended,3/4 Oct 1985,17 attended,15/16 Oct 1985,18 attended,4/5 March 1986,9 attended,22/23 April 1986,16 attended,30/31 July 1986,14 attended,3/4 Dec 1986 (Specialist Health Professions),14 attended,15/16 Dec 1986,14 attended,31 March/1 April 1987,11attended.
Other Conferences/Seminars
1982, "Regional Representative Structures", King's Fund Centre, London.
1984, "Grading and Organisation", King's Fund Centre, London.
1984, "Organising District Psychology",
1984 , S-E Thames Region, David Solomans House.
1984, "Planning Organisational Structure", Oxford Region Seminar,Warneford Hospital.

Physiotherapy Organisation-Research 1980-84
A)Project Title: Chartered Society of Physiotherapy Organisation Project
B)Dates:Phase 1 Jan 1980-June 1980,C).Interviews: 14 District Physiotherapists ,17 senior physiotherapists in Enland and Scotland,E).Other researchers involved:Dr. Warren Kinston (BIOSS).
B)Phase 2 July 1980-July 1982,(role of senior physiotherapsists) C).D).Workshops: 1 day,on site,attended by senior members of all departments in each region,conducted by the researcher alone,
North-West Thames (19/1/82)17 attended,South-West Thames (10/2/82),19 attended, South-Western (26/2/82),22 attended,North-Eastern (11/3/82),18 attended,Oxford (31/3/82),23 attended,Wessex (15/6/82),19 attended,Trent workshop (6/6/81),21 attended.
Other Workshops,chaired with Dr. Warren Kinston.
"Integrating Education and Clinical Services",3/4 Feb 1982, 9/10 March   1982, and 17/18 March 1982.
"Senior Practitioner and Superintendent Workshop",June1984(attended by 27 staff from Nottingham and Norwich departments).
Brunel Workshops,chaired with Dr.Warren Kinston.
"Managing Physiotherapy in the New Districts" (20/21 Sept 1984).
"Managing Physiotherapy in the New Districts" (1/2 Nov 1984).

Research 1986-1990
MULTIDISCIPLINARY TEAM ORGANISATION AND COMMUNITY SERVICES FIELD RESEARCH AND WORKSHOPS

On-Site Workshops
78 events held between 1984 and 1991 in most Regions of the UK

National Workshops at Brunel on Multidisciplinary Team Organisation
30,31 January, 27,28 June, 15,16 July,1986
9,10th April ,5,6th May ,29,30 September,23,24 November 1987
16,17th May 1988,27,28th September 1988,7,8th December 1988
9,10th March 1989,2,3rd November 1989
12,13th February 1990,25/26th October 1990.

ORGANISATION AND MANAGEMENT OF THERAPY SERVICES

National Workshops at Brunel
22/23rd March 1988, 6/7th June 1988,1/2nd December 1988
11,12 October 1989,
22/23rd March 1990,31May1June 1990,27/28th September 1990

On-Site Workshops from 1990
Warrington DHA 7,8 Feb 1990,East Birmingham DHA 19,20 March 1990,Bolton 5,6th April 1990,NE Thames
Region Psychologists(Contract Management) 12/13th June 1990, Basildon 16,17 December 1990.

Appendix 3: Research into Physiotherapy and Clinical Psychology Organisation 1968-1988

INTRODUCTION

This appendix presents the author's field research into the management structures and autonomy of physiotherapy and clinical psychology between 1980 and 1990. Research into three areas is reported, 1) the overall management structure of each profession within an employing authority; 2) the role and institutionalised authority of head profession-managers, and 3) the autonomy of practitioners after qualifying, and after 20 years of practice.

The focus is institutionalised structures, authority and autonomy (roles, relationships and rules which are explicit, agreed and instituted by employing authorities).

RESEARCH FINDINGS - PHYSIOTHERAPY

Between 1980 and 1987 the author carried out four different programmes of research into physiotherapy organisation. The first was research for the Chartered Society of Physiotherapists (CSP) between 1980 and 1982. The project investigated the organisational problems of senior practitioners and newly-established District Physiotherapists and clarified the different management structures which existed at that time. The research is documented in fourteen revised and cleared field reports, which drew together field interviews with approximately thirty-six physiotherapists at different levels in different parts of the country. These formulations were discussion-tested and other structures were clarified in eight regional workshops attended by senior physiotherapists from throughout the country. The workshops were held between June 1981 and June 1982, involving approximately 130 senior physiotherapists from districts in each region (research documents on each workshop were summarised in Doc. 3300). The research was summarised and reported in a series of publications in the professional journal "Physiotherapy" (Øvretveit et al (1980) Nos. 1 - 6), and in a detailed report to the CSP (Doc. 3119).

The second programme of research was investigations into physiotherapy organisation forming part of wider field projects in four districts on the development of Unit management between 1980 and 1984. The third was a series of National Workshops at Brunel for District Physiotherapists, held between 1983 and 1987. Finally, between 1980-85 the author traced the development of professional autonomy in the profession by drawing on previous field research and reports, and published the findings in Øvretveit (1985 a).

The following first presents findings about the role and authority of district physiotherapists, and the overall management structure of physiotherapy within different districts between 1980 and 1987. Research into practitioner autonomy is then presented, drawn mostly from the 1980 - 1982 study.

District Physiotherapist Role and Authority

Initial interviews in the 1980-1982 CSP research revealed that District Physiotherapist posts had been established in the twelve districts where the interviews were undertaken. In addition, district physiotherapy management structures existed, made up of a number of physiotherapy departments managed by the District Physiotherapist and headed by Superintendent and Senior I Physiotherapists (Doc. 3119 and Doc. 3097).

The interviews revealed variations between districts in terms of the role and authority of the District Physiotherapist. All interviewed combined their district role with the day-to-day management of one department (Notes, 10 March 1980), and all but one had full-management authority in relation to "their" Superintendents (Doc. 3097, Doc. 3090). One District Physiotherapist described her authority, "to move physiotherapists between hospitals and alter staffing arrangements" (Notes, 10 March 1980), but her budget for staffing was set by the DMT and she had no formal authority to negotiate budget levels with the DMT or district officers.

The exception was an Area Physiotherapist (single District, "designated" post) who did not have full-managerial authority in relation to the three other Superintendents in the Area (Doc. 3099 (Rev.)). Physiotherapy was organised as a district service through the Area Committee of Superintendents, and ,"all claims for funding and staff from the Superintendents are made through the Area Superintendent", who had "formal access to the Area Team". However, the Area Superintendent did not have, "authority to move staff . it appears a joint decision between superintendents would have to be made". (Such a committee structure is similar to those reported earlier amongst heads of physiology departments in a district). The Area Superintendent also had less than full-managerial authority in relation to senior staff within her own department. Although ,"basic grades were contracted with the Area, and could in principle be moved" (Notes, 11 March 1980), the Superintendent and consultants had agreed to develop physiotherapy sub-specialities, and senior staff had established their practices on the understanding that they would not be moved.

One District Physiotherapist role was discovered with "direct accountability to the DHA" (Doc. 3090, p 6), and "direct access to the DMT", rather than accountability to the District Community Physician or District Administrator, who then presented physiotherapy reports or proposals to the DMT (as proposed in the DHSS circular HC(79)19).

At the same time the author was involved in research into preparations for Unit Management in four districts. In one district a District Physiotherapist post had not been established, and the reasons for the post were closely questioned (Doc. 3096 and 3215). In the other districts management links were being developed between physiotherapy district structure, and the newly-emerging Unit structures. Although the research did not specify existing structure but outlined possible future arrangements, it is of relevance because it shows non-physiotherapy managers moving the balance of control from a District Physiotherapist to Unit management.

Thus in one field project the future possible District Physiotherapist role (DP) was described as "Manager of Superintendents within Units", and as "Controlling the District physiotherapy budget in the sense that the budget would be agreed with the DMT after consultations between the DP and the Units". (Doc. 3270). It was viewed as important that Unit management had some influence over staffing, whereas previously District management had decided - this represented a counterbalance to physiotherapy management autonomy and control. (The District Physiotherapist subsequently reported that this arrangement was established).

The same issue was addressed from a different perspective in another study, where it was recognised that both Unit administrators and District Physiotherapists would have personnel authority in relation to physiotherapists within Units. (Doc. 3262 p 3). The details of the authority of each were not specified in these studies, but it was recognised that a head physiotherapist in each Unit would manage all physiotherapists within the Unit, and be accountable to both the District Physiotherapist and the Unit Administrator for different matters (Doc. 3262).

Evidence of structures which were established after the NHS reorganisation in 1982 was gained from national workshops for District Physiotherapists between 1984 and 1987. District Physiotherapists reported no longer being supplied with plans and information about future developments and not knowing how and where to propose plans for extra staff; not being involved in District and Unit planning teams, and being referred by district managers to Unit teams for decisions. (Workshop Notes ,BWN.17(20/8/84)).

Most reported having to get agreement from Unit management to transfer staff or finance between Units (BWN.18). The conclusions were that District Physiotherapists' authority in relation to staff had been reduced by the new Unit management arrangements. These workshops established that the management structures for most physiotherapy services in the country could be represented in general terms by one of the three models represented below.

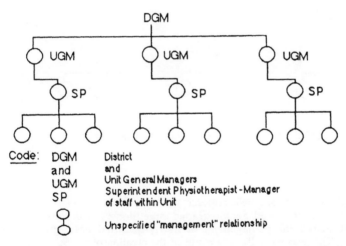

Code: DGM   District
       and   and
       UGM   Unit General Managers
       SP   Superintendent Physiotherapist-Manager
               of staff within Unit

       Unspecified "management" relationship

Model A: Unit Services (No district role or organisation)

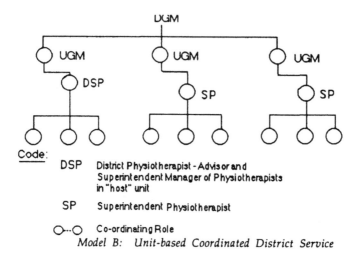

Code:

DSP   District Physiotherapist - Advisor and
       Superintendent Manager of Physiotherapists
       in "host" unit

SP   Superintendent Physiotherapist

O--O   Co-ordinating Role

Model B: Unit-based Coordinated District Service

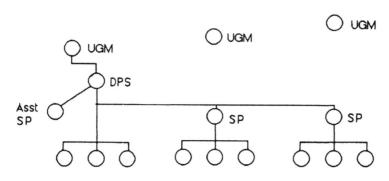

Model C: Unit-based District Managed Service

Practitioner Autonomy

One of the findings of the 1980 field research was that, in comparison with their roles in the early 1970s, experienced Senior graded practitioners had considerably more autonomy, and shared the management of newly-qualified basic grade staff with Superintendents. This was partially as a result of the creation of the Senior grade in the later 1970s [Halsbury Report (1975)].

Field interviews and the later workshops established that Superintendents distinguished between Basic Grade staff, who were supervised and could be moved between specialities or were on "rotation schemes", and Senior graded staff, who usually worked whole-time in one speciality and who could not be moved. In addition, rather than all staff being directly managed by Superintendents, it was found that Senior grade staff "supervised" groups of basic grade staff within specialities and were becoming an intervening management level in the structures (C 3300).

In practice, although not formally recognised, Superintendents exercised less than full-managerial authority in relation to Senior staff in specialities (Doc. 3093). Senior staff autonomy was not only independence to practice within a particular area or group of wards, but also involved independence from case-work review by superintendents and doctors (e.g. "It would be improper to interfere with the clinical judgments of a senior practitioner" (Doc. 3093 p 3); "A Senior practitioner will not tolerate interference with the exercise of his clinical judgment. A senior regards himself as an "expert" and, as long as he acts within legal, ethical and policy bounds, cannot be instructed by another physiotherapist, and certainly not by an outsider, as to how to treat any particular case." (Doc. 3090, p 3).

However, two Senior Physiotherapists interviewed were not clear about "the exact authority to make decisions over type and duration of treatment. There can be conflict within the profession and between members of the profession and doctors over treatment decisions and over who holds full authority for physiotherapy treatment." (Doc. 3112 p 1). They reported that in some cases "treatment decisions depend on the personal confidence and forcefulness of the individual physiotherapist", rather than on agreed and institutionalised authority. (Doc. 3112 p 4). Some seniors were also unclear about their responsibility for treatment decisions made by newly-qualified basic grade staff whom they supervised (Doc. 3100b p 3).

These issues were examined further in workshops for Senior practitioners in eight Regions between 1981 and 1982 and in 1984. (Documented in C.3300, C.3284, C.3290, C.3296, C.3297, C.3304, C.3312, Doc. 3435, and workshop notes).

The workshops revealed that physiotherapy managers usually did not fully-manage Seniors in the sense of deciding case allocation aand reviewing cases. However, this did not mean that Seniors had autonomy to decide where and how they worked. Referrals and requests, mainly from consultants, were high and Seniors were prevented from starting waiting lists and managing their own practices. "Some Seniors struggle at breaking-point under excessive workloads because they are not aware that it is Superintendents' responsibility to regulate workload. Some Superintendents abdicate their responsibility for this work, often burdening Seniors with extra demands." (Doc. C.3300, p 2). The finding was that a failure of physiotherapy managers to exercise their authority to regulate referrals resulted in practitioners' autonomy being decreased rather than increased. The large amount of work which they were required to undertake resulted in a reduction in the discretion practitioners were able to exercise over treatment decisions and location and type of work.

There were exceptions. In one workshop three practitioners reported Superintendents' exercising authority over what they viewed to be clinical decisions: "monitoring number of patients treated, organising patient lists, deciding treatment policies, and changing allocation of work". (Doc. 3296 p 3). This is the only documented evidence showing that Seniors in some districts had less autonomy than was generally reported (Doc. 3093).

The workshops revealed widespread conflict between Superintendent managers and Seniors; not so much about case-work decisions but more about management decisions which Seniors made regarding how they ran their individual practices or their departments, where Senior staff "supervised" basic grade staff (Doc. 3304 p 2). The above research is summarised in chapter 3.

RESEARCH FINDINGS - PSYCHOLOGY

Findings are reported from three main types of research into psychology organisation undertaken by the author between 1982 and 1987. The first type was small-scale short-term field studies of district psychology services involving discussions with heads of services, followed by workshops with the psychologists employed in the service. The second type of research involved thirteen national and two regional workshops each with representatives from 15 - 22 different services, who reported and discussed organisational structures and roles within their services. Other findings, mainly concerning practitioner autonomy, are drawn from a wider range of sources, including workshops for multidisciplinary teams which involved psychologists, and from conferences on organisation arranged by psychologists, as well as from a variety of governmental and professional documents.

The main findings of each field study and workshop are reported below, in each case prescriptive statements about overall organisation and about the head psychologist practitioner roles are presented, followed by descriptions of aspects of organisation provided by participants in individual or group discussions. Critical incidents providing examples of managers exercising, or being prevented from exercising, forms of authority or autonomy are also presented.

District Field Studies

The field studies which are reported involved an initial analysis of employing authority prescriptions, and descriptions by the head psychologist, followed by discussions with the head psychologist to clarify aspects of structure not described. This was followed by two-day workshops involving all the psychologists within the organisation to identify their areas of concern and their understanding of their organisation. The studies were undertaken over a four-year period, involving services of size from 8 to 27 psychologists in urban and rural districts in England and Wales with populations from 110,000 to 360,000.

The outcome of the discussions was documented in field notes, but no detailed research documents were produced and the notes were not checked or revised by the participants, which was normal practice in longer-term social-analytic field research.

Northumberland Field Study
The only prescriptive statements in health authority documents defined the district psychologist as a "budget manager" and as "responsible for the day-to-day operation of the service and accountable to the budget holder", the latter being the unit administrator (UA). Unit Management Groups (UMGs) were described as "monitoring budgets", and the district psychologist as having authority ,(a) to carry over annually all planned savings, as long as the UMG was informed in advance, and ,(b) to carry over "fortuitous savings" only to the next year (NP.01).

Preliminary discussions with the district psychologist revealed that he was provided with information on all staff salary, travel and equipment costs, and that Units did not have detailed information on costing. The authority of the district psychologist either to switch staff sessions between Units, or to change a post if recruitment was difficult, had not been tested. In the past session changes had been carried out "informally", without the District Management Team(DMT) being informed.

The district psychologist was concerned that UMGs might oppose changes if they were told, and that Unit budgeting would both provide information about session changes and "complicate changes" and reduce the district psychologist's and other psychologists' autonomy.

The purpose of the workshop was to clarify existing organisation and future possible options, in order for the district psychologist to present a report to the District Management Team (DMT) about the future of the service and its organisation. The motivation for the workshop was the district psychologist's and the other psychologists' concern that the district psychologist's imminent departure would lead to his not being replaced, and to a "unitised" service being created, which would have reduced psychologists' group autonomy, and their influence at district levels.

Overall Structure
The statements about structure to follow are taken from discussions with the district psychologist, from his report to the health authority (NP.01), and were checked with workshop members(NP.FN) Members of the workshop agreed that the district psychologist as the "administrative and professional head of service" had the "responsibility and authority to ensure that the services are coordinated and are being provided as agreed, and has the power to use the Authority's disciplinary procedure where there is a breach of professional conduct". As well as being the head of the district service, the district psychologist was head of one of the three specialist groupings of psychologists, the other two groupings comprising four and five psychologists respectively. The workshop members agreed that the following provided a simple representation of overall structure:

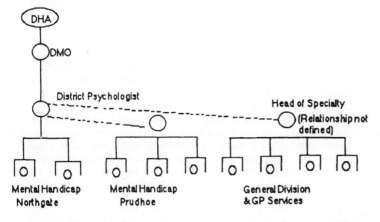

Northumberland Psychology Department Divisional Structure(1982)

A "district committee" of all the psychologists met monthly to share information and discuss proposals for new posts and services. Psychologists in the general division each specialised in work for particular client groups,and had developed greater independence in their community and GP work to choose the type of work which they undertook. Workshop members took the view that each psychologist was "independent with respect to his or her clinical practice". When questioned as to the limits to their autonomy the collective view was that the prescribed limits were defined in a job description which ,"specifies main areas of work and sometimes the balance expected between different kinds of work", and in health authority statements on priorities set by planning groups and management teams.

No examples were given of situations where individuals had not observed the general limits which were prescribed. It was felt that in "extreme" situations the head could institute disciplinary procedures.

The head's report stated that ,"psychologists' clinical practice is not"managed" in the way that nursing or social work are. It is essentially a personal service to people. Referrals from doctors and social workers and nurses come on the whole to named psychologists with whom these practitioners have personal contact". (NP.02).

Case Autonomy
In working towards specifying the structure which would,"reconcile the need to preserve the clinical independence of individual psychologists with the need for an identifiable individual to carry out duties on behalf of the Authority" (NP.03), the workshop based its discussions on a paper by a member of the department (Kat (1980)). This described the responsibilities of the previous area coordinator, responsibilities which had been taken over by the district psychologist. The paper noted that," The acceptance of clinical psychologists as independent practitioners by area officers has been tested in several difficult and unpleasant episodes ", and a workshop member cited one critical incident where psychiatrists had objected to psychologists taking direct referrals from GPs, and the health authority had resolved the issue in favour of the psychologists.

The conclusion to the incident was an agreed procedure which described,"What happens if the GP is unhappy about some aspects of the psychologist's work or behaviour ".The paper continued:". qualified clinical psychologists are accepted as independent clinicians. Whilst in training their clinical judgments are subject to the supervision of a Senior or Principal grade psychologist; having qualified, their clinical judgments are not subject to the direction of any other person. Hence if it is some aspect of the psychologist's judgment in a particular case which is at issue, the first person to take the matter up with is the individual concerned. Clinical psychologists are very conscious of the importance of providing a high standard of service to patients and if the GP suspects gross misjudgment it would be in order to raise the matter with the individual's immediate colleagues. If the GP's concern is with some other aspect of the psychologist's conduct, it may be appropriate for him to contact the Area Coordinator of psychology services who has the power to involve the Area Health Authority's disciplinary procedure if necessary." [Kat (1980 (NP.03)].

Management Autonomy
The workshop agreed with the description of the district psychologist's authority in relation to psychologists as being: "to advise on the appointment and grading of staff; to undertake disciplinary actions in accordance with the authority's agreed procedure, and to monitor the adherence of psychologists to the established policies and procedures of

the Area Psychology Committee and AHA. This does not include authority to direct the clinical work of individuals, but does imply the right to enquire into it." The area coordinator and the district psychologist were nominated by the psychologists and ,"designated by the Authority", and received, "copies of the management team agendas and were invited to attend team meetings for relevant items."

In summary, although the details of the service organisation were not fully specified, the short field study provides evidence that psychologists were organised as a group in a "district psychology committee", were monitored and coordinated but not fully managed by the district psychologist, and clarified some of the limits to each practitioner's autonomy. It did not resolve how changes were to be made to psychologists' sessions to enable a district psychologist to ensure a more balanced service (members would not agree to the district psychologist being able to impose changes) or whether the district psychologist had the authority to overrule a committee view about priorities for new posts. The workshop did establish that the district psychologist had disciplinary authority to act in cases of breach of contract and negligence; did not have authority to "direct the clinical work of individuals", and that referrals were to a named psychologist providing a personalised service.

Manchester Field Study
Initial discussions with the district psychologist established that his post had recently been created as a result of pressure from psychiatrists, who felt that,"there was no leadership in psychology and that each psychologist did what they wanted " (MPFN). The new district psychologist wanted to bring together two traditionally separate psychology departments in mental health, and in child and family services, as well as his own speciality in mental handicap, to provide a "district service". The psychologists saw their new head as being able to prevent consultant doctors from "bringing psychologists back into consultant teams" as a result of new Unit organisation, and as being there to maintain their current independence. The district psychologist, on the other hand, saw the purpose of the workshop as being for the psychologists to agree ways of working together to provide a district service, and to agree and define more clearly his role and authority.

The workshop established that the employing authority had delegated authority to the district psychologist to appoint staff once posts were agreed, and to apply disciplinary procedures for breach of contract or unprofessional conduct (MPFN). Units had not been provided with budgets, and the district psychologist had authority to use "up to 50% of savings in his budget for non-recurrent items without DMT approval". His authority to change psychologists' deployment was unclear.

Each of the two separate departments was headed by principal grade psychologists who were described as carrying a ,"strong coordinating role in relation to psychologists in each department". (Seven and four psychologists in each department). Actual examples of these heads exercising authority in relation to psychologists are not documented.

One outcome of the workshop was to define the head of specialties' authority to "ensure psychologists adhered to contract and department policies and to report sustained divergencies to the district psychologist for disciplinary action as necessary" (MPFN), and that the district psychologist would have authority to define the overall policies and type of service to be provided by each specialty, after consultation.

In summary, the workshop provided evidence of the formation of a management structure for all the psychologists in the district, headed by a district psychologist with delegated budgetary and disciplinary authority, as well as agreed policy-making authority to define the overall type and balance of services if agreement could not be reached within the group. It did not provide evidence of incidents or specification of consultants' or unit management group's authority in relation to psychologists: the district psychologist's view was that complaints or requests would come to him to resolve, and that higher management (DMT) would arbitrate if he supported the psychologists' independence.

Eastbourne Field Study
In contrast to services in Northumberland and Manchester, the department in Eastbourne was based and managed within one unit of management and the district psychologist was accountable to the unit administrator for "managing" the psychology budget and service. Discussions with the district psychologist established that the authority's new unit management arrangements (EP.01) made it more difficult for the district psychologist and other psychologists to change or develop the services they provided outside of the base unit, and hence restricted their previous individual and group autonomy.

The district psychologist confirmed the general description of his role as outlined in the health authority document as being, "accountable for the management of all the professional staff within the department, whatever unit they may be based in", and that "day-to-day matters" were to be "sorted out" by the senior person in each unit (EP.01). The unit administrator (UA) was described as ensuring that,"adequate appointment and disciplinary procedures are observed by the district head", and that they may be "involved" in various personnel matters, but the head reported that the UA had never exercised his authority or "interfered" with the head's decisions on personnel matters.

The unit administrator's budgetary authority was a source of concern for the head :changes to sessions across units, or new posts had to be agreed by the relevant UAs. Previously psychologists had met requests to provide services without informing higher management outside of psychology, and new posts had been agreed or turned down by district management. The new arrangement was that each unit was provided with information about the cost of psychologists' time, and any changes required costing and financial transfers between units and the agreement of UAs: "Where services are provided to other units, then proposed changes must involve the district head plus the relevant UMTs at an early stage." (EP.01).

The district psychologist was concerned that where his views and those of his colleagues about new posts or changes were different from those of a UMG, the DMT would decide in favour of the unit, hence reducing psychologists' ability to decide the future shape and type of service. This possibility was noted (but not decided)in the authority's statement that, "One unit may wish to expand a service and another unit to contract it in complete contradiction to the professional opinion of the district head as to what constitutes a balance." (EP.01). No "test cases" had occurred clarifying the authority of the head.

The main purpose of the workshop, however, was for members of the department to agree a "decision-making process for the department as a whole". In particular the concern was: "Given limited resources, how do we make decisions and cope with competition between different members' needs and areas of interest, allowing for the personal and professional differences?" (EPFN1). Related issues were clarification of the role of department chairman,who was elected by the group, and the role of the district psychologist.

The workshop discussion revealed that new posts in different specialties had been created in a "disorganised" way when funds became available, with each psychologist practising in different fields and "coordinated" by the district psychologist. No incidents were cited where the head had required a psychologist to take on a case or undertake new work against their own judgment. Discussion revealed that the main limits to practitioners' autonomy were vaguely-worded job descriptions, and "informal peer group pressure" at departmental meetings. After a few years in the department each psychologist decided, within the terms of their job descriptions, how many sessions they would spend on which activities and where they would work their sessions. They would report major changes to the department meeting "to keep others informed".

The problems faced by the group, which were not resolved, were how the group could decide amongst themselves what work should be undertaken by new post holders, and how each member could change their work to provide services to areas in the district which did not receive psychology. The district psychologist was reluctant to require individuals to make changes because he supported the notion of freedom from "interference in clinical matters" which he and the group took to include decisions about the siting and type of work. He was also unsure about his authority to impose changes. Workshop discussions, however, revealed that junior members of the department were sometimes asked to change their sessional arrangements and did not have freedom to decide changes in the siting and balance of work.

In summary, the Eastbourne field study provided evidence of a psychology organisation based and managed within one unit of management, headed by a district psychologist who was accountable to a unit administrator rather than to a district officer. Psychologists' previous independence to change setting and type of work was not constrained by the head's authority in relation to them, but by his lack of structural authority to ensure that budgetary and administrative changes in other units were made to allow the psychologists to make the changes which they saw to be necessary. The workshop provided further confirmation that within the terms of their employment contract senior psychologists had a certain "practice freedom", whilst junior psychologists were instructed as to setting and time spent on certain types of work, but were not supervised in their clinical work.

Macclesfield Field Study
Further evidence of the degree of practitioner independence and of the authority of the head of service was gained in a workshop involving all psychologists and the three unit general managers (UGMs) of the district. The district psychologist post had been established in 1980 to develop a district service (McPFN), but with the creation of units of management in 1982 and new unit general managers in 1985, there was concern amongst psychologists that units would not fund new posts, and might require or oppose session changes.

For their part the UGMs were concerned about psychologists deciding to stop sessions for or referrals to the Units for which the UGMs were responsible without consulting the UGMs.The UGMs were worried about how they would deal with complaints from consultants if psychology services were reduced. The UGM responsible for the Unit in which the psychology department was based expected to be ,"held accountable by the DGM for the performance and effectiveness of the district psychology service". He wanted to know what this would mean, and how he and psychologists were to undertake the unfamiliar task of accounting for service effectiveness.

Preliminary discussions with the district psychologist established that psychologists' patterns of work had emerged as each had reacted to requests and referrals and had pursued their particular interests. Most had "manipulated demand" by "selling their services" and by "educating" GPs and other consultants to send them referrals which were within their area of interest and expertise. The district psychologist wished to agree a plan for a more "balanced service", and a structure which would ensure that such a service was provided - she felt her task was to respond to the statement in DHA's strategic plan that,"It is considered that the District Psychology Department is in need of rationalisation given that staff developments have tended to take place in an ad hoc fashion without reference to the overall structure of the service and the needs of the district." [Macclesfield DHA (p.1.9)].

The district psychologist also wished to agree how to institute one aspect of the operational policy she had drafted, "Each member of the Department will have their performance reviewed by Staff Appraisal from their immediate Head of Service, Heads of Service being appraised by the Head of Department. (District Psychologist)" .

This was viewed by some staff as entering the"grey" area between managerial and professional matters, and as a review of clinical practice. Discussion at the workshop focussed on the degree of freedom of individual practitioners to pursue different types of work at different sites, how psychologists as a group were to agree the specialty divisions of the service and which new posts were required, and how new posts were to be funded and existing posts changed through units of management.

One conclusion was that the district psychologist would consult other psychologists before proposing a specialty division structure and plan to UGMs for agreement. In the presence of the three UGMs the psychologists decided that if they could not agree the future structure, the head would have authority to decide and propose a structure, within the next month.

No psychologists had job descriptions and the discussion clarified the existing boundaries to their practice. The formal institutional limits were reported to be those of professional ethics and standards, and contractual statements concerning holiday entitlement. No formal statements existed which restricted any individual to a particular site or even field of work, and the consensus of the meeting was that the main restriction on practice would result from the district psychologist taking action on a consultant's complaint about a psychologist's refusal to take a referral. No examples were cited.

The picture which emerged, much to the astonishment of the UGMs and to the embarrassment of the psychologists, was of a considerable degree of freedom for each psychologist to pursue their practice as each saw fit, and of no mechanisms or policies which ensured that their work was coordinated or monitored. The main constraint to their independence was the need to reduce sessions or services to some consultants and units which had been built up through "custom and practice" over the years, in order that each could take on new areas of work which each decided was of greater importance. The district psychologist did not have prescribed structural authority to direct psychologists to work in certain areas, although it was clear from the workshop that UGMs and the DGM would support her in requiring changes and in directing psychologists as to types and fields of work.

The budgetary arrangements which were agreed gave an indication of the district psychologist's management autonomy. She was required to agree new posts in each of the three Units with each UGM, and she or the UGMs could veto the proposal to be arbitrated by the DGM. The UGM who agreed the post was then to propose it as part of their plan to the DGM for final agreement, and funding would be channelled through the "host" Unit. This represented a reduction in the district psychologist's autonomy as previously posts had been agreed and funded direct from district level with no formal check by units. The host UGM confirmed that the arrangement had been instituted at a later Brunel workshop where the service was presented as an example unit-based district service. (BWN.12).

In summary, the workshop provided evidence of few constraints to practitioners' autonomy and a reluctance to move to explicit arrangements where individuals could be formally held to account for the work which they undertook. This was demonstrated by a refusal of three psychologists even to state at which sites they worked. The district psychologist clarified her authority in relation to psychologists and to UGMs, and the group agreed that she had "policy-making authority" in relation to sites and broad fields of work. These and other aspects of structure examined at the workshop were adopted as health authority policy for the department two months later.

Dudley Field Study
This field study involved preparations and a workshop for the nine psychologists of the Dudley district service and the six psychologists of the Bromsgrove and Reddich district.

Discussions with the Dudley district psychologist revealed that the district service was to be managed within one unit of management and cross-charging arrangements were to be established with other Unit General Managers receiving services. Here concern was that the 'host' UGM, to whom she was "managerially accountable', would question or oppose the level and type of service which psychologists provided to other Units, and that recipient UGMs may also wish to influence the level and type of services they received. (i.e. the authority of the head in relation to UGMs was unclear and the head was concerned that new budgetary arrangements could limit her managerial autonomy). The general health authority prescription was that UGMs had "theright to decide how to use their resources .. whilst professional control is vested in the District Officer." It was clear that UGMs could significantly influence a district management decision about whether a new psychology post should be created and could influence the content and type of work to be done.

It was not possible to agree the limits to and extent of the district psychologist's managerial autonomy because no UGMs were present, but the district psychologist concluded that in the future it would be necessary to describe to UGMs in more detail the type and amount of work each psychologist undertook in each Unit for costing purposes, and to explain to each UGM why the work was undertaken. It was thought that case law would clarify the DP's authority by her taking proposals for changes to services which were not agreed by UGMs to the DGM for arbitration.

Evidence of practitioner autonomy was revealed in the workshop discussions concerning how decisions were made about where and what type of work each psychologist undertook. The department policy stated that,"All trained psychologists in the department are autonomous professional practitioners . who are administratively accountable to the District Psychologist who initiates the disciplining procedure. After due consultation the District Psychologist will set limits on resources and set priorities between specialties. Thus each specialty will have clearly-defined limits within which each Principal (with responsibility for that specialty) will operate. They will be responsible for monitoring and coordinating work within that specialty."

Discussions of management information, staff performance appraisal and clinical responsibility clarified some of the limits to practitioner autonomy. Where a practitioner within a specialty disagreed with the Principal head of specialty about whether the practitioner should change the siting or type of work, the district psychologist would decide, and would use disciplinary procedures to enforce the decision (DPFN). (No actual or likely instances were cited). Each practitioner was expected to provide workload statistics returns and to fill out a detailed two-week time diary. This provided the district psychologist (and UGMs) with information to question the practitioner's use of time and one example was given of where the district psychologist had done so. Finally the district psychologist was proposing to carry out "performance appraisals" where each member would provide a general review of their year's work and discuss their future plans - no case work reviews were to be undertaken.

Oxford Field Study
This field study provided evidence of the constraints to management autonomy in a district with a large number of psychologists (27) practising in different specialist areas, and with eight Units of management. The workshop was undertaken at the instigation of the district psychologist and heads of specialties in order to consider existing and future alternative structures for the department, how specialisms would relate to Units, and head of department roles.

The department documentation and preliminary discussions established the existence of six specialty areas of work with "heads of specialty" with varying responsibilities and authority (confirmed at the workshop). The district psychologist coordinated the heads of specialty, who each decided the type of service to be provided. Psychologists in each specialty provided services to a number of units of management.

Psychologists were concerned that they would be allocated to different Units for management purposes (possibly managed by UGMs) and budgeted for within these Units without regard to their cross-unit working. The district psychologist was concerned to establish a structure and process to ensure a more balanced service and to strengthen his coordinating authority.

Preliminary discussions and the workshop revealed that each practitioner had responded to and generated demand according to their specialist interests. Heads of specialty had made suggestions to the district psychologist about the siting of new posts and had dealt with the various requests of practitioners, but had not actively monitored practitioners' work nor proposed changes in siting or methods of work. It was changes to Unit structures which prompted the district psychologist and heads to examine their structure and their management role, and to begin to define the authority which each reequired in order to be held accountable for providing a district and a specialty service.

The agreement which was reached was that four head of division posts would be established to "monitor" psychologists in each division, and would be coordinated by the district psychologist. The authority of divisional heads in relation to psychologists in the division was not specified further than the "monitoring role" [Øvretveit (1985)] (i.e. limited to specific field of work), but it was agreed that disagreements between divisional heads about new posts were to be resolved by the district psychologist's decision.

This study revealed limits to the district psychologist's management autonomy in large departments with long-established specialties, each of which had separate power bases within institutions. Each head of specialty's concern about what they perceived as "the threat of Unit management" led them to join forces to establish a coordinated district service for "protection". (OPFN).

Other Research Findings

The above field studies provided evidence of forms of organisation which balanced (a) the views of each practitioner about the type of work they should be doing and how best to spend their time, with (b), an overall view of the psychology service as a whole and how each person's skills could best be used. Other national and regional workshops conducted by the author and conferences organised by psychologists focused on this issue and provide further evidence of group and practitioner autonomy, of the roles of heads of service, and of the functioning of departmental meetings or committees.

Bexley Department

One of the longest-running and best documented examples of ,"committee group management" is the Bexley Department. The author discussed the structure with the head of department in two informal meetings in April 1983 (NETCN) and in 1984 (SETCN), at the Brunel Workshop attended by the head (BWN.03), and with groups of psychologists at two conferences. The description of the department by the head (Field, May 1980) was used as a basis for these discussions.

Group management in this instance involved all the psychologists who worked in a hospital department. With the creation of a district service and the appointment of psychologists to posts based outside the hospital, the hospital group model of organisation was extended to manage the district service. The critical issues concerned the role and authority of the district psychologist with respect to the group meeting and to individual practitioners,in particular his ability to decide changes to use of time and sessions where there was no consensus, or where he disagreed with the group or with individuals.

In discussion the head confirmed the description of the case autonomy of practitioners, "Clinical decisions are the direct responsibility of each psychologist and he or she cannot, in clinical matters, be overruled by any office holder or by any meeting of the department." [Field, May (1980)].

He knew of no situations where practitioners' case decisions had been overruled by himself or others. When questioned about the exact meaning of "clinical matters", it emerged that a practitioner's decision to provide teaching or consultancy to a new area, or to accept referrals from a new source, was: "more a service matter than a clinical matter, for discussion at the meeting". [Field, May (1980)].

In situations where practitioners were likely to make "major changes" to their use of time, a departmental discussion was required, with the possibility of a vote. The rules were: "major policy decisions affecting the long-term running of the department require two-thirds majority and three-quarters of department members as a quorum". Documentation is not available of "critical incidents" where a practitioner's proposed change was opposed by the meeting.

The district psychologist reported that practitioners did in fact make changes which did not breach contract, which sometimes later came to light in departmental discussions, and the fact that the group had not known about or agreed the changes was ignored. His concern was that the group was not grappling with the task of ensuring an overall balanced service because each member wished to maintain their own independence. His authority extended only to monitoring adherence to contract and to implementing department policy, and he had not sought the group's sanction to discipline a practitioner for not reporting and discussing session or referral changes. In fact the organisation made such actions unlikely - each department meeting was chaired by each member in succession and the district head was originally elected and only later appointed by the authority as a "district officer".

The district psychologist reported that there had been no conflict in the previous single-specialty department, but with new posts outside the specialty and different views about developments and service priorities, as well as requests for psychology input from across the district, the district psychologist experienced pressure on him to overrule meeting decisions to ensure a balanced district service. (NETCN).

In summary, the Bexley Department organisation provides evidence of psychologists organised as a group with a committee structure, headed by a district psychologist who was accountable to the group for implementing its policies, and to the district administrator for monitoring and coordinating practitioners. Individuals were reported to have autonomy over case decisions.They were also formally required to gain committee agreement to changes in their practice, but their practice did not follow the written policy.

South Birmingham

The author conducted a two-day workshop for 18 psychologists from 12 districts in the West Midlands, and took the South Birmingham service as a typical example for defining and discussing problems of organisation of concern to the participants. Previous discussions with the district psychologist and one head of specialty, as well as analysis of the service description(BP.01), provided a description of the organisation and details of psychologists' management and practitioner autonomy in this district.

The health authority was divided into eight Units of management with five psychology specialties, each staffed by two psychologists with sessions spread across most Units. The psychologists were organised as a "district service", headed by the district psychologist who chaired service meetings of all the psychologists and put forward proposals for new or changed services to the DMT. (BPFN). With "unitisation" in 1982 the district psychologist reported having to take proposals for changes in referrals, sessional arrangements, and new posts to each relevant unit administrator for agreement. She described this as "reducing flexibility" for herself and the psychologists concerned, and as making it more difficult to get new posts established because it required "support from unit administration". (BPFN).

Evidence of practitioner autonomy was provided by discussions of statements in the service description (BP.01, p.3),"Qualified psychologists are independent professionals and as such are not accountable to each other for their clinical work. They are responsible for the management of their own time. Psychologists only have management authority over other psychologists if that is part of their job description." The' district psychologist and others at the workshop reported that head psychologists did not examine psychologists' case decisions, unless there was a complaint. Two occasions were described where psychiatrists had complained to head psychologists about a psychologist's conduct of case-work, and on each occasion the head had not overturned the psychologists' decisions because they had satisfied themselves that the individual was within professional standards.

Other aspects of autonomy were examined by the researcher suggesting situations where a psychologist might decide to spend half of their time on, for example, research. Discussion showed that research proposals were "discussed at department meetings". (BPFN). In addition, the view was that most heads did in fact have disciplinary authority to ensure that psychologists kept to their employment contract, and if a psychologist's decision about their use of time led to a breach of contract, a head would be responsible for noting the fact and acting on it. Again, no incidents were reported where heads had exercised formal disciplinary authority over such matters.

This brief study and the workshop discussions provided evidence of psychologists in one district organised as a group, headed by a district psychologist who was having increasing difficulties in arranging changes to sessions and new posts on behalf of her colleagues in the department because of the number of new units of management. It provided another example of a situation where once psychologists were appointed, the main limits to their autonomy were those of their job description (if they had one) and subsequent psychology service policies which were agreed by group. No examples of heads imposing policies without group agreement were provided, nor of heads overriding case decisions.

Hampstead Psychology Service
Psychology organisation in this district was described by the Chairperson of the Heads of Department Committee at a conference on organisation [23.6.82) (noted in BPS, June (1982)], at a workshop conducted by the author (13-14.2.85, BWN.07). The twenty-eight psychologists in the district were managed in three separate departments, each with a head of department. The elected chairperson of the committee reported that psychologists in each separate unit refused to change sessions to provide services which the committee decided were needed, and the committee itself did not always agree priorities for new posts (NETCN),"It was felt to be impractical to appoint a District Psychologist because no single person could effectively participate in the management of these complex and separate units." [BPS, June (1982)]The chairperson reported requests to her from the district administrator to arrange for psychology services from

one of the units to be provided for people with a mental handicap. As elected chairperson she had no authority to require one of the heads to provide a service when agreement was not reached. As a result the district administrator considered appointing a district psychologist with clearly defined authority to change sessions, but chose the cheaper option of funding a new post in mental handicap instead.

This example and the form of organisation adopted show an arrangement where there was no single group management or clear head of service. As a result the autonomy of psychologists as a group and their ability to plan and act to pursue the interests of the profession was less than in other districts. However, the sub-groupings and individual practitioners maintained their autonomy. No details of the limits to practitioner autonomy were available.

Brunel   Workshops
Up to 1988 twelve national workshops were conducted by the author at Brunel University which were attended by over 200 psychologists from most districts in the UK . The workshops provided further evidence of a separation of ,(a) the managerial monitoring functions of district psychologists who were accountable to DMOs i.e. DAs, from,(b) roles of chairpersons of district committees of psychologists appointed by them to represent psychologists' views. These workshops also provided further evidence of the limits to practitioner autonomy and of two types of autonomy - case and practice autonomy. The following situations and "critical incidents" were described at the workshops.

23/24 Nov 1983 (BWN.01)
A district psychologist with a district budget and management responsibility for 24 psychologists reported difficulties in getting heads of department to agree and implement changes to their services (BWN.01). Another district psychologist (11 staff) reported "difficulty in ensuring that psychologists came to department meetings", and was unaware of her authority to ensure that they did so even though it was a requirement of departmental policy. Another reported that once the department had agreed priorities and the need to change psychologists' use of time, the base Unit management group had opposed losing the sessions, and district management had not ruled on the matter. Most reported the requirement to inform and agree with Unit management any proposals for redeploying sessions. This proved to be one widespread constraint to profession-management autonomy which was noted in the field studies reported earlier.

Discussion of a problem raised by one district psychologist regarding, "what to do if a psychologist makes a bad clinical decision", showed general agreement that the district psychologist had authority to check both adherence to contract and that professional standards were met, but not to override the decision if these requirements were met, and that the district psychologist would not be legally liable if procedures had been followed.

9/10 Feb 1984 (BWN.02)
Many of the district psychologists and heads of department attending were concerned about how to change psychologists' use of time to meet what they and higher management saw to be service priorities. This focused their attention on their authority in relation to other psychologists and to unit management (UMGs or UAs). One district psychologist described wishing to direct a psychologist to provide sessions

to a small local mental handicap hospital, but was opposed by the unit administrator and consultants in the psychologist's unit because they were losing the psychologist's sessions. The district psychologist had not tested his authority in the situation by taking the matter higher to the district administrator for a ruling, because he felt it would undermine the cooperation which existed amongst the psychologists in the department. Another described having to present their case for new posts to the Unit Management Group instead of, as previously, to the DMT. They felt this reduced their chances of gaining new posts. Another district psychologist described a situation where previously he had been able to decide to increase the sessions of a part-time practitioner to make up for not being able to recruit into a new post. With the new unit budgets he had wished to continue the arrangement, but the UMG had opposed the arrangement in order to make use of the psychology savings in other areas. These and other instances provided evidence of the head's authority and the limits to management autonomy in the profession.

One district psychologist raised a problem common to most concerning what influence he could bring to bear on practitioners whom he thought were not making the best use of their time, even if they were complying with contract. The example he gave was of a practitioner undertaking mostly long-term individual psychotherapy, where he felt the practitioner should undertake more group and service development work. Other workshop members took the view that they and the district psychologist could not and should not require the practitioner to change but could exert "informal peer-group pressure". If the department agreed a policy about limiting individual case-work [e.g. Victoria DHA (12 sessions before departmental agreement)] then it was felt that the district psychologist could act, but no examples were given where this had occurred.

23/24 Feb 1984 (BWN.03)

Participants described two types of management arrangements: where the district psychologist was accountable to a district level officer (South Birmingham, Bolton, South Lincolnshire, Southend, Bexley, and Winchester), and where there was no district psychologist and heads of specialties were accountable to Unit management (Waltham Forest, Borders Health Board, Islington, and Barnsley) (BWN.03). One district administrator at the workshop reported a structure of planning where Unit management put forward proposals as to where new psychology posts should be provided, on advice from psychologists. The two separate psychology departments had not developed joint management arrangements and the "district psychology coordinator" was required to settle all routine matters with each Unit management team.

This latter example provides evidence of a situation where all psychologists in the district were not grouped together, and separate departments were accountable to, and managed by, unit management. As a result psychologists' power to influence the siting and creation of new posts was less than where the whole group represented their views direct to district management, and psychologists' practice autonomy was constrained by unit management control. The two psychologists from each department who attended the workshop were in favour of creating a single department headed by a district psychologist, but the district administrator wanted "his Units"to be the main focus for management and planning in the district.

The district psychologist from the Bexley department described the department organisation and the particular problems he faced in attempting to move posts and sessions between units. These were, firstly, opposition from units losing services, and difficulties in transferring funding brought about by new unit budgetary arrangements, and, secondly, opposition from individual psychologists who were required to change sessions, and a lack of structural authority to overrule them. These factors defined some of the limits to the district psychologist's actual management autonomy.

13/14 Sept 1984 (BWN.04)

Five district psychologists at this workshop reported difficulties which they experienced in undertaking their different roles, and uncertainty about their authority in relation to unit management and to other psychologists. One had been appointed to "advise the DHA on service developments and to manage staff in the department"; another had been "designated" district psychologist pending a decision to appoint to a fully-funded post, and a third had been termed a "district coordinator" by the district psychology advisory committee, although the DHA had not "recognised" the position. The other two were appointed to develop a district service, but reported difficulties in gaining new posts and in transferring staff. The differences in district psychology roles and the absence of the role in the other nine districts represented at the conference showed a reluctance on the part of some DHAs to provide district psychologists with authority to manage and extend the service, especially if it might conflict with unit management. District Psychology Advisory Committees in North-West Surrey and Hillingdon were described as "pressure groups" for representing psychology views and plans to district management.

Most psychologists felt that a district psychologist and a district service was the best way for the profession to increase its staffing and develop its service, and considered to whom and how they might put their case to sceptical management teams who wished to strengthen unit management. A head of department in mental handicap (N W Surrey) described trying to provide psychology time to GPs and primary health care teams, and reported an inability to gain funds from unit management to do so, and medical consultants vetoing her proposals to change the sessions of a psychologist on the community mental handicap team. Most heads' managerial authority was either unclear, untested, or limited by unit management. There is no documentation from the workshop on details of practitioner autonomy.

27/28 Sept 1984 (BWN.05)

District psychologists and heads of department reported a variety of Unit arrangements and different links with district management. One district psychologist (Essex) described himself as being "managed" by the district administrator and as being instructed to introduce annual staff appraisals. He described arrangements he was introducing to discuss with each staff member their work and future plans, but reported that he was not going to review case-work, and had not, and would not, override case-decisions. There was agreement at the workshop over the latter point, but disagreement over whether staff appraisal should be implemented and, if so, how detailed the appraisals should be. There were no examples of systems in operation.

A second example relevant to practitioner autonomy was a head of department's description of his authority to ,"check that psychologists follow the policies and procedures laid down by the district psychologist". He described requiring psychologists to follow administrative procedures for record keeping and travel claims and being prepared to apply disciplinary procedures for their failing to do so. There were no policies requiring psychologists to undertake teaching or research, or which specified other details of "clinical practice'. Discussion examined whether policies should do so and how district psychologists should respond to expected pressures from new general managers to "manage psychologists more closely". Workshop members, as usual, were ambivalent about their management role, and usually had not and did not wish to exercise their structural authority (where it was specified) to impose changes. They felt this would make it more difficult to exercise their "informal powers" and could lose them the respect and support of their colleagues.

Evidence of the management practices of existing heads showed little monitoring of staff activities. Two were able to report where staff sessions were sited, but most did not know how many sessions were spent in which units or specialties. The evidence suggested that most psychologists who were "managed" by these heads decided where and how to spend their time, and were not questioned about their activities unless complaints were made.

By February 1985 the pressure to develop management information systems in the NHS had increased. Workshop members examined how to introduce such systems and the implications for practitioner autonomy and heads' management authority. A workshop in February 1985 (BWN.08) provided evidence of two departments which had required their members to record details of their work activities as an experiment for management information systems (e.g. time spent on "direct" and "indirect" patient contact, administration, research, teaching, etc). All departments represented at the workshop intended to complete similar statistical returns as part of the new Korner minimum data sets.

This evidence of moves to provide detailed information on each individual's activities is relevant to the issue of practitioner autonomy. Previously little detail was known about where and how each practitioner worked, but with details on these matters, questions could be, and were, asked by heads and administrators about whether certain activities were the best use of psychologists' time. (Indeed, the purpose of the systems was to make this possible). The availability of this information placed subtle and "informal" constraints on practitioner autonomy. As one psychologist put it - "If I spend too much of my time on individual therapy and not enough on group work, it looks bad on my returns and the head starts asking questions." (BWN.08). In such situations there are implicit limits or assumptions held by heads about psychologists' use of time, and informal rather than explicit structural authority is brought to bear on practitioners to account for their use of time, or to make adjustments. For their part, the problem raised by heads in this and other workshops was, "What do we do if psychologists refuse to change?" This suggested that they had not enforced their views, were uncertain of their structural authority to do so, and reluctant to exercise such authority even when it was clear that higher management wished them to do so.

Documentation from other workshops provides further descriptions of organisation and critical incidents which are evidence of the extent of management authority and the limits to practitioner autonomy. (30/31 Oct, 1984 (BWN.06); 31 Jan/1 Feb, 1985 (BWN.07); 13/14 Feb, 1985 (BWN/08); 4/5 Oct, 1985 (BWN.09); 30/31 Oct, 1985 (BWN.10); 4/5 March, 1986 (BWN.11); 22/23 April, 1986 (BWN.12); 30/31 July, 1986 (BWN.13).A district psychologist (Brent (BWN.06)) reported that his DMO had instructed him to hold monthly, rather than weekly, department meetings because the DMO viewed it as a "poor use of psychologists' time". The district psychologist had refused to change and the DMO had not taken the matter to a higher authority.

A district psychologist (Gwent (BWN.08)) reported saving funds as a result of being unable to recruit a psychologist, but being prevented from using the "fortuitous savings" by a unit management group. The UMG had received budget statements on costings of all staff in the unit and on realising that the staff member was not appointed, applied to the DMT to use the savings for a ward upgrading. (The district psychologist thus did not have authority over a staff budget).

A workshop conducted with members of a psychotherapy unit which included psychologists (Derby, June 1984 (DPFN)), established that the consultant doctor, "regularly reviewed the overall management of cases" to satisfy himself that therapists were "taking proper steps to ensure client safety". No trained members reported the consultant directing them to take different actions from those they would otherwise have done, or of removing them from the case. No long-term field work or observation was undertaken to confirm these reports.

Northern Region Workshop (1986)
The structure of the Sunderland psychology service, as reported by the district psychologist (and drawing on previous team field research), was examined in the workshop. Evidence of management and practitioner autonomy was provided by the incidents, negotiations and problems reported by the district psychologist. The psychology service was sited in the Mental Health Unit of Management, which was the base for six of the eight psychologists in the district, the two other psychologists working in two other Units of Management. The district psychologist described his negotiations with district management to ensure that the budget for all psychologists was channelled through the Mental Health Unit, rather than splitting budgets between Units and reducing management autonomy.

It had been agreed that the district psychologist would agree levels of service for the coming year with UGMs in the annual planning cycle and cross-charge the costs to the host unit budget. This agreement had formalised and increased UGMs' influence over the provision of psychology within their units and decreased the district psychologist's management autonomy.

The district psychologist raised two problems which demonstrated some of the limits to practitioner autonomy and the nature of management authority in relation to psychologists. The district psychologist was concerned that one member of the department who had for some years undertaken a specialist "technician" role would be opposed to more flexible working in the community. The district psychologist was reluctant to change the siting of work but described the strategies of persuasion he was to use before instructing the member of the department.

The second issue was the conflict of views between one member who spent a large amount of time practising long-term individual psychoanalytic therapy with a small number of patients, and the district psychologist who viewed this as an inefficient use of time on a treatment where there was no evidence of effectiveness. The district psychologist and workshop members concluded that the district psychologist would be unwise, and possibly unable, to exercise his formal authority to change the member's practice, but could require the member to provide evidence of effectiveness. Again, the workshop members drew a distinction between the siting of work and the use of time in therapies within the sessions allocated.The above research is summarised in chapter 3.

Appendix 4:Co-Management of Therapy Practitioners

Many therapists working in multidisciplinary teams come under the direction of a team leader (eg team coordinator), and a profession-manager, who is not usually a member of the team. They are frequently described as being "managerially accountable" to the team leader and "professionally accoutable" to the profession-manager. This is not usually sufficient, and to avoid common problems it is necessary to agree the responsibilities and authority of each over key areas of the practitioner's management (Øvretveit(1987)). The following framework has proved useful to working out who does what and to agreeing their authority from the three type listed.

- What authority does the Team Leader and the Professional Superior need to meet their responsibilities for the seven key areas of management? Choose from three types of authority:
A: Right to propose or be consulted, B: Right to veto (must be joint decision); C: To decide.
- What should each be accountable for?

	Team Leader's Authority	Professional Superior'sAuthority
1. Drafting Job Description:		
2. Interview & Appoint:		
3. Assign work, a) Casework:		
b) Other work:		
4.Review work a) Outcome:		
b) Details of individual Cases:		
c) Other work:		
5. Perfromance Appraisal:		
6. Training:		
7. Disciplinary action:		

CLARIFYING A THERAPY MANAGER'S ROLE- DETAILS

1) Responsibilities
What are the ongoing duties in the original job description and which have been assigned since? What are the limits to the reponsibilities of the post?What level of management work is expected of the post?

2) Accountability
To whom is the person in post accountable to for carrying out these responsibilities? How are they held to account? Only if something goes wrong? Is there regular performance apprasal? Through contracts?
In relation to practitioners the person in post manages, how are practitoners held to account for meeting their responsibilities:
a) an individual showing that they observed and followed procedures, policies and prescriptions (adhered to prescribed limits or "following orders"), and,
b) an individual explaining the reasons for their decisions within prescribed limits and being held to account for the quality of the discretion which they exercised.

The convention in many professions has been to call a practitioner to account for a), and possibly b) only on specific occasions, for example where there has been a complaint. Good management practice requires routine poisitive monitoring to ensure that policies, job contracts and other prescribed limits are adhered to by staff.(i.e, routine monitoring systems for a)).

3) Authority
The other aspect of working relationships which need to be defined is the degree of authority of an individual or group in relation to another individual or group over specific matters.Authority is the sanctioned power of a role to:
- commit or deploy resources (e.g. staff time or materials) and to assign tasks;
- exercise negative sancitons (e.g. levels of disciplinary action);
- to give positive incentives and rewards.
Sanctioned authority is different to personal power or management style. Degrees of authority may be specified over different matters, ranging from authority to request information, to persuade, to veto a proposal and finally, to decide.

181

Appendix 5: Guidance and Data Formats for Formulating Strategy

This appendix gives more detailed guidance for formulating a strategy for a therapy service comprising of a number of therapy sub-services (see chapter 8). A therapy manager will need to define a timetable and a process for involving therapists in developing and revising strategy. Analyses of sub-services should be delegated to sub-service heads.

FORMULATING STRATEGY - Steps in the Process

Step 1   **Service Mission**

Step 2   **Aims & Objectives**

Step 3   **Current Services**
Sub-services(deliver one or more "products")
Competitors, Comparitors.

Step 4   **Market & Capability Analysis for each sub-service**

4a Data   Assessing current and future demand, market shares
4b gathering   Our current & future capability to respond, costs
Current and future competitors
4c Analysis   SWOT for each sub-service.

Step 5   **Strategic Decisions**
Understanding sub-service interdependence/synergy.
(eg could a sub-service be fully-independent?)
Corporate issues
Combining analyses of each sub-service to decide,
which to expand/contract

Step 6   **Change Strategy & Business Plan**
Details, justification, and basis for control/ressessment,
for markets, capability and finance.

Step 7   **Implementation**
Timetables, landmarks and responsibilities

Step 8   **Review-Return to "Aims & Objectives"**

Chapter 8 discusses the principles and concepts underlying this guide, and details of steps 1 and 2.

Step 3: Current Services

This step is to agree and list the key sub-services, where there is a need and the prospect of a purchaser. this step also lists local competitors, and services against which the sub-service can be compared. A format is given on the next page.

Step 6 questions whether the sub-service defintion and structuring is the best way of packaging responses to need in the future. (eg There may be specialties within services which should be developed as services in their own right, or specialties may be better as parts of other services).

Step 3 Format

Operational Sub-Services List	Competitors	Comparitors	Purchasers

eg   *Acute services.*   *Next district   national figures*   *Own district*
     Mental health services   *NE area GPs*
     Elderly services
     Rehabilitation,ect.

For each operational sub-service,
Who makes the purchasing decisons, and what influences these decisions?

Step 4a Market Analysis - Introduction
(Concerned with the "Demand" part of the equation (chapter 8))

        a) "Needs" Data Gathering & Analysis = "Needs Potential"
        b) Purchasing Power = "Income Potential"
        Needs Potential + Income Potential = Market Attractiveness

The purpose of this part of step 4 is to,
- gather data about perceptions of needs for each sub-service, for the past, and extrapolating into the future,
- assess what proportion of the total the sub-service currently meets (market share)
- assess what proportion is met by other services/competitors, and is unmet.
- assess the purchasing power of the market for the sub service, and what needs purchasers will pay to be met, and decide how to influence.

Use the format on the next page to organisa the maket data.

(NB The two parts of the "Demand" picture are: a) Needs as assessed from different perspectives, b) What purchasers will buy. Remember:
- The market for the service is not just needs, however assessed.
- A market can be defined as "the total volume of business transacted between buyers and sellers in a particular sector", ie purely in terms of purchasing power.
- There may be the needs, but no purchasing power.
- A strategy based only on needs analysis will be different to one based on an analysis of purchasing power.
- Expanding into a market with high needs but no purchasing power is commercial suicide.
- It may be possible to use needs data to persuade a purchaser to buy more, but purchaser's budgets are fixed and the finance will have to come from other services. Is effort better spent seeking other purchasers?)

Thus the market analysis must build a picture of needs, a picture of who might pay for needs to be met, and of the potential purchasing power of the market.

If the are the needs there is a market opportunity; if there is the purchasing power there is also market potential - to decide if the market is attractive there must be both an opportunity and a potential.

The market data is used later to clarify,
- critical success factors in this market,
- diversification options for each service/potential new markets.
- in the "responses" analysis, the critical limiting factors (constraints) preventing increasing volume of service provided, (usually not needs but purchasing power and investment finance)

(Step 4b ("responses") gathers data and analyses each sub-service's capability to respond to needs, and that of competitors.

Step 4c (Analysis) draws on this data to carry out a SWOT analysis for each service, and reach conclusions for the overall strategy.)

Step 4a Format for Market Data

"Demands" Data Sheet for Service...
Type of client/needs served...

OUR SUB-SERVICE

PAST   **FUTURE**

1) Demand Met   Estimate demand will meet
(Volume served)   (assuming little change)

2) Estimate Need not met by service   Estimate
(Nos.)

OTHER SVCS/COMPETITION

3) Of this (2), demand met by other   Estimate in 2 years time
services
(Nos)

MARKET SIZE

4) Estimate need not met by anyone   Estimate in 2 years time
(Nos)

PURCHASING POWER

5) Who will pay for these needs to be met? (list purchasers)

6) What is total Nos/Volume purchasers will wish to contract for?

OBJECTIVITY CHECK
Any different estimates which might be given by purchasers, GPs, or clients or others.
(Would they all agree with our perceptions?)

Analysis/Summary of Step 4a

6) Draw pie charts of our and competitors' shares of,
a) total unmet need   b) purchasers' purchasing power

7) From the proportion of the market the sub-service holds of both of the above representations of the market, assess the market potential for the service.

8) What are the possible diversifications/new markets for this service?
(related needs which the service could meet?) Mergers?

9) Note the principle constraints/limiting factors to our,
- ability to create/develop new markets?
- capacity to respond/expand profitably and increase market share?
(to be considered more fully later under"Response" analysis).

Step 4a Market Analysis Summary Format

Market Assessment for sub-service: ....
Place the sub-service on the following grid, only in terms of the market potential

MARKET ASSESSMENT

Good

Service to develop
high risk from
competition

High volume service
with strong position

Market Growth

Poor growth potential *High volume service*
Low share   *low growth potential*

Poor

Low   **Market Share**   High

Note

1) The Market is both needs ,and the finance available to buy services. Thus,

-"Market share" refers to both the proportion of needs met, and to the proportion of the total purchasing power which is income for the service. Market share is usually summarised as % of market volume in £.

- "Market growth" refers to both the forecast rise or decrease in need/demand, and to the forecast rise or decrease in purchasing power.

2) We are here only concerned with the market (needs and income potential)

The service's capacity to respond and investment finace is part of the "Response" side of the equation to be considered next. (eg the market may have high potential and be attractive, but the service's capacity to respond may be weak (eg costs too high to compete)).

Step 4b Responses - Data, Us & Others

The purpose of this part of the data gathering is to appraise the capacity and costs of the sub-service to respond to needs, and that of competitors or comparison services.Note that part of the future capacity to respond depends on securing investment finance to maintain or expand capacity-an assessment of this must be part of the data on future response.

Step 4b Responses - Data Format

	OUR SERVICE		OTHER SVCS/COMPETITION	
	PAST	FUTURE	PAST	FUTURE

1) Utilisation of capacity
Nos of clients/patients served, and estimate future(no change)

2) Capacity
How many more clients could have been served with the resources (Nos)

Costs/Contribution to Overall Service/Finance
2) Cost per case av and range:
(est. Budget/Volume)
Rate how compares with ideal: (% of 100)

Rate competition by comparison
to us estimates, where ideal is 100%

3) Capital Costs
(est. % of total space/equip)
Rate how compares with ideal:(% of 100)

4) Proportion of total service income contributed by sub service(%)
Again, Rate % of ideal

5) Profitability/Loss
(how much income for each £100 expenditure(inc capital costs))
(as % return on expenditure)

6) Required Investment Finance (To maintain capacity and quality)
Assess likelyhood of securing this and more investment finance
Assess ability to generate investment finance through profit (eg higher prices)

For a more detailed assessment of the sub-service's capicity to respond now and in the future , also consider the floowing

Quality- Key aspects, eg:

7) Waiting times for first consultation
Again, Rate % of ideal

8) Effectiveness of treatment/service & outcomes as percieved
Again, Rate % of ideal

9) General level of complaints & satisfaction (clients,GPs,purchasers)
Again, Rate % of ideal

10) Other Quality aspects (eg Audit/QA) Again, Rate % of ideal
Staffing

11) Numbers (Again, Rate % of ideal)

12) Grade/Skills. (Gaps?)(Again, Rate % of ideal)

13) Buildings/Equipment
Rate how compares with ideal:(% of 100)

14) Systems
Rate how compares with ideal:(% of 100)

15) Other Critical Aspects of our/others capacity to respond
Rate how compares with ideal:(% of 100)

Step 4b Response - Summary Analysis

Summarise the data on capacity to respond by listing strengths and weaknesses of the sub-service in comparison to competitors, or as percieved, or in relation to comparable services.
Be objective, consider what others would say. Use as headings for each answer:

Our view,   clients,   our staff,   referrers,   purchasers

STRENGTHS

- What is special about this service/What do we do well?
- What do others value about the service/ What are the Unique Selling Points?
(basis for differentiation)
- as perceived by clients,
- referrers,
- purchasers,
- others.
- What resources do we have which we do not make the most of/unrealised assets?
- What single thing is our biggest strength?

WEAKNESSES

- What do we think we could/should do better?
- What do others think we do badly/would welcome improvement?
- clients,
- referrers,
- purchasers,(- others).
- What aspects of our service are vulnerable to decline?
- Can we pay for future necessary investments by raising prices or profits now?
If not, how sure are we that we can cover the cost of borrowing through higher prices/profits? Can we persuade financiers of this?
What single internal weakness hampers us most?

Step 4c Overall Business Analysis for the Sub-Service

This draws together the assessment of the market and response capability in steps 4a and 4b. It relates market potential to capabilities & strengths
considering the risks and weaknesses

OPPORTUNITIES
1) In addition to the market attractiveness (needs and income potential), and undeveloped internal strengths already considered, are there any other opportunities?

THREATS/RISKS/VUNERABILITIES
2) In addition to internal weaknesses noted,
-What are the threats to maintaining or increasing market share?
-Which aspects of the service are most vulnerable?
-Where are the risks? (eg dependence on suppliers, on labour markets, on one purchaser, negligence/compensation)

RELATE MARKET POTENTIAL TO SUB-SERVICE CAPABILITY
3) Draw on the summaries of market attractiveness and of strengths and weaknesses in capacity to respond to place the sub-service on the following grid:

Summary of Overall Business Analysis for the Sub-Service
High

	Seek new markets	*Expansion*

CAPABILITY
(see strengths&
weaknesses summary)   *Reduce service Improve*

Low

Low	High

MARKET ATTRACTIVENESS/POTENTIAL
(See Market summary: Needs & Income Potential)

4) CONCLUSIONS FOR SUB-SERVICE FUTURE
a) Does it have a future as a stand-alone sub-service, or as part of another?
b) To make a better future,
- what weaknesses should be minimised?
- strengths developed/maintained/publicised?
- threats addressed/risks reduced?
- opportunities seized/potential developed?

Step 5   *Strategic Decisions & Overall Analysis, for the whole service*
The purpose of this step is to:
- decide which sub-services to develop, consolodate, reduce/close, or contract.
(after overview of prospects for all, and assessment of likely investment finance and management capability/time)
- reassess best structuring of sub-services,(mergers, off-shoots etc.)
- reassess needed internal support services (contract?)

1) COMPARE MARKET POTENTIAL FOR EACH SUB-SERVICE
From the assessment of market potential for each sub-service, place each sub-service on the grid below for the overall service:
MARKET ASSESSMENT

Good   *Service to develop*   *High volume service*
              high risk from   *with strong position*
              competition

Market Growth

              Poor growth potential High volume service
              Low share   low growth potential
Poor
              Low   **Market Share**   High
2) FOR THE SERVICE AS A WHOLE

BIGGEST OPPORTUNIES
Arising externally
Arising internally (eg to lower costs, new ideas)
BIGGEST THREATS/RISK
External
Internal

3) CORPORATE ISSUES:
Sub-Service interdependence/synergy.
a) Do we understand why all sub-services need to be grouped together within the service?
(Synergy: additional benefit to each service as a result of combining/cooperating or being part of a larger entity)
b) Should any support services be reduced/contracted-in?
c) Any supply problems affecting all sub-services?
In light of above,

4) COMPARE MARKET POTENTIAL & CAPABILITY FOR EACH SUB-SERVICE
Referring back to the summary analysis for each sub-service, place each sub-service on the grid:

High

Seek new   *Expansion*
markets

CAPABILITY

(see strengths&
weaknesses summary)   *Reduce service Improve*

Low

Low   High

MARKET ATTRACTIVENESS/POTENTIAL
(See Market summary: Needs & Income Potential

And Summarise SWOT Analysis to reveal strategy:

OPPORTUNITES

Improve Service   *Expand Service*

Reduce Service   *Seek New Services*
THREATS

WEAKNESSES   STRENGTHS

5) CONCLUSIONS
Given the limited investment finace and management time, and the markets and our ability to respond and compete,
what would provide the best return on investment, and which sub-services should be reduced or merged?

The next steps are to gather the details for a Business Plan, and to consider the change strategy of the service-primarily how to change attitudes and working relationships.

Appendix 6: Review of Research into Professions

DISTINGUISHING THE PROFESSIONS: EARLY TWENTIETH CENTURY STUDIES

Professions were peripheral to the concerns of nineteenth century social scientists, but the perspectives they established formed the basis for later studies which considered the place and development of professions in modern society. In the first part of this century social scientists attempted to understand the emergence of professions as a social force, mostly by describing the development of professions and by attempting to define what constituted a profession.

The earliest serious attempt at definition was by Flexner (1915) who asked, "Is social work a profession?", and proposed six objective criteria for distinguishing a profession: professional activity was intellectual and carried great personal responsibility; it was learned, based on considerable knowledge and was not routine; it was practical rather than "academic"; its technique could be taught and formed the basis of professional education; a profession was strongly organised internally; and professionals were motivated by altruism, viewing themselves as working for the good of society. (Source: Becker (1962) p 88).

However, Flexner went on to qualify this definition, possibly feeling that his audience - social workers at a "National Conference of Charities for Correction" - would be unhappy with the answer to the question. He ended by emphasising the "vocational" aspect, "What matters most is professional spirit. All activities may be prosecuted in the genuine professional spirit. Insofar as accepted professions are prosecuted at a mercenary or selfish level, law and medicine are ethically no better than trades. Insofar as trades are honestly carried on, they tend to rise toward the professional level......The unselfish devotion of those who have chosen to give themselves to making the world a fitter place to live in can fill social work with the professional spirit and thus to some extent lift it above all the distinctions which I have been at such pains to make."

The idea that an attitude of "professionalism" could raise an occupation above "trade status" and overcome "objective factors" combined the aspirations of many occupations of the time with social scientists' liberal interest in possible social structures which were alternatives to communism and fascism. Thus Tawney (1972), like Durkheim, argued that "professionalism", which stressed the ethics of a "moral community", could counter extreme economic individualism.

Similarly, Carr Saunders and Wilson (1933), in a landmark study, put forward professions as a defence against, "crude forces which threaten steady and peaceful evolution", and as a major force for stability in society. They saw scientific advances as inevitably leading to more professions and that, "the extension of professionalism over the whole field seems in the end not impossible", (p 494). For Carr Saunders the, "chief distinguishing characteristics of the profession" were, "the application of an intellectual technique to the ordinary business of life, acquired as the result of prolonged and specialised training" (p 491).

Parry and Parry (1976) suggest that at the time the belief in the moral superiority of professionalism was a peculiarly English phenomenon, which perpetuated elements of the 19th century medical profession's wish to attain "gentleman" as opposed to "businessman" status. Certainly it is true that American social scientists did not take up quite the same crusading stance. At this time (1930) Parsons was drawing on the perspectives of Weber and Durkheim to develop a structural-functionalist theory of society. In his perspective professionals and workers in other occupations shared the same values and orientations of a market society.

For Parsons "service orientation" or "altruism" was of secondary importance, a set of additional norms which was required to regulate the intimate relationship between professional and client (Parsons (1964), originally (1939)). Parsons (1951) suggested that professional ethics were specific to the relationship and not generalised to the wider society. Parsons' wider theoretical perspective in part prevented him from reproducing some of the ideologies of the professions, the latter being a weakness of the "trait" studies which followed.

Later examples of the "trait" approach to defining professions are Cogan (1953), Greenwood (1957), and Goode (1957). Such studies started with a general discussion of the meaning of the term, noted typical "man-in-the-street" conceptions ,and attempted to offer more precise definitions, testing them against empirical examples to decide whether or not an occupation was a profession according to the proposed definition.

Functionalist studies proceeded in a similar fashion but confined their analysis to those traits which were thought to make a functional contribution to establishing a relationship between professional and client or to the maintenance of society. Thus Barber (1963) described as the four "essential attributes of professionalism", "A primary orientation to community interests rather than individual self-interests; a high degree of self-control of behaviour through codes of ethics internalised in the process of work socialisation, organised and operated by the work specialists; and a system of rewards (monetary and honorary) that is primarily a set of symbols of work achievement and thus ends in themselves, not means to some end of individual self-interest." He went on to propose that the attributes, "define a scale of professionalism, a way of measuring the extent to which it is present in different forms of occupational performance."

Millerson's (1964) summary of the definitional studies proposed that, although few authors cited exactly the same characteristics, there was agreement on certain typical characteristics of professions. These included: a theoretical knowledge base (both pure theory and theory of practice); a required education and training, and adherence to a code of conduct; and loyalty to an occupational organisation and to an ideal of altruistic service. Hickson and Thomas' (1974) analysis also noted common elements and summarised the elements included in most of the main studies.

Continuum of Professionalism

Goode's (1960) and Millerson's (1964) papers marked a point where studies moved from trying to define what was, or was not, a profession, to trying to assess to what extent certain key characteristics were present or absent. This "scale" or "continuum" approach addressed the question, "How professionalised in identifiable respects is a particular occupation?" [Hall (1968)].

A series of studies drew on the definitional studies to examine "professionalisation' and the historical stages by which occupations become professions. Caplow (1954) proposed a four-step process. Wilensky (1964) studied eighteen occupations to demonstrate a typical five-stage historical process of professionalisation. He traced the dates at which the occupations first became full-time occupations, then acquired training schools and university schools, formed local and national professional associations, were "protected" by law, and ultimately adopted formal codes of ethics.

Pavalko's (1971) more recent work also applied the continuum approach to analyse a wide variety of occupations. He proposed that the "voluminous" literature had produced a consensus about, "key features of work groups that appear to occur in combinations and clusters that function to differentiate "occupations" from "professions" ". His aim was ,"not to develop a scheme whereby some kinds of work can be labelled "occupations" and others "professions" ", but rather to focus on ,"differences of degree" and to ask, "To what extent is a particular work activity a profession?" A page later, however, he proposed, "eight characteristics of work that can be considered as crucial in differentiating occupations from professions". (Theory or intellectual technique, relevance to basic social values, training, motivation, autonomy, commitment, sense of community, and code of ethics). All studies of professions have at some point to deal with the question of definition.

Hickson and Thomas (1974) noted the lack of systematic research on the subject, and suggested that, "The continuum might well form a scale in terms of the characteristics of professions commonly cited. Yet it has remained hypothetical, agreed but not demonstrated, and comparisons along it have been couched only in fairly general terms."

They tested the adequacy of the concept of "professionalisation" as a unitary variable or continuum by operationalising the concept to provide a measure of "professionalisation", and by applying it to a number of professions. One finding was that the age of the qualifying association was strongly related to "professionalisation". The study noted that the assumed causes of "professionalisation" had not been studied empirically, and an international comparison using the measure was suggested.

Goode (1969) proposed that there were limits to the extent to which certain occupations could "professionalise", mainly because society did not accept that some occupations had sufficient of the two core elements of knowledge base and service ideal .Goode's (1960) study proposed that the two "core characteristics" were ,"a prolonged specialised training in a body of abstract knowledge and a service orientation", and that as occupations become professionalised they manifest features of these core characteristics. He listed ten which formed a "continuum of professionalism".

In addition he argued that the "four great person professions" of law, medicine, the ministry, and university teaching, in an important sense, "get inside the client" (p 307). He suggested that the client was "more likely to get emotionally involved with their professionals", and would be more vulnerable, which in turn required a strong adherence to a set of norms and ethics. The "semi-professions" did not have the knowledge, skills or service value to exchange for the public trust.

For Goode, "the crucial difference is whether the substance of the task requires trust and therefore autonomy, and therefore some cohesion through which the occupation can in fact impose ethical controls on its members." Consequently, "If we place the various professions along this continuum - the extent to which the client must allow the professional to know intimate and possibly damaging secrets about his life if the task is to be performed adequately - a fairly clear ranking emerges."

Moore (1970) proposed that the professional role could be conceptualised by a series of traits, each of which was a component of a complète continuum, with professionalism at one end and non-professionalism at the other. He held that the concept (ideal type) of "professional" was a useful sociological category and defined a profession as involving the existence of, 1) a full-time occupation, 2) a calling which implied "the treatment of the occupation and all of its requirements as an enduring set of normative and behavioural expectations", 3) a formalised occupational organisation, 4) specialised education based on the acquisition of useful knowledge and skills, 5) a service orientation, and, 6) personal and collective organisation "restrained by responsibility".

Putting Moore's definition together with the many others, it is possible to regard "calling" and "organisation" as derivative of 4), 5) and 6), and closely related to the assumption of autonomy, or "trust" granted by the public [Hughes (1963)]. In short, that the fundamentals of the ideal type appear to be a knowledge base, a service ideal, and autonomy or public trust.

Conclusions

At first sight the literature reviewed seems to be unable to agree over "essential traits", regardless of whether the purpose of defining these traits is to arbitrate between "real professions" and "other occupations", or to construct an ideal type or the end of a continuum. However, the disagreement is more apparent than real, and mainly concerned with deciding which trait or characteristic is more essential, and which are derivative.

The studies reviewed in fact have much in common. There is a tendency to accept the claims of several self-appointed traditional professions, rather than to carry out research into their practice and organisation. There is a lack of awareness of the continual changes to which occupations have to adapt, and of how they continually negotiate their relationships with other occupations. Many of the "essential characteristics" cannot be isolated. More serious is the lack of attempts to theorise about the relationship between the elements. The decision about which elements to include depends on which profession is viewed as having professional status, and is largely arbitrary.

In these studies there is little distinction made between "a profession" as a social institution with an association, and the attitude or characteristics of "professionalism" and of a "professional". Øvretveit (1985) also argued that whilst many occupations show similar tendencies and developments, the professionalisation perspective implies a single and inevitable process towards an ideal type. (c.f. Goode's (1969) "Natural history of professionalisation"). Conscious imitation by aspiring professions, rather than any structural or other causative process could explain this tendency. Finally, as Johnson (1972) showed, "the professionalisation process" is historically-specific and culture-bound.

Typologies of Professions

One development which took place in the 1960s was to separate categories of occupation. General studies of occupations in society distinguished between fields and types of occupations for the purpose of presentation and analysis. Those specifically concerned with professions distinguished between types of professions. Recognising some of the limitations of the trait approaches, some studies distinguished certain types of professions and focused on their particular features. The "continuum" and historical studies already mentioned distinguished "would-be-professions" from "new professions", "near-professions" and "professions" (Carr Saunders (1955)); Marshall (1965) distinguished "new" from "traditional" professions; Goode (1969) categorised a group of "aspiring professions"; and Hughes (1958) classified "professions", "near-professions", "enterprises", "missions", "arts", "crafts", and "jobs".

Etzioni [(1964) and (1969)] defined the "semi-professions" of nursing, social work, and teaching, whose, "claim to the status of doctors and lawyers is neither fully established nor fully desired .... Their training is shorter, their status is less legitimated, their right to privileged communication less established, and there is less of a specialised body of knowledge and they have less autonomy from supervision or societal control than "the" professions." [Etzioni (1969) p v] He later notes, as an aside, that almost all "semi-professionals" are employed in organisations, and are women.

Forsyth and Danisiewicz (1985) further subdivided two types of semi-profession: the "client-autonomous "(education), and the "organisation-autonomous" (nursing and social work). They also added a category of "mimic professions", which ,"may have a code of ethics and other trappings of professions but they have no power".

Etzioni's typology, whilst continuing to judge occupations in relation to "real professions", was part of a trend towards developing social scientific categories for analysing occupations which did not depend on a concept of an ideal-type of profession, or on the claims of the traditional professions.

Halmos' (1970) categorisation of "personal", as opposed to "impersonal", service professions cut across the conventional "true" versus "non- profession" distinction. He proposed that the principal function of clergy, doctors, nurses, teachers and social workers was to, "bring about changes in the body or personality of clients", and that this group were importantly different from lawyers, accountants, engineers and architects. We note that Halmos' thesis is in direct disagreement with Goode's (1969) definition of "the four great person professions", and Goode's proposition that, unlike these professions, the semi-professions did not need to "get inside the client" and win trust.

Bennet and Hokenstad (1973) also argued that a different way of conceptualising occupations to the professional/non-professional approach was more likely to advance knowledge. They proposed, 1) that the nature of "human services work" (first defined as such by Reissman & Pearl (1965)) raised questions about the trait and continuum approaches, 2) that the "professional model" was not appropriate for describing "modes of people working", and, 3) that "progress" in human services could not be assessed in terms of a rank on a single continuum of professionalisation.

They suggested that "people working professions" were a distinct group because the object of their work was, "the client himself, his personality, behaviour or relationships, rather than a third party or thing" [Halmos, Ed(1973), p 34)]. Fundamental to their distinction was Benne's (1970) notion of "expert", "rule" and "anthropogogical" authority, the latter involving submission to authority in the hope of becoming like the bearer of that authority. They developed this notion to suggest that the knowledge of "people working professions" is about producing change in clients in order that clients may themselves solve their own problems in the future.

Bennet and Hokenstad's categorisation therefore differed from Halmos's (1970) in excluding many doctors who, "deal with parts of the body in rather impersonal ways". They, like Etzioni (1967) and Hall (1968), noted that, "people workers" functioned in bureaucratic settings and were salaried employees rather than entrepreneurs. At first sight the nature of the work of "people workers" would appear to require a type of relationship with clients which was in conflict with this type of work setting. This issue is considered as part of the "bureaucratic-professional conflict".

Freidson's (1970) theory of professional dominance was not intended as a categorisation or typology as such. However, he did distinguish between "dominant professions", such as medicine and law, and a range of subsidiary or "para-professions", whose work was structured around, and ultimately controlled by the dominant profession. This theory is one of the studies of this period which proposed a subdivision in the study of professions, but unlike most others, was also linked to a theory of the structuring of professions, rather than the mainly descriptive approach of the typologies mentioned above.

The conclusion of the review so far is that, in general, the way in which professions are categorised depends on the purpose of the study: the "professionalisation" and "continuum" approaches categorise new and aspiring professions as opposed to established or traditional professions; other studies such as Halmos's separate a group of occupations which share elements in common which are more important than their ranking on the scale; and Freidson's category of "para-professions" is linked to a theory of a professionally-ordered division of labour. Such typologies are an advance over earlier studies in, a) documenting new groupings of occupations, b) developing categorisations which promise to open up new areas of investigation and are less influenced by the claims of professions themselves, and, c) beginning to link empirical research to theories of professions.

PROFESSIONS AS OCCUPATIONS: THE INTERACTIONIST AND POWER PERSPECTIVES

The nineteen-sixties marked a time when both social scientists and the public adopted a more critical stance towards professions. Social scientists' theoretical perspectives and research revealed some of the similarities between professions and occupations, rather than the qualitative difference which had been emphasised by earlier studies.

The Chicago school of symbolic interactionism produced the most well known of the earliest studies which took a "debunking" approach. The perspective focused on individual practitioners and clients, and examined the meanings of certain situations for the actors and how understandings were negotiated - as Dingwall (1976) describes it, how "profession is accomplished in interaction".

Becker's interpretive approach proposed that "profession" should be regarded as a symbol, and that social scientists should not confuse the symbol with reality [Becker (1956)]. He proposed an answer to the paradox of, on the one hand, an apparent unanimity to definitions of "profession", and on the other hand, the continuing disagreement about an "authoritative" definition. His answer was that laymen used the term in a "morally evaluative" sense with "unselfish devotion as the key criterion", but that social scientists constructed a concept to isolate an "objectively discriminable class of social phenomena". The attempt on the part of social scientists to incorporate common usage into the social science concept would inevitably lead to problems, as common usage would continually change,"the laymen's sense of which occupations are "really" professions continually changes".

Becker's(1962) answer to the question of definition was to view, "professions simply as those occupations which have been fortunate enough in the politics of today's work world to gain and maintain possession of that honorific title." In this view there is no "true" profession and no set of characteristics necessarily associated with the title. Becker proposed that social scientists should study "profession" as a "collective honorific symbol" or "folk concept". He outlined a general characterisation, emphasising the interrelation of the oft-noted elements, and considered the role the symbol performed in society. He noted that the symbol contained an ideology which provided a justification and rationale for "complete autonomy": only professionals could judge how good their work was, and whether unsuccessful work was due to incompetence or other causes.

In comparing the symbol with reality, Becker noted that, in practice , medicine and law failed to match the symbol because neither held a monopoly over esoteric knowledge or functions. He suggested that the symbol had become not only inaccurate but harmful in ignoring, "the lack of homogeneity within professions, frequent failure of clients to accept professional judgments, the chronic presence of unethical practitioners as integrated segments of the professional structures, and the organisational constraints on professional autonomy".

Hughes' (1958) early work took a largely interactionist perspective and laid the basis for much of the later American occupational sociology. Taking a broad range of occupations he considered the relationships between individuals, their personal careers, and their occupational groups and employment settings. His approach was to note the problems and tensions created by work and social situations and to consider how the worker dealt with the problems. "Deviant" occupations were of particular interest because a study of the coping strategies which they used could illuminate the strategies of individuals in conventional occupations.

Trust and Confidentiality

Hughes' (1963) article on professions emphasised the service and trust components of professional practice over the knowledge aspects.He proposed that, in the ideal situation, the professional asks to be trusted and is granted this trust- rather than the business motto of, "let the buyer beware" (caveat emptor), that of the professional is ,"let the buyer trust" (credat emptor). Related to trust is one of the distinctive features of a profession mentioned by Hughes, the "licence to delve into the personal affairs of others, or to make "impositions" on them, which are not normally acceptable." Hughes related the community mandate of a profession (the willingness of a community to allow practitioners to do their work unsupervised) to the degree of licence allowed. Thus if a group had no independence from community or organisational evaluation and control, it would also not have the sanction to delve into personal areas. In essence it was a community's acceptance of the profession's claim to expertise (the faith which they profess), and the community's granting the profession a mandate, which was fundamental. Freidson was later to develop this insight in his theory of professional autonomy.

A more recent and critical discussion of trust within the client-professional relationship can be found in McKinlay (1973), who questioned the grounds for professionals' claims to trust. He argued that the view that it was safe to trust professionals because they had been specially selected, or "called" to profess a faith, was not borne out. In McKinlay's view the "calling" in the USA was the call of cash, and the "special selection" was as much a market control mechanism as a safeguard of quality. Secondly, "altruism and service orientation" was not central to professional practice: work practices were usually for the convenience of professionals. Thirdly, the view that the unique training of professionals warrants extra trust could not be sustained: the training may be longer, but in McKinlay's view it is not different to many service occupations. Finally, there was the view that trust should be accorded because the public was unable to evaluate professional work. However, although the public may not be able to evaluate process, McKinlay argued that consumers could and did evaluate outcome.

In questioning whether clients could or did trust professionals, McKinlay's discussion tended to minimise perhaps the most important feature of trust in the professional-client relationship: that the professional requires the client's trust (and faith) to carry out their work (and to provide their livelihood), and that professions establish a variety of conditions to achieve client trust. As Bidwell (1970) noted,"For the professional, trust as the sole basis of his moral authority, is essential for effective performance. Unless he enjoys his client's confidence, he may be denied access to the client's person, or to the full range of necessary but often covert information about the client, while the client may not follow the professional's directives or counsel. Hence the professional cannot fulfil his responsibilities to the client, or to his peers for the client's welfare, unless the client trusts him. Thus the responsible professional must reject the client who will not trust him." (p 40).

Trust is central to professional work and the important question is, how is it achieved? The traditional professions (medicine, law, the ministry) view client confidentiality as a necessary requirement for establishing and maintaining trust in the relationship. Whilst there are good reasons for this condition, it is also important to note the consequences of this requirement. Chief amongst these is that absolute confidentiality protects professionals from evaluation, and enables them to escape accountability and justifying their actions to anyone apart from the client, who already trusts them. It maintains a particular type of autonomy. It also creates dependency in the relationship: the client has disclosed intimate secrets and thereby comes under the power of the professional. Although the professional has sworn not to break confidence, the client is dependent on the professional's decision not to do so - the professional has gained power where he had none.

A study of confidentiality in social work and in multi-disciplinary teams [Øvretveit (1986a and 1986b)] showed that absolute confidentiality was rare, and that professionals, as a matter of routine, exchanged "confidential" material. They only invoke "confidentiality" in their own interests; not in the interests of clients (e.g. when insisting that other professionals act on the information , but that they can not disclose the professional source because it would supposedly damage that professional's working relationship with the client).

The professional-client relationship is best conceptualised as one of mutual dependence. An understanding of how trust is established and maintained in the relationship and of how the power of both parties is regulated, may reveal differences between occupations.

Hughes and the Chicago school, then, recognised the drawbacks of addressing the question of, "is this occupation a profession?", and instead asked, "what are the circumstances in which people in an occupation attempt to turn it into a profession and themselves into professional people?" (Hughes (1963)). Two strands developed out of this approach.

The first concentrated on socialisation and individual interaction (Strauss et al (1963), Becker (1961)), and tended to neglect wider historical processes and structural issues. One such study was by Goldie (1977) who considered how occupational groups in the mental health division of labour defined their work situation. His study showed the different ways in which members of the same occupation would deal with recurring "problems" such as medical direction.

The second strand used insights developed within the interactionist frame of reference to understand wider social processes. Bucher and Stelling (1967) used the perspective on a broader structural level to consider the diversity and conflicts of interest between "segments" within supposedly homogeneous professions.

Power Perspective

Freidson,who was originally a student of Hughes, took professional autonomy to be of fundamental significance, and laid the foundations for what was later to be loosely termed a "power" perspective for the study of professions. Freidson's (1968) study advanced Hughes' ideas about the service and trust reciprocation at the centre of professional practice. Freidson used the term "profession" to refer to a way of organising work rather than to refer to an orientation towards work (professionalism) or a body of knowledge (Freidson (1970a) p.155). From this starting point he distinguished between "dominant professions", who directed others in a division of labour and who were autonomous, and other "para-professions".

Freidson (1970a, 1970b) and Johnson (1972) initiated an approach to the study of professions which focused on the structures and processes at the societal level by which occupations acquired and maintained power. They viewed professions not as occupations which exhibited many elements of an ideal-typical "full profession", but as a means of controlling an occupation: "occupational organisation and practice are to be understood only in terms of the prevailing type of control to which an occupation is subjected." [Johnson (1972), p 90].

A similar approach was taken by Krause (1971). For Krause, as for Durkheim, the significance of the study of occupations for the social sciences was their function as the main mediators between the individual and society. His basic question was, "What changes have there been in the historical role of major occupational groups?", a question which he explored from four standpoints: the historical, the biographical (e.g. "socialisation" and career), the functional, and the conflict-of-interest approaches.

The study drew on Durkheim's analysis of the division of labour to highlight the interdependence of occupational groups, and to consider the function of the group for society as a whole and its consequent power. Krause suggested that professions shared with all occupations the features of, "central skills, code of ethics, group culture, occupational authority, and permission to practise on the part of the community", but had these features to "a very high degree". What distinguished them was firstly, that they were,"functionally powerful, or near to "key places" in the division of labour", and this was reflected in their political power, prestige, and material rewards", and secondly, that they dealt with basic needs, where the absence of their skills would lead to individual or social crisis. From this perspective "professionalisation" was only possible where an occupational group had a crisis-serving function, autonomy and power bestowed by the community, and the capacity to manipulate the work situation and the laws governing practice to its own advantage.

Drawing on these four standpoints, Krause analysed various "occupational fields", and came to a number of conclusions. The first was the importance of how and why a group identifies itself as an occupation, and used the concept of "occupation" to act as a cohesive group. The second was that the state and "power elites" opposed the functional power of occupations. For Krause the concept of functional power, as the potential of an occupational group to coerce a society through the withholding of its services, had to be refined with the understanding that," "functional" occupational group power and "state" power may be ideal types rather than actually different, and we may need to look at the picture in terms of the "occupational quality" or the "governmental quality" of a type of power. In general, far more research needs to be done on the definition and specification of power as it relates to the functions of occupational groups in the social system." (p 351).

Krause's third conclusion was that in modern society occupational groups could not be understood in isolation from technological change and work organisation. Social changes altered the meaning of "functional power" for different professions.

The studies of Freidson, Johnson and Krause established a new and more critical approach to the study of professions. Subsequent work using this "power perspective" examined the political and historical processes through which occupations are created, develop ,and maintain their claim to being a "profession" [(Jackson (1970), Eaton and Webb (1978), and Larkin (1982)]. Parry and Parry's (1976) historical study of the medical profession considered the profession in terms of class mobility, viewing "professionalism" as, "a strategy for controlling an occupation in which colleagues, who are in a formal sense equal, set up a system of self-government."

These studies criticised the assumptions of the earlier trait and functionalist studies. They proposed that it was not special features of professional work or of professionals which were important, but how professionals and professional associations use certain features to advance or maintain their interests. They held that to search for distinguishing features was to perpetuate the ideology of professions that their work and values are intrinsically special, and to ignore the strategies by which an occupation uses these features to its advantage.

The "Deprofessionalisation" and "Proletarianisation" Theses

With the abandonment of "profession" as an ideal type, and as a result of changes in the work setting, studies also took a different view about the future of professionalism. In contrast to the eulogistic and optimistic tone of studies such as Carr-Saunders and Wilson in the first part of the century, more recent studies note trends which not only limit the professionalising aspirations of new occupations, but "deprofessionalise" the traditional professions. Trends which have been viewed as undermining the professions are the development of corporate capitalism, the use of management sciences to increase productivity and control of professionals employed in capitalist and other enterprises, and the increasing reliance of professionals on expensive technology.

Haug (1973) proposed a "deprofessionalisation" hypothesis, citing as contributing factors the computerisation of academic knowledge, the accessibility of experiential knowledge to "less schooled persons", and the challenge to professional detachment and the erosion of professional autonomy through client review. Haug suggested that, although organisational accountability and evaluation were difficult because, a) professionals' actions were not easily observable, b) there were unclear goals and techniques, and, c) unclear connections between methods and outcomes [c.f. Daniels (1972)], the effective power of clients to criticise the professional and to hold him accountable had increased. Haug explained this change in terms of the bureaucratic content of work and large-scale services aggregating clients and providing conditions for client organisation, as well as because of a developing consumer ideology and clients being more ready to challenge expert authority and autonomy.

Oppenheimer (1973), in a similar vein, proposed that the "autonomous professional" was becoming "proletarianized", that is , subject to an increasing division of labour, where many aspects of practice were determined by higher non-professional authorities, where they were remunerated on a salary basis, and were increasingly forming unions to defend working conditions. The study noted that the increasing bureaucratisation and rationalisation of work, methods for measuring professional output and quantitative criteria to replace qualitative (professional) criteria, high unemployment, and relative reduction in income, all created "proletarian" conditions. As a result professionals tended to join trade unions or influence their professional associations to assume trade-union-type activities.

In considering the proletarianisation thesis it is necessary to distinguish between a process for rationalising work, associated with the ideas of "de-skilling" (Braverman (1974)), work fragmentation, and loss of control over the labour process by the worker, and a process by which previously self-employed professionals become employees and adopt working class strategies such as unions. The latter is consonant with the Marxist thesis of increasing class polarisation; the former describes a process by which "rational" and scientific techniques are applied to professional work as to any other work in order to increase productivity, and, in a capitalist society, profit. This process, as described by Braverman (1974), turns work which was skilled and relatively autonomous into fragments, and removes control from the worker. It involves a separation of the intellectual facets of work, involving creativity and planning, from the worker, leaving him to execute the ideas and plans of others. (hierarchical fragmentation).

There are certainly processes outside of the control of professionals which affect the work which they do and their occupational structures. One of these processes is the use of management techniques to increase productivity (in state welfare services) and profit (in capitalist organisations). Managerial rationalisation, however, does not necessarily lead to work fragmentation and de-skilling for professionals (and consequently union opposition); indeed it may enhance professions' status by encouraging professions to delegate "menial work" to assistants to "make cost-effective use of their skills and training". Some professions are in fact instigators of "work rationalisation" processes, and the process of professionalisation can in some instances be complementary to and supportive of increasing productivity.

Where de-skilling does occur, and professions adopt an oppositional and union-stance, it does not necessarily follow that "proletarianisation-as-polarisation" follows. In many instances private practice is a viable alternative, and the individualist ideology of the professional leads to alternative action. In short, in the case of the professions, managerial rationalisation is a complex phenomenon and does not automatically lead to either "proletarianisation-as-polarisation", or "de-professionalisation".

SUMMARY

This appendix used the question which all studies implicitly or explicitly addressed,"what is a profession?", to organise a review of the literature. Common usage shows a multiplicity of meanings which have changed over time. It is of note that social scientists have tried, perhaps more than with other definitions, to remain faithful to common meanings. When we also note that aspiring occupations capitalise on features which are associated with traditional professions, and that their rise depends on their ability to gain a mandate and trust from the public and clients (Hughes (1963)), we see that the use and change in meaning of terms is not purely a question of philology. In remaining close to common meanings, perhaps early social scientists recognised the significance of the public's understanding of what constituted a profession and a professional for a social scientific understanding of the nature of professions. That the early social scientific definitions proved an important resource for professions advancing their claims perhaps also shows that professions had a clearer understanding of their own nature and place in society : a profession is an occupation which the public are prepared to trust, and the public's conception of "professional" is crucial to acquiring this trust.

An historical review shows that social changes influenced the concerns of social scientists and their approach towards the study of professions. Professions were not a significant force in Marx's day and did not figure in his analysis of society. However the theoretical perspective established by Marx has been used to understand the rise of professions and the economic base of their power. From this perspective the debates have centred around whether professions constitute a distinct class, and whether social change has or will lead to the "proletarianisation" of professionals.

The Weberian perspective, whilst recognising the significance of the economic concept of class, introduced the concepts of status and power which were to prove important to later understandings of professions. Durkheim's analysis of the division of labour highlighted interdependence in complex societies and the possible basis for social cohesion centering on occupational organisations. His perspective was developed by later functionalist writers. A number of writers drew on his ideas to advance the notion of professions as a liberal, progressive and scientific social force which upheld the value of the individual, in opposition to communism and fascism

The social scientists of the first half of the century generally accepted professions' claims about the degree and significance of their differences to other occupations. More than with any other conception the "ideal type" of "profession" became a moral rather than an analytic category.

Many post-second-world-war social scientists also were in broad agreement that a profession was defined ("trait" theories) or characterised ("continuum" theories) by skill based on theoretical knowledge, required education and training, adherence to a code of conduct, and loyalty to an occupational organisation and an ideal of altruistic service. The disagreement was over which traits were more fundamental and which derivative, and whether professions were qualitatively different from other occupations in these respects, or whether the difference was one of degree. With an increase in the number of "professionalising" occupations, the traits turned into continuums and social scientists considered the "process of professionalisation", the limits to this process, and the meaning of "professionalism".

The nineteen-fifties and sixties saw the development of specifically social scientific categories for research into professionalisation, and an attempt to develop theories which were capable of explaining the power and significance of professions in modern society.

The first of the more critical studies arose out of the interactionist perspective as applied to the world of work. These studies highlighted the differences between professional claims and practice, and the similarities between professionals and other workers in the dilemmas each faced and the strategies each adopted. These "naturalistic" and sometimes "debunking" studies were limited, however, in focusing on individual interaction and ignoring social change, stable social institutions, and political power.

Another development was to focus on certain types of professions such as "semi-professions", "para-professions" or "people-professions", noting common features of the work content and context of these professions. With the increasing employment of professionals in bureaucracies, another field of research addressed the question of whether professionalism was antithetical or compatible with bureaucratisation.

Along with consumer and managerial challenges to professions in the late sixties, social scientists reassessed the concepts of professions, professional and professionalism. Probably the most important development was the "power perspective". This approach considers the political and social process through which professions maintained and advanced their interests. This perspective views a profession as a particular way of organising certain work and workers, and shows how professions manipulated public belief to achieve positions of power and to maintain their occupational advantages by organising and controlling markets and practitioners. This view holds that the particular attributes of the occupation or the worker are less relevant than the way in which these attributes are used, and the social structures and processes which create and sustain the special position of the profession and professional: a profession is first and foremost a social creation. The general historical review closed by considering the deprofessionalisation/ proletarianisation debate.

Conclusions

One conclusion of the above review is that typologies of the client practitioner relationship more often described the relationships practitioners wished to achieve to minimise "problems" and maintain autonomy, than the realities of modern practice in large organisations, and the institutional arrangements regulating the relationship. The notion of independent professional and individual client is a professional ideal with an ideological function, rather than an accurate representation of modern professional practice. As Freidson (1975) noted in his study of doctors in a health insurance funded group medical practice, "Living in a period when private practice was the taken-for-granted normal mode... their conception of solo, entrepreneurial practice established many of the parameters of what was normal and acceptable about their work". It was this conception which led them to see themselves and their patients, "locked into an "unnatural" situation in which neither had any freedom of choice, in which both were in some sense trapped."(p 41)

The author's research [especially Øvretveit (1986)] found that the client-practitioner relationship in many instances in UK welfare services is not an isolated relationship but is part of a relationship between two groups or networks: on the one hand the practitioner as part of a multidisciplinary team, taking into account other professions' contributions and referring to them constantly; on the other, the individual client is part of a system or network of family group or community, or the client is another professional or the client's carers. Professions are increasingly concerned with changing the client's social, psychological or physical environment to support or maintain whatever changes they may have effected in their direct relationship with the client. There are primary and secondary clients (the client's main carers), and sometimes "a system" is the client (e.g. family therapy). The social sciences,and the professions,have yet to recognise the multiplicity of interdependencies and relationships in these situations.

This review revealed that there are certain core questions addressed by social scientists studying professions: do "the professions" constitute a new class?, What is the significance of professions in the social division of labour - are they particular kinds of monopolies for pursuing self interest, or do they restrain trends towards the competitive pursuit of individual economic self interest?, Is there a hierarchy of dominance of professions in fields such as health and law?, Are professions compatible with, or an opposing force to, bureaucracy?, Will the western "post industrial" or "information" society be ruled by professions with their monopoly over knowledge? (the "professionalisation" thesis), and will professional experts be increasingly integrated into large organisations and, backed by bureaucratic authority, become even more powerful in relation to clients, or will other forces reduce professions to the status of "skilled workers", and the concept of profession become obsolete (the "deprofessionalisation" thesis)?

The author's main conclusions from the review were:
-there is not a qualitative difference between a profession and an occupation or between a professional and other types of worker;

-like any social group, any group of workers will develop ideologies which emphasise their differences from other groups, in part to affirm identity and self-worth within the social group, in part to differentiate their product as a marketing strategy;

-differentiation is accentuated by the length and depth of common experience, the commitment to a career, and often by full-time "occupational organisers";

-both for occupations aspiring to be professions, and for established professions, certain attributes are particularly important to emphasise in order to gain the trust of clients and the public, and to acquire the advantages which derive from this trust;

-the nature of such attributes are irrelevant as long as they enable the individual client to extend their trust and submit to the authority of the professional, and, more importantly, convince the public that it is safe and necessary to institutionalise that trust in a mandate for the profession alone to carry out certain social functions;

-trust and the client-practitioner relationship are central to an understanding of professions and their organisation; new conceptions of client-practitioner relationships and of service and labour markets are needed to understand professions in state welfare services. "Service recipients" and "users", with entitlement to services, are more appropriate concepts than "consumers" or "customers" who usually pay directly and have a choice;

-in the current state of development of knowledge, the study of a range of occupations within a particular field is more likely to generate new insights than either a study of occupations in general, a comparison of "professions" with other occupations, or an historical study of one occupation.

The main conclusion, however, was that previous research had not found anything inherent in the work of professions which distinguished them from other occupations, or which enabled clear distinctions to be made between the work of different occupations.

This conclusion is borne out by the existence and severity of the problem experienced by professions and professionals in defining the practitioner's role and work responsibilities. This "problem" and the strategies used by professions and professionals to define their work is central to an understanding of professions. The available research suggests that the definitions of work which do exist are the result of a complex social process of negotiation and continual redefinition.

Social scientists who have attempted definitional typologies have themselves introduced new elements to this process, which are frequently referenced by aspiring professions. It is the particular way in which the occupation defines its work and regulates workers and clients which distinguishes different occupations, rather than intrinsic features of the work itself.

REFERENCES AND BIBLIOGRAPHY

Akers, R. & Quinney, R. (1968), "Differential organisation of health professions: a comparative analysis", American Sociological Review, Vol. 33, pp 104-109.

Alaszewski, A. W. (1977), "Doctors and paramedical workers: the changing pattern of interprofessional relations", Health and Social Services Journal, Centre 8 Paper, B1-4, 14. Oct.

Alaszewski, A. W. (1979), "Rehabilitation, The Remedial Therapy Professions and Social Policy", Social Science and Medicine, June, 13A, No. 4, pp 431-443

Anciano & Kirkpatrick (1990) "CMHTs and clinical psychology ; the death of a profession?", Clinical Psychology Forum, April ,pp9-12.

Armstrong, D. (1976) "The decline of the Medical hegemony: a review of government reports during the NHS". Social Science and Medicine, 10, 3-4, Mar-Apr, pp 157-163.

Becker, H. S. (1977) "The nature of a profession", In: Becker H.S. (1977) Sociological Work: Method and Substance. Transaction Books, New Brunswick, N.J.

Bexley Psychology Department (1980) "The evolution of democracy in an NHS psycholgy department", Clinical Psychology Forum May 1980, pp 24-30.

Boyce, R. (1991) "Hospital Restructuring - The implications for allied health professions", Australian Health review, 14,(2) pp147-153.

Brown, C. A. (1973) "The division of labourers: allied health professions", International Journal of Health Services, 3, p 435.

Bryant, R. J. S. (1979), "The physiotherapy profession", Health Services Manpower Review, Vol. 5, No. 5, May, pp 13-15.

Burt Report (1973), The Council for Professions Supplementary to Medicine: Report of Remedial Professions Committee, CPSM, London.

Buxton M., Packwood, T. &Keen J. (1989) "Resource Management: Process and Progress", HERG, Brunel University, Uxbridge.

Cang, S. and Rowbottom, R. (1978), National Health Service Reorganisation, HSORU Working Paper, Brunel University.

Church M. (1990) "Managerial capability and organisational complexity: an uncotolled study of

Cogan, M. (1953)"Towards a definition of a profession", Harvard Educational Review, 23, pp 33-50.

Cope Report (1951), Report of the Committees on Medical Auxiliaries, April, HMSO, London.

Day,P. & Klien, R (1987), Accountablilities , Tavistock Publications, London.

Department of Health and Social Security, Grey Book (1972), "Management Arrangements for the Reorganised NHS", HMSO, London.

Department of Health and Social Services, HSC (IS) 101 (1974), "The Remedial Professions and Linked Therapies", DHSS, London.

Department of Health and Social Security, (1974), "Third Report of the Joint Working Party on the Organisation of Medical Work in Hospitals", HMSO, London.

Department of Health and Social Services HRC(74)35"NHS Reorganisation Circular" HMSO, London.

Department of Health and Social Services (1975), "Better Services for the Mentally Ill", (Cmnd.6233) HMSO, London.

Department of Health and Social Services (1976) (1980), "Health and Personal Social Service Statistics", HMSO, London.

Department of Health and Social Services HC (77) 33, "Relationship between the Medical and Remedial Professions - A Statement by the Standing Medical Advisory Committee", Sept 1977, DHSS, London.

Department of Health and Social Security Report (1977), (Winterton/Perry Report), "Report of the Sub-Group onthe Organisation of the Remedial Professions in the NHS", DHSS, London.

Department of Health and Social Services HN (77) 124 (1977), "Nursing and Remedial Professions - Joint Working Party Report", Aug 1977, DHSS, London.

Department of Health and Social Services HC (79) 19, "Management of the Remedial Professions in the NHS", Oct 1979, DHSS, London.

Department of Health and Social Services, HC (80) 8, (1980), "Health Service Development: Structure and Management", DHSS, London.

Department of Health and Social Services, July (1981), "Care in the Community. A consultative document on moving resources for care in England", HMSO, London.

Department of Health and Social Services, (1981), "Care in Action. A Handbook of Policies and Priorities for the Health and Personal Social Services in England", HMSO, London.

Department of Health and Social Services, HC (84) 13, "Implementation of the NHS Management Inquiry Report", HMSO, London.
Department of Health and Social Services (1986), "Health Services Management - Resource Management (Management Budgeting) in Health Authorities". Health Notice, HN (86)34, HMSO, London.
Department of Health (1987) "Promoting Better Health", HMSO, London. (new GP contracts ap 1 91)
Department of Health (1989a) "Working for Patients", HMSO, London.
Department of Health (1989b) "Caring for People", HMSO, London.
Department of Health (1989c) "Working Paper No1. Self-governing Hospitals", HMSO, London.
Department of Health (1989d) "Working paper No2. Funding and Contracts for Hospital Services", HMSO, London.
Department of Health (1990)"Community Care Act", HMSO, London.
Department of Health (1991)."The Health of the Nation- A consultative document", (Cm 1523), HMSO, London.
Dingwall, R. (1976), "Accomplishing profession", Sociological Review, 24, pp 331-349.
Dingwall and Lewis (Ed.) (1983), The Sociology of the Professions: Lawyers, Doctors and Others, Macmillan, London.
Dixon (1989) IHSM, London.
Dyson, R. and Spary (1979), "Professional Associations", In: Bosanquet, N. (1979), Industrial Relations in the NHS, King's Fund, London.
Etzioni, A. (Ed.) (1969), The Semi Professions and their Organisation, The Free Press, New York.
Forsyth, P. & Danisiewicz, T. (1985), "Toward a theory of professionalization, Sociology of Work and Occupations, Vol. 12, pp 59-76.Freidson, E. (1960), "Client control and medical practice", American Journal of Sociology, LXV, Jan., pp 374-382.
Foster, J. (1971) "Enquiry into the practice and effects of scientology", London, HMSO.
Freidson, E. (1963), The Hospital in Modern Society, Free Press, Glencoe, Ill.
Freidson, E. (1970a), Professional Dominance: The Social Structure of Medical Care, Atherton Press, New York.
Freidson, E. (1970b), Profession of Medicine: A Study of the Sociology of Applied Knowledge, Dodd, Mead & Co., New York.
Evans, R. (1991) "Bath capitalises on Merging Skills", Therapy Weekly. Sept 12th, p.4.
Freidson, E. (1971), "Professions and the occupational principle". In: Freidson (Ed.) (1971), The Professions and their Prospects, Sage, Beverly Hills, California.
Freidson, E. (1973), "Professionalisation and the organisation of middle-class labour in post-industrial society", Sociological Review Monograph 20, University of Keele.
Freidson, E. (1975)Doctoring Together: A Study of Professional Social Control, Elsevier, New York.
Freidson, E. (1977), "The Future of Professionalism", in Stacey et al. (1977), op. cit.
Freidson, E. (1985), "The reorganisation of the medical profession", Medical Care Review, Vol. 41, No. 1, Spring.
Galley, P. (1977), "Physiotherapists as first-contact practitioners - new challenges and responsibilities in Australia", in Physiotherapy, August, Vol. 63, No. 8, pp 246-248.
General Medical Council (1977), Professional Conduct and Discipline, GMC, Tavistock Square, London.
Goode, W.J. (1969), "The theoretical limits of professionalization", In: Etzioni, A. (Ed.) (1969), The Semi Professions and their Organisation, The Free Press, New York, pp 266-313.
Greenwood, E. (1957), "Attributes of a profession", Social Work, 2, pp 45-55.
Griffiths Report (1988) "Community Care: Agenda for Action", HMSO, London.
Hall, R.H. (1968), "Professionalization and bureaucratization", American Sociological Review, 33, (Feb), pp 92-104.
Ham C.(1990) "Holding on while letting go", Kings Fund Project Paper 86.
Ham, C (1991) "The New National Health Service", Radcliffe Medical Press, Oxford.
Heywood, S. (1990),"Professions Allied to Medicine: Contracts for Services,' HSMC No 18, University of Birmingham.
Halmos, P. (1965), The Faith of the Counsellors, Constable, London.
Halmos, P. (1970), The Personal Service Society, Constable, London.
Halsbury Report (1975), Report of the Committee of Inquiry into the Pay and Related Conditions of Service of the Professions Supplementary to Medicine and Speech Therapy. HMSO, London.

Harding Report.(1981), Harding, W. & Frost, W. (May 1981), "The Primary Health Care Team", Standing Medical Advisory Committee & Standing Nursing and Midwifery Advisory Committee, DHSS, London.

Haug, M. (1973), "Deprofessionalization: an alternative hypothesis for the future", in Halmos, P. (Ed.) (1973), op. cit., pp 195-212.

Health Services Organisation Research Unit (1977), Organisation of Physiotherapy and Occupational Therapy in the NHS, HSORU Working Paper, Brunel University.

Henly, J. & Harrison, S. (1981), "Remedial Professions in the Corporate Management Structure", Unpublished document, Nuffield Centre for Health Services Studies, University of Leeds.

Hickson, D. & Thomas, M., (1974) "Professionalization in Britain: A Preliminary Measurement", Administrative Science Quarterly.

Lee, R.H. (1975), "Medical rehabilitation: policy-making in the English health service", in Social Science and Medicine, Vol. 9, pp 325-332.

Jackson, J.(Ed.)(1970) Professions and Professionalization Cambridge University Press, Cambridge.

Jaques, E (1947)"Social therapy: technocracy or collaboration", Journal of Social Issues, 3, pp 59-66.

Jaques, E.(1976), A General Theory of Bureaucracy, Heinemann, London.

Jaques, E.(Ed.) (1978), Health Services: their nature and organisation and the role of patients, doctors, and the health professions, Heinemann, London.

Jaques, E.(1982), "The Method of Social Analysis in Social Change and Social Research", Clinical Sociology Review, Vol. 1, pp 50-58.

Johnson, T. (1972), Professions and Power, Macmillan, London.

Jones, Corke & Childs (1990), "Working for Whom?", Forum No.27 June 1990,pp 28-31.

Kat, B. (1985), "The Emergence of clinical psychology as a profession", presentation for the 1985 "May Davidson" award.

Kinston, W. & Øvretveit, J.(1981), "The physiotherapist as a bureaucrat; Physiotherapy Organisation: 2", Physiotherapy, June, Vol. 67, No. 6, pp 168-170.

Kinston, W., Øvretveit, J.& Cleland, S. (1982), "The origin, significance and future of the district physiotherapist role; Physiotherapy organisation: 6", Physiotherapy, April, Vol.68, No. 4, pp 118-123.

Kinston, W., Øvretveit, J.,& Teager, D. (1981), "Levels of work in physiotherapy; Physiotherapy Organisation: 3", Physiotherapy, August, Vol. 67, No. 8, pp 236-239.

Kinston, W., Øvretveit, J.,& Williams, J. (1981), "The nature of the district physiotherapist role; Physiotherapy Organisation: 4", Physiotherapy, Nov., Vol. 67, No. 11, pp 329-333.

Kinston, W. and Rowbottom, W. (1983), The New NHS Districts and their Units, HSORU Working Paper, Brunel University.

Koch, H (ed) (1986) Community Clinical Psychology, Croom Helm, London.

Larkin, G.V. (1983), Occupational Monopoly and Modern Medicine, Tavistock, London.

Larson, M.S. (1977), The Rise of Professionalism: A Sociological Analysis, University of California Press, London.

Larson, M.S. (1979), "Professionalism: rise and fall", International Journal of Health Services, Vol. 9, 609.

Lee, R.H. (1975), "Medical rehabilitation: policy-making in the English health service", in Social Science and Medicine, Vol. 9, pp 325-332.

Levitt, R. (1979), The Reorganised National Health Service, Croom Helm, London.

Liddell, A. (Ed.) (1983), The Practice of Clinical Psychology in Gt. Britain, Wiley, Chichester.

Morgan, J & Marchment, M (1990) "A framework for assuring quality in contracts", NAQA Papers on Quality in Contracts, NAQA, Birmingham.Ω

Marzillier, J & Hall, J (eds)(1988) What is Clinical Psycholgy?, Oxford University Press, Oxford.

McMillan Report (1973), The Remedial Professions: A Report by a Working Party set up in March 1973 by the Secretary of State, HMSO, London.

McPherson, I. & Sutton, A. (Eds.) (1981), Reconstructing Psychological Practice, Croom Helm, London.

Mercer, J. (1980), "Physiotherapy as a Profession", Physiotherapy, June, Vol. 66, No6, pp 180-184.

Monopolies Commission (1970), A Report on Restrictive Practices in the Supply of Professional Services, Cmnd. 4463, HMSO, London.

MPAG (1990) Manpower Planning and Advisory Group Report on Clinical Psychology, DSS Leaflets Unit, PO Box 21, Stanmore, Middlesex.

Oddie Report (1970), The Council for Professions Supplementary to Medicine, Report and Recommendations of the Remedial Professions Committee, CPSM, London.

Øvretveit, J. (1984),"Organisating Psychology in the NHS," HSC Working Paper, BIOSS, Brunel University.

Øvretveit, J. (1984),"The Accountability of a Head of Department to the DHA", BPS, DCP Newsletter No,.45, September,pp.17-22.

Øvretveit, J. (1985),"Medical Dominance and the Development of Professional Autonomy in Physiotherapy",Sociology of Health and Illness, Vol.7,No.1, March,pp.76-93.

Øvretveit, J. (1985),"Grades and Planning Psychology Services and Organisational Structure",BPS, DCP Newsletter ,

Øvretveit, J. (1985),"Monitoring and Evaluation for Service Management", BPS, Clinical Psychology Forum, No.1, February, pp.12-15.

Øvretveit, J. (1985),"Health Service Budgeting", BPS, Clinical Psychology Forum, April.

Øvretveit, J. (1986),"Management and Democratic Teams",BPS Clinical Psychology Forum, October.

Øvretveit, J.(1986),"Organising Multidisciplinary Community Teams," HSC Working Paper, BIOSS, Brunel University.

Øvretveit, J.(1988), "Management and Multidisciplinary Teamwork",Scottish Division of Educational and Child Psychology Newsletter for 1988.

Øvretveit, J (1988),"A Peer Review Process for Developing Service Quality",BIOSS Working Paper,Brunel University,Uxbridge,Middlesex.

Øvretveit, J.(1988) "The Griffiths Proposals for Community Care - A summary and some implications",Clinical Psychology Forum,No.16,August,British Psychological Society,Leicester.

Øvretveit, J.(1989),"The Future of Paramedical Professions in the NHS",The Health Service Journal,24 August

Øvretveit, J.(1989),"Future Organisation of Psychology Services",Clinical Psychology Forum,December,1989.

Øvretveit, J.(1990) "Implications of the NHS Review proposals for Speech Therapy", College of Speech Therapists Bulletin, April 1990,pp2-3.

Øvretveit, J.(1990), "Improving Primary Health Care Team Organisation", Research Report, BIOSS, Brunel University, Uxbridge, Middx.

Øvretveit, J.(1990),"What is Quality in Health Services", Health Service Management,June, pp 132-3

Øvretveit, J.(1990),"Quality in Service Contracts", Bulletin of the College of Speech Therapists,June,No 459,p6-7.

Øvretveit, J.(1990),"Health Service Quality", Bulletin of the College of Speech Therapists,July,No 459,pp 6-7.

Øvretveit, J.(1990), "Quality Health Services," Research Report, BIOSS, Brunel University, Uxbridge, Middx.

Øvretveit, J.(1991),"Why Teams Fail",in Lindesay (ed) (1991) Working Out: Setting-up and Running Community Psychogeriatric Teams, RDP,134 Borough High St. London SE1 1LB.

Øvretveit, J.(1991),"Organisation options for speech therapy services", College of Speech Therapists Bulletin, March 1991.

Øvretveit, J.(1991),"Future Organisation of Therapy Services", Health Service Management, Vol 87, No. 2, April, pp 78-80.

Øvretveit, J.(1991),"Quality Costs- Or does it?", Health Service Management, August.

Øvretveit, J.(1991), "Case Management and Psychologists", Clinical Psychology Forum, September.

Øvretveit, J.(1992), "Health Service Quality,", Blackwells Scientific Press, Oxford.

Packwood, T., Keen, J. & Buxton, M. (1991), "Hospitals in Transition: The Resource Management Experiment", Open University Press, Milton Keynes.

Paxton (1990), "After the NHS Bill, Psychology as a Trading Agency?," Forum No.29 October 1990,pp11-13.

Parry, N. & Parry, J. (1976), The Rise of the Medical Profession: A Study of Collective Social Mobility, Croom Helm, London.

Piper & Webb (1990) "Evaluation Report of a Clinical Psychology Service", Loughbrough University.

Ritzer, G. (1975), "Professionalisation, bureaucratization and rationalization: The views of Max Weber", Social Forces, 53, 4, pp 627-634.

Rowbottom, R.W. et al (1973), Hospital Organisation, Heinemann, London.

Rowbottom, R.W. (1977), Social Analysis, Heinemann, London.

Secretary of State for Social Services (1972), "National Health Services Reorganisation: England", Cmnd. 5055, HMSO, London.

Sheaff, R (1991), "Marketing for Health Services", Open University Press, Milton Keynes.
Sieghart Report (1978), Statutory Registration of Psychotherapists HMSO, London.
Stamp, G. (1988), "Longitudinal Research into the Methods of assessing Managerial potential", US Army Institute for Behavioural and Social Sciences, Alexandria, VA 22333, USA.
Stamp, G. (1989) "The individual the organisation and the path to mutual appreciation", Personnel Management, July.
Stevens, R. (1966), Medical Practice in Modern England: The Impact of Specialisation and State Medicine, Yale University Press, New Haven, Conn.
Strick, P. & Bennun, I (1990) "Clinical Psycholgy within the Torbay Health Authority: A four-year follow-up", Clinical Psychology Forum, Feb 1991,pp 6&7.
Trethowen Report (1977) The Role of Psychologists in the Health Service, HMSO, London.
Tunbridge Report (1972), Rehabilitation: Report of a Sub-committee of the Standing Medical Advisory Committee of the Central Health Services Council, HMSO, London.
Tunbridge Statement (1972). Statement from the Committee on the Remedial Professions to the Secretary of State, HMSO, London.
Vollmer, H.M.& Mills, D.L.(Eds.)(1966), Professionalization, Prentice-Hall, Englewood Cliffs, N.J.
Wallis, M. (1987) "Profession and Professionalism and the Emerging profession of Occupational Therapy: part 1", Br. J. Occupational Therapy.
Ward, A. (1979), "Physiotherapists - career patterns and attitudes", Health Trends, Vol. 11, pp 14-17.
Watson (1990) "Another perspective on CMHTs and clincal psychology", Clinical Psychology Forum, Oct ,p27-8.
Watts, F.N. (Ed.) (1985), New Developments in Clinical Psychology, B.P.S., Leicester.
    "   "   "   (1988),   "   "   "   Volume 2 " "
Watts, F.N. (1985), "Clinical psychology", Health Trends, Vol. 17, pp 28-30.
Webster, R & Skilbeck, C (1991), "Psycholgy Agencies in the NHS and Contracts for Psychology Services", South Tees Health Authority, Middlesborough.
West, J & Spinks, S. (eds)(1988) Clinical Psychology in Action, Wright, London.
West Midlands Regional District Chiropodists (1990), "Quality assurance for a district chiropody service", Association
Whittington, C. & Bellaby, P. (1979), "The reasons for hierarchy in social services departments: A critique of Elliottt Jaques and his associates", Sociological Review, Vol, 27, No.3, pp. 513-517.
Wickings, et al. (1983), "Review of clinical budgeting and costing experiments", British Medical Journal, Vol. 286, pp 575-577; 12.2.83.
Wicksteed, J. (1974), "The Growth of a Profession".
Wilensky, H.L. (1964), "The Professionalisation of Everyone", American Journal of Sociology, Vol. 70, No. 2, pp 137-158.
Willis, E. (1989), Medical Dominance, Allen & Uniwin, Melbourne.
Zangwill Report, R.C.Psych., R.C.N. & B.P.S. (1980), Behaviour Modification: Report of the Joint Working Party to formulate Ethical Guidelines for the Conduct of Programmes of Behaviour Modification in the N.H.S., HMSO, London.

Professional Associations

Society of Chiropodists, 53 Wellbeck Street, London, WIM 7HE. 071-486-3381.
British Dietetic Association, Daimler House, Paradise Street, Birmingham, BI 2BJ. 021-643-5483.
College of Occupational Therapists, 6/8 Marshalsea Road, London, SE1 1 HL. 071-357-6480.
Chartered Society of Physiotherapy, 14 Bedford Row, London, WC1R 4 ED. 071-242-1940.
British Psychological Association, Division of Clinical Psychology, 48 Princess Road East, Leicester, LE1 7DR. 0533-549568.
College of Speech and Language Therapits, Harold Poster House, 6 Lechmere Road, London, NW2 5 BU. 081-459-8521.

INDEX

www.ingramcontent.com/pod-product-compliance
Ingram Content Group UK Ltd.
Pitfield, Milton Keynes, MK11 3LW, UK
UKHW041840280225
455677UK00010B/265